CHARLES KINGSLEY
1819-1875

CHARLES KINGSLEY
in his study in Eversley Rectory, painted by Lowes Dickinson, 1862

Courtesy of the National Portrait Gallery

CHARLES KINGSLEY
1819-1875

MARGARET FARRAND THORP

1937
PRINCETON: PRINCETON UNIVERSITY PRESS
LONDON: HUMPHREY MILFORD • OXFORD UNIVERSITY PRESS

COPYRIGHT 1937, PRINCETON UNIVERSITY PRESS

PRINTED AT PRINCETON UNIVERSITY PRESS
PRINCETON, NEW JERSEY, U.S.A.

For

W. T.

PREFACE

TWO of Charles Kingsley's most agreeable characteristics were his generosity and his interest in the plans and projects of others. So strong were these traits that they seem to have descended to those connected with him in even remote degree. In no one are they more pleasantly evident than in his grandniece and literary executor Miss Gabrielle Vallings. The family papers which Mrs. Kingsley entrusted to her younger daughter Mrs. Mary St. Leger Harrison (Lucas Malet), Mrs. Harrison, on her death in October 1931, left to Miss Vallings. Miss Vallings has permitted me to go through the large collection of letters, notebooks, commonplace-books, and marked copies of books belonging to Charles Kingsley and his wife, and to copy, practically without restriction, anything which seemed to be of interest and importance. She has also given me permission to publish or republish these and letters now in other hands, including those in the British Museum.

E. P. Stapleton, Esq., of Barkston Gardens, London, has given me access to a large body of family letters written to and by the Kingsleys. Mr. Stapleton's grandfather was that Augustus G. Stapleton, Esq., who was chiefly responsible for the appointment of Charles Kingsley as rector of Eversley and one of whose sons was for a time Kingsley's curate. The letters, therefore, are rich in details of parish and family life not accessible elsewhere. E. F. Johns, Esq., headmaster of Winton House, Winchester, has put at my disposal an interesting collection of letters written to his father and mother by Mr. and Mrs. Kingsley. The Rev. A. C. Johns, a lifelong friend of Kingsley, was headmaster of Winton House when Kingsley's son Grenville was a pupil there.

For oral information, both personal impressions and family tradition, I am indebted not only to Miss Vallings, Mr. Stapleton and Mr. Johns but to Miss Mary Hughes, the late G. Lowes Dickinson, Mrs. Lowes and Miss Lowes Dickinson, the late S. M. Ellis and to Mr. and Mrs. J. Hautonville Cope of Finchampstead Place, Berks.

I wish to express my appreciation of the courtesy of George Macmillan, Esq., of Macmillan and Company, who has permitted me to make use of some hitherto unpublished letters which passed between Kingsley and Alexander Macmillan, his publisher. I am under obligation also to Wilfred Partington, Esq., who has put at my disposal some copies of Kingsley family letters to which he had access.

To the authorities of the British Museum who have allowed me to make use of a very large body of uncatalogued Kingsley material I am indebted for this and for other courtesies too numerous to recount; to Professor Tucker Brooke of Yale University, for the kind of criticism and encouragement which cannot be reckoned in concrete terms; and to M. L. Parrish, Esq., for the pleasure of using his remarkable Kingsley collection in the library of Dormy House, Pine Valley, New Jersey.

TABLE OF CONTENTS

			PAGE
Chapter	I.	A Bugle Strung Sable	1
Chapter	II.	"The Inspiration of My Life before I Met You"	5
Chapter	III.	"Paroxysms of Pain and Petulance"	14
Chapter	IV.	"Amamus"	18
Chapter	V.	"Village Sermons"	29
Chapter	VI.	"If It Shall Deter One Young Man"	41
Chapter	VII.	"Esau Has a Birthright"	50
Chapter	VIII.	"I Am a Church of England Parson—and a Chartist"	59
Chapter	IX.	"Tailor and Poet"	72
Chapter	X.	"The Three Fishers"	82
Chapter	XI.	"Employment for My Pen"	91
Chapter	XII.	"How to Train not Scholars but Men"	99
Chapter	XIII.	"Emersonian Anythingarianism"	108
Chapter	XIV.	"A Sanguinary Book"	117
Chapter	XV.	"I See One Work to be Done ere I Die"	126
Chapter	XVI.	"All of Me Which Will Last"	137
Chapter	XVII.	Chaplain to the Queen and to the Prince of Wales	143
Chapter	XVIII.	"The Only Course Fit for a Gentleman"	153
Chapter	XIX.	"As Great a Talker as Any Man in England"	162
Chapter	XX.	"Muscular Christianity, a Clever Expression"	169
Chapter	XXI.	"At the Service of the Good Citizens of Chester"	175
Chapter	XXII.	"At Last"	182
Bibliography of Charles Kingsley's Works			191
Index			205

CHAPTER I

A BUGLE STRUNG SABLE

AND HE spake three thousand proverbs: and his songs were a thousand and five. And he spake of trees, from the cedar tree that is in Lebanon even unto the hyssop that springeth out of the wall: he spake also of beasts, and of fowl, and of creeping things, and of fishes. (1 *Kings* iv. 32, 33.)

The Dean of Chester chose this text for his obituary sermon on Charles Kingsley, a singularly comprehensive characterization, for almost the only missing element in the portrait is supplied by implication: Canon Kingsley always admired the Song of Songs as a great hymn in praise of monogamy. So satisfactory was Dean Howson's sermon to the cathedral audience which had enthusiastically loved Charles Kingsley that it was published at length in *Good Words* (March 1875) for the pleasure and consolation of that huge national audience who looked up to the preacher and novelist with reverence and with love because he had met the great Victorian problems at first hand and solved them happily.

Born in the same year as the Queen, Kingsley typifies the Victorian man as closely as she presents the Victorian woman. He shared most of her fundamental principles. He believed in England, in the Empire, in the Established Church; in the ennobling influence of womanhood and the sanctity of the home; in a good God guiding the universe and each of its individual inhabitants; in the spiritual brotherhood of men within a benevolent aristocracy; in evolutionary progress and the compatibility of science and religion. Most of the great literary figures of the nineteenth century were rebels against or thinkers in advance of their time. Kingsley's influence was due in large part to his not being a thinker at all. He suffered all the torments endured by the average man of the period in his struggle with a changing universe; he differed from the average man in the courage with which he faced the problems of the day and the volubility with which he discussed them. He made for himself solutions which were shallow but convincing to hundreds because of their power for comfort and because of the enormous vitality and sincerity behind his presentations. His power in his time and his significance to succeeding generations lies in this, that he was not so much an artist as a fluent English gentleman.

All the Kingsleys were gentlemen, a good old family of no particular distinction. They claimed descent from the Kingsleys of Kingsley, or Vale Royal, in Delamere Forest, Cheshire, and from Rannulph de Kingsley, "Grantee of the Forest of Mara and Mondrem from Randall Meschines, ante 1128," whose "bugle strung sable" they still bear in their arms. Fighting blood they had too. They stood with Cromwell at Naseby and Marston Moor and lost broad acres for their Puritanism, and they reckoned as most illustrious of their line General William Kingsley who commanded the 20th Regiment of Foot Guards, fought at Minden and had his portrait painted by Reynolds.

Charles's father was born in 1781 at Battramsley House, New Forest. While still fairly young he was left an orphan, and that part of a decent fortune which was not dissipated by the hands of careless guardians quickly vanished under his own when he came of age, so that he found himself at thirty faced with the melancholy prospect of adopting a profession. By this time he was unfortunately too old for the army and so, since he had had a good education at Harrow and Oxford and was blessed with friends who owned church property, he decided to take orders. He seems to have been a thorough sportsman about the whole affair, to have entered with real seriousness into his new calling and to have turned his fighting and athletic talents to practical effect in his ministry. He sold his hunters and land and took his young wife up to Cambridge where he read at Trinity Hall. There, by his enthusiasm for German literature, he attracted the attention of Dr. Herbert Marsh, Lady Margaret Professor, who, when he became Bishop of Peterborough, procured for Kingsley a cure in the Fens and made him his examining chaplain. "A magnificent man," Charles wrote of this father, "in body and mind, and was said to possess every talent except that of using his talents."[1]

Of his mother Charles speaks at one time as "a second Mrs. Fry, in spirit and act" (I, 149) and again as having "a quite extraordinary practical and administrative power," combined, even at seventy-nine, with "my father's passion for knowledge, and the sentiment and fancy of a young girl." (I, 4.) Mary Lucas came of a family which had been "West Indian" for generations; she herself was born in the Indies but brought up in England. Her father, Nathan Lucas of Rushford Lodge, Norfolk, had been a judge in the Barbadoes, was a great traveller, a "scientist" and the friend of scientists, and had had all sorts of adventures which enchanted his grandchildren. Charles's "love of travel, science and literature, and the romance of his nature," he inherited therefore from his mother's side of the house, as, attempting to be scientific, he thanked his father for his "love of art, his sporting tastes, his fighting blood." Certainly Mary Lucas Kingsley had a romantic passion for scenery and was particularly charmed by the beauty of the West Country where her husband was stationed at the time their second son was born. She was convinced that if before his birth she took delight in the beauties of that countryside they would enter into his soul and be dear to him all his life. She proved her theory to the hilt, for there was never a more passionate lover of scenery than Charles Kingsley and it was his ability to describe it, especially Devon, with elaboration and detail which so deeply delighted his contemporaries.

In short, so much vitality, imagination and nervous energy did these parents transmit to their children that only one of them succeeded in becoming a conventional Englishman.

The eldest son, Gerald (1816-44), died at twenty-eight a gallant useless young naval death. Charles, who was born on July 12, 1819, began life as a socialist clergyman who wrote letters to Chartists and preached God's love to the working man but became a Queen's chaplain, Macmillan's most profitable novelist and a Canon of Westminster. Herbert, the third son, died of brain fever (1834) while still a boy, and we know nothing of him. George Henry

[1] *Charles Kingsley: His Letters and Memories of His Life.* Edited by His Wife. Henry S. King & Co., London, 1877, I, 4. Further references to this work will be given simply as I, 1, II, 1, etc. Later abridged editions contain some material not included in the first editions. References to this are to the 1890 edition published by Macmillan and are given simply as 1890 ed., p. 1, etc.

(1826-92) studied medicine in Edinburgh, was wounded on the Paris barricades in '48, explored the South Seas and the Rocky Mountains as doctor-companion to various young noblemen, was at one time librarian of Bridgewater House, edited Thynne's *Animadversions* upon Chaucer and turned out, whenever he cared to take the trouble, translations or highly amusing original sketches of travel. He seems to have enjoyed life more thoroughly than any of the rest of the family but he married beneath him and was too thoroughgoing a Bohemian to be perfectly satisfactory to his parents. George's "awful temper" was an accepted fact in the family but the Canon, says George's daughter, the explorer Mary Kingsley, "understood this brother of his, and, understanding, loved him." (Memoir in George Kingsley's *Notes on Sport and Travel,* London, 1900, p. 3.)

Henry (1830-76) left Oxford without a degree to seek gold in Australia. Returned, without the gold, to England he achieved respectability and some money, though he seems never to have had quite enough, by writing a long series of novels, some of which it is now the fashion to prefer to his brother's, interspersing them with magazine editing and war correspondence. Charles was constantly stretching him a helping hand in his literary career, and Mr. S. M. Ellis in his vindication of Henry Kingsley (*Henry Kingsley,* London, 1931) has made definite the friendly relationship between the novelist brothers.

Charlotte (Mrs. John Mill Chanter, 1828-82), the only daughter, correctly married a clergyman but managed also to publish a book on ferns, some stories for children, in collaboration with her husband, and a very melodramatic novel of her own.

CHAPTER II

"THE INSPIRATION OF MY LIFE BEFORE I MET YOU"

ONE of the earliest literary references to Charles Kingsley is contained in a letter from Harriet Martineau with whom—she was twenty years his senior—he carried on in the summer of 1852 a lively and intimate correspondence. She tells him that she has just heard from a friend an account of a stormy passage of the river Trent in flood when Mrs. Kingsley's chief anxiety was for her "little delicate Charles" whom she wrapped in her shawl, going without it herself.

As a small boy Charles had the delight in words so common in precocious children. He composed poems and, not unnaturally, preached sermons, which his mother took down and showed to the Bishop of Peterborough. Dr. Marsh predicted a great future for the child and begged that they be preserved. One of them, preached at four to a congregation of nursery chairs, throws some light upon the theology and pulpit style of the Rev. Charles Kingsley, Sr., while one or two of the poems are interesting as social documents of the 1820's:

It is not right to fight. Honesty has no chance against stealing. Christ has shown us true religion. We must follow God, and not follow the Devil, for if we follow the Devil we shall go into that everlasting fire, and if we follow God, we shall go to Heaven. When the tempter came to Christ in the Wilderness, and told him to make the stones into bread, he said, Get thee behind me, Satan. He has given us a sign and an example how we should overcome the Devil. It is written in the Bible that we should love our neighbour, and not covet his house, nor his ox, nor his ass, nor his wife, nor anything that is his. It is to a certainty that we cannot describe how thousands and ten thousands have been wicked; and nobody can tell how the Devil can be chained in Hell. Nor can we describe how many men and women and children have been good. And if we go to Heaven we shall find them all singing to God in the highest. And if we go to hell, we shall find all the wicked ones gnashing and wailing their teeth, as God describes in the Bible.

If humanity, honesty, and good religion fade, we can to a certainty get them back, by being good again. Religion is reading good books, doing good actions, and not telling lies and speaking evil, and not calling their brother Fool and Raca. And if we rebel against God, He will to a certainty cast us into hell. And one day when a great generation of people came to Christ in the Wilderness, he said, Yea ye generation of vipers! (I, 8.)

SUNDAY MORNING

> Now the bells are ringing loud
> People rising very early—
> Boys and girls are dressing now,
> And now they go to Sunday School
> To Church—and then come back again.
> To reading Bibles they return
> Everybody does not work,
> But idle people do not read their Bible
> And God punishes them.
> Now Sunday evening thus comes
> Everybody goes to bed.
> Boys and girls still remain reading their Bibles
> Till the time they go to Bed
> Then Monday morning
> Men and women return to work.

The country scenes in which most of Kingsley's childhood was spent furnished him with richer poetic materials. He was born in Holne Vicarage, "under the brow of Dartmoor, Devonshire," where his father was curate in charge from June to August when he went to a curacy in Burton-on-Trent. In 1821 he became Vicar of North Clifton, near Newark.[1] From 1824 to 1830 he held, as a warming-pan for Bishop Marsh's son, the pleasant living of Barnack near Stamford in the Fens. The rectory was a fine old fourteenth century house with a haunted room, to intimate acquaintance with which Charles later traced his firm disbelief in ghosts. The Fen country touched his young imagination almost more deeply than Devon so that he wrote of it always with an affection which forty years later urged him to his last novel, *Hereward*. In the Fens, too, he developed the family taste for field sports

---

[1] Mr. W. Henry Brown (*Charles Kingsley, The Work and Influence of Parson Lot*. Pioneer series no. 4, Manchester, 1924) who has taken much pains to trace the senior Kingsley's clerical movements, feels that this constant shifting indicates some difficulty in settling to his new profession, and this seems not improbable.

when on shooting days he was mounted on his father's horse in front of the keeper, to bring back the game bag. And with his sportsmanship developed, for he thought them really interdependent, his lifelong passion for "natural history."

When he was forced to relinquish the Barnack living Mr. Kingsley, who had caught ague in the Fens, was advised to try Devonshire. He stayed for a time at Ilfracombe and in 1831 was presented to the living of Clovelly which he held for the next five years. Here he seems to have endeared himself to his people by some of the "muscular Christianity" which his son so ardently preached despite his dislike of the term. Mr. Kingsley, according to his daughter-in-law, could steer a boat, shoot a seine or haul a herring net as well as any of his parishioners, and they responded accordingly to his ministrations.

Charles Kingsley, Jr., was to put Clovelly upon the map of every tourist itinerary. He and his brothers delighted in the little town. They had their boat, their ponies, a shell collecting neighbour who excited their enthusiasm for conchology, and any number of friends among the fisher folk, who thoroughly liked their father. The West Country took romantic hold upon the two future novelists and twenty-five years later Charles's and Henry's "word pictures" of Devon scenery were admired by Mudie's best subscribers. "Now that you have seen the dear old Paradise," said Charles to his wife in 1854, "you know what was the inspiration of my life before I met you." (I, 20.) Two of his novels are laid in Devon; many of the poems have their springs there and a long prose idyll on North Devon was one of those "beloved," so the *Athenaeum* said (January 10, 1874), "and deservedly, of undergraduates." There he describes the merry beach beside the town "covered with shrieking women and old men, casting themselves on the pebbles in fruitless agonies of prayer, as corpse after corpse swept up at the feet of wife and child."

It may have been this youthful close acquaintance with death which set the Devon scenes so deeply on the minds of the Kingsley boys. Mrs. Charles Kingsley tells us that "when the herring fleet put to sea, whatever the weather might be, the Rector, accompanied by his wife and boys, would start off 'down street,' for the Quay, to give a short parting service at which 'men who worked,' and 'women who wept,' would join in singing out of the old Prayer Book version of the 121st Psalm." (I, 17.)

Young Charles saw death close again and in a particularly horrible form when he and his younger brother Herbert were sent to a preparatory school in Clifton. Twenty-seven years later, lecturing at Bristol, he described the riots of 1831 with that minuteness of visual memory which played so large a part in his science and his novel writing:

It was an afternoon of sullen autumn rain. The fog hung thick over the docks and lowlands. Glaring through that fog I saw a bright mass of flame—almost like a half-risen sun.

That, I was told, was the gate of the new gaol on fire. That the prisoners in it had been set free; that—But why speak of what too many here recollect but too well? The fog rolled slowly upward. Dark figures, even at that great distance, were flitting across what seemed the mouth of the pit. The flame increased—multiplied—at one point after another; till, by ten o'clock that night I seemed to be looking down upon Dante's Inferno, and to hear the multitudinous moan and wail of the lost spirits surging to and fro amid that sea of fire. . . .

It was on the Tuesday or Wednesday after, if I recollect right, that I saw another, and a still more awful sight. Along the north side of Queen-square, in front of ruins which had been three days before noble buildings, lay a ghastly row, not of corpses, but of corpse-fragments. I have no more wish than you to dilate upon that sight. But there was one charred fragment—with a scrap of old red petticoat adhering to it, which I never forgot—which I trust in God that I never shall forget. It is good for a man to be brought once at least in his life face to face with fact, ultimate fact, however horrible it may be; and have to confess to himself, shuddering, what things are possible upon God's earth, when man has forgotten that his only welfare lies in living after the likeness of God.

Not that I learnt the lesson then. When the first excitement of horror and wonder were past, what I had seen made me for years the veriest aristocrat, full of hatred and contempt of these dangerous classes, whose existence I had for the first time discovered. It required many years—years, too, of personal intercourse with the poor, to explain to me the true meaning of what I saw here in October twenty-seven years ago: and to learn a part of that lesson which God taught to others thereby. ("Great Cities and their Influence for Good and Evil," *Miscellanies,* 1859, Vol. II.)[2]

[2] References to Kingsley's own works are given with short title only. Complete titles will be found in the bibliography on p. 191.

"The Inspiration of My Life before I Met You"   9

The Rev. John Knight, Charles's headmaster at Clifton, described him as "affectionate, gentle, and fond of quiet" so that he often left the boys' schoolroom and took refuge with his tutor's daughters and their governess. This constitutional shyness Charles himself believed would have been cured by a public school and he regretted all his life that his parents' evangelical-Tory principles prevented them from placing him under Dr. Arnold. The idea of Eton was also abandoned and in 1832 Charles and Herbert were sent to the Grammar School at Helston under the Rev. Derwent Coleridge who was undoubtedly responsible for much of Charles's lifelong enthusiasm for German philosophy. He encouraged his pupil, too, in verse writing and the second-master, the Rev. Charles A. Johns, fed his passion for botany. Charles was not popular as a schoolboy but he formed some real friendships, the most enduring that with Cowley Powles who thirty years later, when he resigned a fellowship at Exeter College, settled at Eversley to become one of Charles Kingsley's parishioners.

The poetry of this schoolboy period, though Powles admired it, Kingsley never thought worth reprinting. A great deal of it still exists in an MS. book entitled *Original Composts, dedicated to Myself*. Composts, Charles explains, in what seems to be intended for a seventeenth century manner, contain much rubbish yet have a vivifying virtue, but the vitality here is neither very great nor very promising. There are some metrical experiments but they are made with small idea of what he is doing. The diction is altogether "poetic." The principal theme is that "I" have not known love and do not expect to but am glad to see it in others; also that Life is pretty difficult. Several verses are addressed to R. C. P. who appears to be having a serious affair, and there is a prose tale by a world-weary man of forty who has seen the lovers, unable to swim, drown in each other's arms despite his efforts to save them. There are lines to Miss S. P. who seems to have loved another, and to C. E., apparently a child. A note in Kingsley's mature hand records that: "All the women in the poems are now married and happy."

For boys like the young Kingsleys with enormous nervous energy, bad health and lively curiosity a Victorian adolescence was a difficult experience. Charles was a highly nervous and excitable child who fell into more than one serious illness. He attributed the stammer which afflicted him all his life to "nerves ruined by croup and brain fever in childhood." In 1834 he had a violent attack of English cholera. From brain fever—what we should call today a nervous breakdown—he suffered severely at sixteen. The cause, it was supposed, was overwork. Control and balance of his energies Charles Kingsley never learned. The admirable results in the occasional periods when he did subject them to discipline show what he might have done; usually he let them pour themselves away in a dozen ill-directed channels. Physically he was capable of immense exertion. He could walk fifty miles in a day or lead the field in a hunt over bad country and dangerous jumps, but he never subdued his long loose-jointed limbs to the accuracy and grace necessary for skill in games and to the end of his life he found it difficult to sit still during a meal. "Unless I get frantic exercise of body," he wrote when he was composing *Hypatia*, "my mind won't work. I should like to have a 'Nicor' to slay every afternoon; wouldn't I write eight hours a day then!" (To Ludlow, June 1852, I, 336.)

His youthful mind raced on like his over-energetic body and the Tory-evangelical ideals proposed for its restraint seemed to his boyhood totally unreasonable fetters. It was only his genuine affection for his father and mother which drove him to fight down the thoughts and impulses he was taught to regard as wicked, and the continual return of those wicked thoughts upon him he could account for only as the malevolence of a personal devil. The single useful direction his youthful mind received was in the "science," the geology and natural history, to which he was encouraged by his father and his schoolmasters. The eternal collecting and classifying gave scope to his quick observation, his accurate visual memory, his eager desire for knowledge on any subject. It taught him, too, that it was right to be curious and he not unnaturally extended that curiosity to the sphere of religion and morals. He began to question and then to doubt the faith of his fathers, and his doubts terrified him. He could not talk to his parents about them; he found no consolation in the Church or in the Bible; he felt unsure of God; he began to be uncertain of his own existence. He saw himself, he put it in one of the poems of the period (*Hypotheses Hypochondriacae*), as

>A speck, an atom—inconsumable—
>Immortal, hopeless, voiceless, powerless!

When he pushed these thoughts out of his conscious mind they sprang up with terrible vitality in his sleep. Those dreams which play so large a part in his novels and those of his brother Henry are not mere literary devices but transcripts from a quivering memory. It was the autobiographical truth of the dream chapter in *Alton Locke* which made Charles Kingsley so insistent on its publication, against the objective criticism of his friends. They took the form, these dreams, of actual spectral illusions, many of them gigantic enlargements of the creatures the boy studied under the microscope, but their most terrible characteristic was the sensation of utter loneliness, of complete detachment from every other being in a cold passionless universe, and that sensation persisted by day. Charles Kingsley never found stability within himself, and it was the memory of that youthful terror which made him cling so closely, once he had learned to know Him, to a personal and loving God, which made him so completely dependent upon the wife through whom he came to that knowledge. He himself diagnosed the visions as maladies of youth, dissipated at last by love and by his discovery of the soothing influence of tobacco, and it was this which made him all his life long annoyingly incapable of understanding the genuine mystic. He was sure that he knew by experience all about that state of mind and that it indicated merely a prolonged immaturity.

During his own immaturity he could find peace only in boisterous hilarity, in feverish activity or in the "vague emotions which were called up by the inanimate creation." Nature, gazed on scientifically or sentimentally, was his great consoler. He was very far from pleased, then, when in 1836 Lord Cadogan presented his father to the comfortable living of St. Luke's, Chelsea.

Only the Queen and the Bishop have London gardens larger than that of St. Luke's rectory but it was a meagre exchange for Devonshire. Nor was Charles delighted by his father's parishioners.

>I find a doleful difference in the society here and at Helston, paradoxical as it may appear. . . . We have nothing but clergymen (very

good and sensible men, but), talking of nothing but parochial schools, and duties, and vestries, and curates, &., &., &. And as for women, there is not a woman in all Chelsea, leaving out my own mother, to be compared to Mrs. Coleridge; and the girls have got their heads crammed full of schools, and district visiting, and baby-linen, and penny clubs. Confound!!! and going about among the most abominable scenes of filth, wretchedness, and indecency, to visit the poor and read the Bible to them. My own mother says the places they go into are fit for no girl to see, and that they should not know such things exist. . . . I regret here, then, as you may suppose, Mrs. D., and Mrs. C.; but, alas! here are nothing but ugly splay-footed beings, three-fourths of whom can't sing, and the other quarter sing miles out of tune, with voices like love-sick parrots. Confound!!! I have got here two or three good male acquaintances who kill the time; one is Sub-Secretary to the Geological Society. . . .

As you may suppose all this clerical conversation (to which I am obliged to listen) has had a slight effect in settling my opinions on these subjects, and I begin to hate these dapper young-ladies-preachers like the devil, for I am sickened and enraged to see "silly women blown about with every wind," falling in love with the preacher instead of his sermon, and with his sermon instead of the Bible. I could say volumes on this subject that should raise both your contempt and indignation. I am sickened with its day-by-day occurrence. As you may suppose, this hatred is πατρόθεν, and the governor is never more rich than when he unbends on these points. (To Cowley Powles, 1836, I, 38.)

Despite his disgust Charles took some share at least in the good works of evangelicalism, for it is on record that he translated Krummacher's sermon on *The Beheading of John the Baptist* for the Religious Tract Society.

Henry built one of his best novels, *The Hillyars and the Burtons*, about the old church at Chelsea and the curious Essex House, now torn down, which stood close to St. Luke's rectory, but the shade of neither Henry VIII nor Thomas More walks Charles Kingsley's pages and there is scarcely a reference to Chelsea in all his writings. His imagination, which was constantly excited by natural scenery, seems to have been almost unmoved by architecture. The descriptions of houses in his novels are not at all like the elaborate affairs one finds in Henry's; they run off usually into historical anecdote.

Charles went to school at King's College in the Strand, walking the four miles from Chelsea, reading, all the way, books taken from his father's excellent library or bought at the second-hand stalls on his route. And because he found in chivalry some of the consolations he was later to find in religion, Spenser's *Faerie Queen* was till the end of his life his favourite book, with Malory's *Morte d'Arthur* not far behind.

CHAPTER III

"PAROXYSMS OF PAIN AND PETULANCE"

IN the autumn of 1838 Charles Kingsley at nineteen matriculated at Magdalene College, Cambridge, an unhappy and bewildered young Victorian. He had strong animal passions and he had been taught that this was something to be ashamed of. He was moved and exalted by beauty, in nature, in art and in woman, and he was uncertain whether these stirrings should be regarded as from God or the devil. He was passionately fond of sport and the family income did not permit of very free expenditure on guns and horses. He wanted to be a soldier but that costly career was out of the question for a younger son of a not too wealthy clergyman. Completely content as he was in the ministry once he had chosen it, Kingsley never lost his romantic enthusiasm for the military life. "It was a constant occupation to him," Mrs. Kingsley tells us, "in all his walks and rides, to be planning fortifications. There is scarcely a hill-side within twenty miles of Eversley, the strong and weak points of which in attack and defence during a possible invasion he has not gone over with as great an intensity of thought and interest as if the enemy were really at hand; and no soldier could have read and re-read Hannibal's campaigns, Creasy's *Fifteen Decisive Battles,* the records of Sir Charles Napier's Indian warfare, or Sir William's Peninsular War, with keener appreciation, his poet's imagination enabling him to fill up the picture and realize the scene, where his knowledge of mere military detail failed. Hence the honour he esteemed it to preach and lecture to the troops at Aldershot, and at Woolwich. His eyes would kindle and fill with tears as he recalled the impression made on him on Whit Sunday, 1858, by the sound heard for the first time, and never to be forgotten, of the clank of the officers' swords and spurs, and the regular tramp of the men as they marched into church, stirring him like the sound of a trumpet." (1890 ed., p. 211.)

But he was destined for the bar and his name was written down at Lincoln's Inn for no particular reason except that law was the other profession open to a gentleman.

Kingsley consequently saw no incentive for labour at Latin, Greek or mathematics beyond the general desirability of taking a good degree. He was irked at the thought of a life of comparative poverty and saw small prospect of anything else. That his ability in writing or drawing might be taken seriously did not occur to him, nor did he think of his enthusiastic shell and plant collecting as anything more than a pastime. He was not concerned about the state of society and the sufferings of the poor; he was too thoroughly occupied with his own state and sufferings.

He began his university career by winning a scholarship and prizes. He was first in the examinations in classics and in mathematics also but he was far from enthusiastic about the university curriculum with its insistence on "the acquirement of confessedly obsolete and useless knowledge, of worn-out philosophies, and scientific theories long exploded." (I, 51.) The only things he thoroughly enjoyed were Professor Sedgwick's field lectures. The old man, mounted on a swift bony nag, proceeded by road to the appointed place of scientific interest while most of his pupils took advantage of the opportunity to do some hard cross-country riding so that the livery stable keepers, who called the exercise "jollygizing," charged more for it than for a day's hunting.

Small wonder then that Kingsley filled his days with riding and rowing, with reckless high-pressure living, only occasionally interspersed with brilliant bursts of study. He speaks of himself at that time as "wicked," and perhaps one is to take as autobiography two passages in *Yeast*:

Love had been to him, practically, ground tabooed and "carnal." What was to be expected? Just what happened—if woman's beauty had nothing holy in it, why should his fondness for it? Just what happens every day—that he had to sow his wild oats for himself, and eat the fruit thereof, and the dirt thereof also. (Chap. I.)

"Had you never the sense of a Spirit in you—a will, an energy, an inspiration, deeper than the region of consciousness and reflection, which, like the wind, blew where it listed, and you heard the sound of it ringing through your whole consciousness, and yet knew not whence it came, or whither it went, or why it drove you on to dare and suffer, to love and hate; to be a fighter, a sportsman, an artist—"

"And a drunkard!" added Lancelot, sadly. (Chap. XVII.)

It seems more probable that what he had in mind when he speaks of wickedness, sensuality and dissipation is the sort of incident he once related to John Martineau. He had gone with some friends on a geologizing expedition which took them so far into the Fens that they stayed for the night at a little country inn. They passed the evening with wine and cards at which a good deal of money changed hands. In the morning when the housemaid came to call Kingsley she brought a hat filled with money which she said she had found in the sitting-room and asked what she was to do with it. He recognized it as his own and then recollections of the night before came flooding back to him. He had won so heavily that he had stuffed his pockets with money and when they would hold no more, filled his hat. The sight of the money and the thought of how he had come by it filled him with a sick disgust and his response was characteristic. He seized the hat and pitched the money out of the window. From that day forth he never played for stakes again and never in his life did he permit a game of cards to be played for money in his house.

Even in scenes less melodramatic than this one Kingsley was usually the central figure of a lively group. His schoolboy queerness had worn away and the qualities which all through life were to make him so singularly beloved by all conditions of men began to appear; he was interested in everybody, curious about everything, ready to take part in any adventure, endlessly ready for talk. "Abounding in conversation," "boundless information," are the phrases his friends use in recalling their impressions of the undergraduate. What manner of man he himself admired at that time one may see in his account of his growing friendship with Charles Mansfield, the brilliant and eccentric young scientist who was expected to be Faraday's successor. Just after Mansfield's premature death in 1855 Kingsley wrote a biographical introduction for his *Paraguay, Brazil, and the Plate,* and the more intimate sketch from which this was elaborated Mrs. Kingsley published in her Memoir. (I, 441.) What attracted Kingsley first in Mansfield was his combination of the graces of body and mind. Physically he had those qualities which Kingsley lacked, skill and beauty of movement. "He was more like an antelope than a man." He shot, he leaped, he rowed, he performed gymnastic feats with daring and precision. And his thinking had the same grace and courage. "He first taught me not to be afraid of truth." Mansfield thought himself at the time a materialist but "his materialism was more spiritual than other men's spiritualism," and the quality by which he fascinated and held his friends in Cambridge and in later life was his earnestness. He had that inner stability for which Kingsley so desperately longed but it was not from Mansfield that he was to attain it.

In the summer of 1839 came the beginning of Kingsley's great revelation. He found the key, the answer to all his riddles, the peace of which he had dreamed. His life was by no means smooth from that point onward but it was secure. He understood, at least dimly, the reason for the universe and he knew how to have faith. From that moment he devoted himself to the proclaiming of his solution to all mankind, for it was the only true solution, the one thing needful which had done all for him and would for any man who would but trust and try it. That he might be wrong never entered his head. He had seen God's truth and God is not mocked. Therein lay his power with his generation; he had suffered in all points like as they had and he kept a continual remembrance and tenderness for that suffering, an understanding and a tolerance so great that he was frequently accused in later life of condoning, even of encouraging, youthful sin, but he had found the way of escape and he preached it with compelling conviction.

CHAPTER IV

"AMAMUS"

CHARLES KINGSLEY and Frances Eliza Grenfell loved at first sight; they found each in the other the solution of their religious doubts; they sustained each other through all vicissitudes, financial and celestial, with much happy companionship along the way; and they wrote upon their tombstone: "Amavimus, amamus, amabimus."

They met first on July 6, 1839. "That," Charles liked to say, "was my real wedding day." Fanny was twenty-five and the daughter of a good many earls; Charles, a Cambridge undergraduate of twenty whose rector father was taking temporary duty at Checkenden in Oxfordshire near Ipsden where Fanny was visiting. There is a family tradition that she saw him first on horseback—he rode uncommonly well—and undoubtedly one may take the opening chapter of *Yeast* as a fairly accurate description of the scene:

That face and figure, and the spirit which spoke through them, entered his heart at once, never again to leave it. . . .

"What a horribly ugly face!" said Argemone, to herself; "but so clever, and so unhappy!"

"His peculiar character," Mrs. Kingsley tells us in her Memoir, "had not been understood hitherto, and his heart had been half asleep. It woke up now, and never slept again. For the first time he could speak with perfect freedom, and be met with answering sympathy. And gradually as the new friendship (which yet seemed old—from the first more of a recognition than an acquaintance) deepened into intimacy, every doubt, every thought, every failing, every sin, as he would call it, was laid bare. Counsel was asked and given, all things in heaven and earth discussed. . . .

"Two months of such intercourse passed away only too quickly." (I, 44.)

Charles at this time she says, was "just like his own Lancelot in *Yeast*," and most commentators recognize in Argemone a portrait of Fanny Grenfell:

> Her features were aquiline and grand, without a shade of harshness; her eyes shone out like twin lakes of still azure, beneath a broad marble cliff of polished forehead; her rich chestnut hair rippled downward round the towering neck. With her perfect masque, and queenly figure, and earnest upward gaze, she might have been the very model from which Raphael conceived his glorious St. Catherine—the ideal of the highest womanly genius, softened into self-forgetfulness by girlish devotion. (Chap. I.)

Except for the colouring the description tallies well with photographs of Miss Grenfell and the impressions of people who knew her. She was not so much beautiful as striking with large features usually described as "Spanish," masses of straight black hair and big dark eyes. Of those eyes a reminiscent letter writer to *The Times* tells a characteristic tale. He was a small boy looking on curiously at an evening party where Kingsley was something of a lion. Suddenly a deep voice proclaimed: "There is one thing I consider more beautiful than anything else in the world." Silence, while the company waits expectant for the wisdom of the great man, who booms: "My wife's eyes." (G. S. Lanyard, *The Times*, June 14, 1919.)

Frances Eliza, born in 1814, was the eleventh daughter of Pascoe Grenfell of Taplow Court, M.P. for Marlow and later for Penrhyn. The Grenfells traced their lineage to the famous Sir Richard Grenville. The fortunes of their particular branch of the family were established early in the eighteenth century by Pascoe Grenfell, merchant, of Penzance, whose grandsons became M.P.'s and justices of the peace and began to find brides in the peerage. Fanny's father married twice, first his cousin, Charlotte Granville, and then the Hon. Georgiana St. Leger, youngest daughter of the fifth Viscount Doneraile. She died when Fanny was four years old. Charles Pascoe, Fanny's elder brother, who became guardian of his sisters on his father's death in 1837, seems to have done uncommonly well by them—two of them married peers—and had no intention of letting Fanny throw herself away. She and Charles were forbidden to see each other but, partly through the sympathetic aid of Charles's mother, they carried on for three years an enormous and mutually formative correspondence. They kept their commonplace-books, too, for each other: "Finish this book," writes Charles in his, "with your own ideas or passages that strike you, and I will finish yours, and we will compare notes either on earth or in heaven."

At the time of her meeting with Charles Kingsley Miss Grenfell was a fairly ardent disciple of Pusey. Like her sister, whom Froude persuaded from a convent, and so many other high-souled young people of the day, she had all but made up her mind to embrace the celibate life, when she fell in love, profoundly and enduringly; but her heart went before her head and Charles Kingsley had to marshal all his logic and the ardour of his own new convictions on the subject to prove to her that she would be serving God more truly in holy matrimony than as a nun. It was for that that he began to write a prose history of St. Elizabeth of Hungary, later reworked into *The Saint's Tragedy*. Each chapter as it was completed was copied into a great folio destined for a bridal gift, and adorned with delicate drawings in pen and ink, drawings which, in their passionately religious voluptuousness, are a good indication of the state of the young man's mind. That book—the wedding day came before it was finished—is now in the British Museum and the Preface gives, especially in some paragraphs not quoted in Mrs. Kingsley's Memoir of her husband, a very clear picture of their mutual attitude; shows, too, why Kingsley felt it so continually necessary all his life to harp upon the theme of sacred matrimony.

You know what first turned my attention to the Oxford Tracts; but you do *not* know that my own heart, too, strangely yearned towards them from the first; that if they had not, I felt from secret warning, struck at the root of our wedded bliss, I too had been ensnared! [He had gone even further than this. He wrote, May 11, 1849: "I have longed for Rome, and boldly faced the consequences of joining Rome." (I, 202.)] Love saved me! Tender Lord! some men's afflictions, but my bliss, has been a guide to heaven! . . . Is human love unholy—inconsistent with the perfect worship of the Creator? Is marriage less honourable than virginity? Are the duties, the relations, the daily food of men, of earth or heaven? Is nature a holy type or a foul prison to our spirits? Is genius the reflex of God's mind, or the self-will of man? These were the heart questions! And in this book I try to solve them. If I succeed, then we are safe! If not, our *honest* home is Popery! Popery and celibacy! You felt it thus, baby, when you said "In that case Romanism *and* a nunnery, must have been my end!"

Bless you for those words! No woman worthy of my love, could marry, holding Popish or Tractarian doctrines, without degradation, and a wounded conscience! Lord! Thou hast saved us! Thou, Thou alone!

But I do not fear! God will look on my prayers, my fasts, my study, my watchings! and we are safe! He will root out from your understanding, as He has done from your heart, all which predisposed you to the sensebound and thankless Manichaeism of Oxford, as He has done for me! He will give you the true faith, darling, by His Holy Spirit, and by my poor words, a reason to give to others, for the hope which is in you!

But this was after his own conversion. At the time when he met Miss Grenfell he was in a period of tormented mental questioning but "before he left Oxfordshire he was so far shaken in his doubts, that he promised to read his Bible once more—to pray—to open his heart to the Light, if the Light would but come. All, however, was dark for a time, and the conflict between hopes and fears for the future, and between faith and unbelief, was so fierce and bitter, that when he returned to Cambridge, he became reckless and nearly gave up all for lost." (I, 45.) The miseries of being a poor man tormented him with renewed vigour and he seriously contemplated emigration, that favourite nineteenth century remedy later to be resorted to by his brother and both his sons. Thirty years later (May 11, 1874) he wrote to his wife:

We are at Omaha! . . . and opposite to us is Council Bluffs!! Thirty years ago the palavering ground of trappers and Indians (now all gone), and to that very spot, which I had known of from a boy, and all about it, I meant to go in despair . . . as soon as I took my degree, and throw myself into the wild life to sink or swim, escaping from a civilization which only tempted me and maddened me with the envy of a poor man! Oh! how good God has been to me. Oh! how when I saw those Bluffs yesterday morning I thanked God for you—for everything, and stared at them till I cried. (II, 433.)

There were long theological struggles to be gone through before he found steady faith, struggles which it is interesting to watch because in fighting them he found a solution for his generation of the great problem religion *vs.* science, a solution which made it possible for him, twenty years later, to meet the *Origin of Species* without terror, though in awe, and to be a friend to Darwin, Huxley and Wallace. He had watched his father struggling to reconcile the carnal life and the spiritual, trying to decide how far he ought to despise the beauty of the world, how far to think it a thing of God, and in a curious MS. document, *The Snake's Book,* part of which later developed into *Yeast,* he analyses this state of mind.

There was in him a genial love of the beautiful, a seeing eye for God's earth. He dared a love of poetry, music, scenery—art of all kinds. And yet all hampered, choked, as being a thing apart, a tertium quid in his life. Carnal he dared not call it—his conscience forbade him. Spiritual he dared not call it—his religious system said nothing about it. His fellow parsons nothing.

Intellectual then it was to be, this love of the beautiful, a word which he himself did not understand, for he was no scholar. And thus divorced from that which he knew to be his highest life, the beautiful was a subject for mere prurient dilettantism, scenery hunting, flower and fossil collecting, sketching and ballad-reading—not without secret novel debauches—and so lived in him, godless, meaningless, a life in death.

This triple tangle the younger Kingsley cut with a blow: the universe is the temple of the living God who is to be worshiped by man with his body as well as his soul; polyps are to be admired as evidences of the divine ingenuity; drains repaired that Christians may have health and strength to serve God; Jesus, the God-man is the archetype of man's divinity.

Many doctrines puzzled Charles Kingsley before he found his reconciling formula. The doctrine of the Trinity was difficult'; so was the Athanasian creed, later one of his bulwarks. He could get no help from the clergy; they seemed to him to have built up upon insufficient Biblical grounds a huge superstructure of their own imaginings, but Miss Grenfell ministered both to his heart and his reason. She sent him books: Coleridge's *Aids to Reflection,* Carlyle's *Miscellanies, Past and Present* and *French Revolution.* Nearly ten years later (April 26, 1849) Kingsley wrote to Carlyle: "At a time when I was drowned in sloth and wickedness, your works awoke in me the idea of Duty; the belief in a living righteous God, who is revealing Himself in the daily events of History; the knowledge that all strength and righteousness, under whatever creed it may appear, comes from Him alone; and last, but not least, the belief in the Perfect Harmony of the Physical with the Spiritual Universe."

With this settling of his spiritual ideas Kingsley began to "reform" in his outward actions also, read seven or eight hours a day, gave up hunting and driving, made a solemn vow against cards, and at last could write to Miss Grenfell: "Saved—saved from the wild pride and darkling tempests of scepticism, and from the sensuality and dissipation into which my own rashness and vanity had hurried me before I knew you. Saved from a hunter's life on the Prairies, from becoming a savage, and perhaps worse. Saved from all this, and restored to my country and my God, and able to believe. And I do believe, firmly and practically, as a subject of prayer, and a rule of every action of my life." (I, 53.)

It was then that he began to hear a still small voice directing him to the Church, to feel more and more daily that it was for a clergyman's life that "both my *physique* and *morale* were intended—that the profession will check and guide the faulty parts of my mind, while it gives full room for my energy." (I, 53.) Charles Kingsley had found the standard against which to brace himself. "Everything I do, in my studies, in my plans, in my actions is now and shall be done in reference first to God, and then to you." (1890 ed., p. 17.)

The energy swung itself at once to the making up in six months of vast arrears of neglected study. He took his degree in the winter of 1841 as senior optime in mathematics with a first class in classics, reading himself ill in the process and spending three weeks after the mathematical tripos in agonies of pain, with leeches on his head.

So violently was Kingsley's mind occupied with his new labours, emotions, beliefs and problems that far less poetry sprang from his courtship than one might expect. *Palinodia* and *A Hope* are the only verses of the time which he ever thought worthy of print. The Commonplace-Book contains some stanzas on *The Birth of Alexander,* headed for Miss Grenfell, "To the pure all things are pure." He believed himself now at an age in which "a man is at once too old and too young to write poetry—too old to write it according to the *empirical* aesthetic standard, by which he wrote it in boyhood—too young to write it by the *rational* aesthetic standard, by which he ought to impart his knowledge in mature manhood."

In February he left Cambridge and went down to his birthplace, Holne in Devonshire, to read for Holy Orders and to recover from his long nervous strain. He felt very old, he wrote his mother, like Manfred. He continued of course to correspond copiously with Miss Grenfell, urging her to read Tennyson, the most beautiful poetry of the last fifteen years; telling her of his increased liking for the Low Church School whose knowledge of the human heart he found refreshing after the cold dogmatism of the High. His opinion, not conviction, for he may be wrong, is that those men are disingenuous, cowardly and false. He was distressed at Miss Grenfell's use of the term "father-confessor." "I am sure that it is unwomanly for woman, and unmanly for man to make any *man* his *father*-confessor. All that another should know of our hearts should be told in the almost involuntary overflowing of love, not in the midst of blushes and trembling to a man who dares to arrogate *moral* superiority over us." (1890 ed., p. 24.)

Early in July Kingsley was ordained at Farnham. He had some hours of agony about the verity of his vocation. Was he desiring to be a deacon in order to serve God or that he might marry his beloved? He prayed that the examiners might reject him if his motives were not pure and "after this what can I consider my acceptance but as a proof that I have not sinned too deeply for escape!" (I, 72.)

On July 17 he conducted his first service as curate in Eversley Church, Hampshire, quieting his nervousness and his terror of offending people by reminding himself that he was speaking not on his own authority but God's. He was daily formulating convictions about the right way of life for a clergyman and he set them all down for Miss Grenfell. The ascetic neglect of health then so much affected seemed to him mere laziness and untidiness. "I could not do half the little good I do do here, if it were not for that strength and activity which some consider coarse and degrading. Many clergymen would half kill themselves if they did what I do. And though they might walk about as much they would neglect exercise of the arms and chest, and become dyspeptic or consumptive." (I, 83.) Everything was for the glory of God. He delighted in composing sermons while he was cutting wood and in talking one moment to one man about the points of a horse and the next to another about the mercy of God to sinners. His chief reading was to be the Bible, read as he had never read it before, but he planned also a study of Maurice, Kant and St. Augustine.

The consistently high moral tone of the letters of this period is due not merely to the earnestness of the young man in his new vocation but to the editing of Mrs. Kingsley who prepared them for her Memoir by omitting every phrase and sentiment which he would not have uttered in the pulpit. When the manuscript originals from which she worked are extant one can see how deliberately this was done, also that while she usually indicates omissions by dots she frequently gives no indication of change of date, of the combination of two letters into one or the alteration of words or phrases which she considered too coarse or undignified for publication. It is possible in many cases to restore the letters to their original state, especially those to Hughes and Maurice, but of the love letters very few are available.

In the summer of 1842 the love letters ceased altogether for a year. A degree and a curacy were not enough to satisfy Miss Grenfell's family. Fanny was sent to the Continent with an elderly friend, Lady Gainsborough, and even correspondence was forbidden. The lovers bowed to the decree with proper reverence but persisted in their belief that Providence would permit their love to flourish one day, in heaven if not on earth. Kingsley wrote a long last letter of instruction and suggestion for the period of separation:

Though there may be clouds between us now, yet they are safe and dry, free from storm and rains—our parted state now is quiet grey weather, under which all tender things will spring up and grow, beneath the warm damp air, till they are ready for the next burst of sunshine to hurry them into blossom and fruit.[1] Let us plant and rear all tender thoughts, knowing surely that those who sow in tears shall reap in joy. . . .

Some minds are too "subjective." What I mean is, that they may devote themselves too much to the subject of self and mankind. Now man is not "the noblest study of man." (What lies the trashy poets of Pope and Johnson's age tell, which are taken as gospel, and acted upon because the idol said so!) God is the noblest study of man. He

---

[1] He liked this figure so well that he used it in *The Saint's Tragedy*, III, 1:
> You might have made this widowed solitude
> A holy rest—a spell of soft grey weather,
> Beneath whose fragrant dews all tender thoughts
> Might bud and burgeon.

is the only study fit for a woman devoted to Him. And Him you can study in three ways:

1st. From His dealings in History. This is the real Philosophy of History. Read Arnold's *Lectures on Modern History*. . . .

2nd. From His image as developed in Christ the ideal, and in all good men—great good men. . . .

3rd. From His works. Study nature—not scientifically—that would take eternity, to do it so as to reap much moral good from it. Superficial physical science is the devil's spade, with which he loosens the roots of the trees prepared for the burning! Do not study matter for its own sake, but as the countenance of God! Try to extract every line of beauty, every association, every moral reflection, every inexpressible feeling from it. Study the forms and colours of leaves and flowers, and the growth and habits of plants; not to classify them, but to admire them and adore God. Study the sky! Study water! Study trees! Study the sounds and scents of nature! Study all these, as beautiful in themselves, in order to re-combine the elements of beauty; next, as allegories and examples from whence moral reflections may be drawn; next as types of certain tones of feelings, etc., but remain (yourself) in God-dependence, superior to them. Learn what feelings they express, but do not let them mould the tone of your mind; else by allowing a melancholy day to make you melancholy, you worship the creature more than the Creator. No sight but has some beauty and harmony!

Read geology—Buckland's *Bridgewater Treatise* and you will rise up awe-struck and cling to God!

Study the human figure, both as intrinsically beautiful and as expressing mind. It only expresses the broad natural childish emotions, which are just what you want to return to. Study "natural language"—I mean the "language of attitude." It is an inexhaustible source of knowledge and delight, and enables one human being to understand another so perfectly. Draw,—learn to draw and paint figures. No one with such freedom of touch in landscape and perception of physical beauty requires anything but a few simple rules, and some common attention to attitudes, to draw exquisitely. If you can command your hand in drawing a tree, you can in drawing a face. Perfect your colouring. . . . It will keep your mind employed on objective studies, and save you from morbid introversion of mind—brooding over fallen man. It will increase your perception of beauty, and thereby your own harmony of soul and love to God!

Practice music.—I am going to learn myself, merely to be able to look after my singers. . . . Music is such a vent for the feelings. . . .

Study medicine. . . . I am studying it. . . . Make yourself thoroughly acquainted with the wages, wants, and habits, and prevalent diseases of the poor wherever you go.

Let your mind freely forth. Only turn it inwards at prayer time, to recollect sins of which you were conscious at the time, not to look for fresh ones. . . .

Let your studies, then, be objective entirely. . . .

Use your senses much, and your mind little. Feed on Nature, and do not try to understand it. It will digest itself. It did so when you were a baby the first time! Look round you much. Think little and read less! Never give way to reveries. Have always some employment in your hands. . . . When you are doing nothing at night, pray and praise!

See how much a day can do! I have since nine this morning, cut wood for an hour; spent an hour and more in prayer and humiliation, and thereby established a chastened but happy tone, which lasts till now; written six or seven pages of a difficult part of my essay; taught in the school; thought over many things while walking; gone round two-thirds of the parish visiting and doctoring; and written all this. Such days are lives—and happy ones. One has no time to be miserable, and one is ashamed to invent little sorrows for one's self while one is trying to relieve such griefs in others as would kill us, if we gave way or fancied about them! . . .

Keep a common-place book, and put into it, not only facts and thoughts, but observations on form, and colour, and nature, and little sketches, even to the form of beautiful leaves. They will all have their charm, all do their work in consolidating your ideas. Put everything into it. . . . Strive to put every idea into tangible form, and write it down. Distrust every idea which you cannot put into words; or rather distrust your own conception of it. Not so with feelings. Therefore write much. Try to put everything in its place in the great system . . . seeing the realities of Heaven and Earth. (Eversley,[1] August 1842, I, 86.)

Kingsley also composed prayers which they were to offer at the same hour during the separation:

After the petition ending . . . "and to turn their hearts," Insert

"That it may please thee to turn the hearts of our families and to teach them thy truth!"

"That it may please thee to allow us to meet in heaven!"

"That it may please thee to join us together in holy matrimony in the days of our youth and health!"

"That it may please thee to preserve us through the miseries and dangers of celibacy, and to sanctify to us this our great affliction that by it we may become more worthy both of each other and of thee."

Miss Grenfell wrote into a thick locked book all the letters she would have sent to Charles and marked it to be given "unread by

---

[1] From this point on I have omitted the place line on letters written from Eversley.

anyone" to him in case of her death before they were united. The separation scenes, then, and the behaviour of the lovers in *Yeast,* which to the twentieth century appear manufactured, are pure realism.

Charles had his mother's sympathy and help during his trial, but Miss Grenfell had to endure her family's opposition and was perhaps instrumental in bringing about the appointment which finally melted it and made her marriage possible. Her sister Emily's husband, the Rev. Lord Sydney Godolphin Osborne, with whom Kingsley later worked so vigorously for sanitary reform, got him the promise, through Lord Portman, of a small living and in the meantime a good curacy, Pimperne, near Blanford.

He was married in January 1844 and was to settle in Pimperne in the spring but before that time the Rector of Eversley died and Sir John Cope, the patron, urged thereto by one of his church wardens, Augustus Granville Stapleton, who had been impressed by Kingsley's labours as curate, presented him to the living.

CHAPTER V

"VILLAGE SERMONS"

SIR JOHN got something quite other than he had bargained for. At least so one deduces from the only literary portrait there is of him, drawn by Kingsley's friend John Malcolm Ludlow in the *Economic Review* (October 1893). Ludlow was the most socialistic of the Christian Socialists and a trained journalist. Copes live still at Bramshill Park today and the neighbourhood is full of their relatives and friends. Personal recollections therefore of previous heads of the family are too numerous and nebulous to make it possible to construct a definitive picture. If Ludlow's is not correct it ought to be, it makes so good a story.

Sir John Cope, who was seventy-six at the time of Kingsley's presentation, hated his nephew and heir, a clergyman, and this gave him a general dislike for the cloth. Moreover he was a hunting squire of the old school, a strict game preserver and a five-bottle man who had been a boon companion of the Prince Regent. He had casually observed the long-legged young curate following the hounds on foot, had heard tales from Cambridge of his hard riding and had imagined that it would be pleasant to have in the rectory a fellow who understood hunting and would drink the evenings away with him at Bramshill. He was astounded to discover that a keen sportsman could also be an earnest young parson who took his work seriously, asked for money to build schools, had no hesitation in saying that some of the tenants' cottages were not fit to live in, devoted his days to parish visiting and his nights to lending libraries and coal clubs. For all his disappointment Sir John helped his young rector materially; he furnished a good many of the features for the portrait of Squire Lavington in *Yeast*.

A less energetic man than Charles Kingsley would have been appalled by the tasks before him. His predecessor had been not only incompetent and negligent but dishonest, decamping at last with a good portion of the parish funds so that the new rector had arrears to pay on the Poor Rates and the curate's salary. There was of course no dilapidation money for the rectory which, set a little below the crest of a hill and surrounded by ponds, was so damp and badly drained that heavy rains caused actual floods in all the ground-floor rooms and master and servants were sometimes up all night bailing with buckets. Expensive drainage work was done but the place was never really healthful and the Kingsleys were often forced to flee to the seaside or to rent a house on higher ground in the village.

The church, too, had been shockingly neglected; the altar cloth was moth-eaten and farmers pastured their sheep in the churchyard. Improvements suggested by the new rector were regarded with the usual rural suspicion. Kingsley was able to institute monthly communions only by promising himself to supply wine for the celebration. There were few rich families in the parish so that the charities fell almost wholly upon the incumbent and it was long before the living, though considered a good one, £600 a year, became remunerative.

His parish with its seven hundred fifty parishioners was, Kingsley used to say, like a dachshund, all at the ends and very little in the middle. It was well that the rector liked to ride and walk. He loved the high bleak moors with their great patches of self-sown Scotch firs. Eversley lay on the borders of Old Windsor Forest and on what had been in the days of the French war one of the regular smugglers' routes to London. Most of the older men in the district had smuggled in their time or connived at it, though they now limited their activities to poaching. It was for this reason that Kingsley himself never took a gun in hand. He declined, too, to be made a magistrate lest he have to sit in judgment on members of his congregation. There was nothing, however, to stand in the way of his being an ardent fisherman and though when he first came to Eversley he could not afford to hunt, his knowledge of horses and dogs was a distinct asset to his ministry. When the first confirmation after his induction was announced and those who wished to be confirmed were invited to the rector's study for weekly instruction, the whips and stablemen at Bramshill—Sir John was M.F.H.—delegated the stud groom to report to the rector that they had all been confirmed once but would be very happy to come again if Mr. Kingsley wished it.

Kingsley really understood these parishioners of his and admired them, the dark-haired ruddy handsome men, swaggering in their youth but in old age stately with a princely courtesy; shrewd, too, thanks to their dash of wild forest blood, beyond the average yokel. He was not alarmed by their superstition, their belief in ghosts "with no heads and jackboots on." Better believe in ghosts than believe in nothing but self. With a wisdom rare in those days among the clergy he tried to make the services in Eversley Church pleasing not to Charles Kingsley but to the "clods" of Eversley village.

If I were inclined [he wrote to Derwent Coleridge, February 12, 1851] to make my own "tastes and thoughts" the test of what should be restored I should have long ago adopted daily service, the Litany read from the nave, ceremonials as gorgeous and intricate as I could afford: lights and censers—the whole machinery almost of St. Barnabas—and emptied my church and driven God's poor back again to wander as sheep that have no shepherd. . . . I not sympathize with St. Barnabas and Mr. Bennet! It has been *the* temptation which I have had most to fight against, to imitate him. Not a Sunday do I enter my own Church without longing to do a thousand things which I *dare not do for the sake of God's people*. . . . The sense of deadness, desolation, unreality (as far as the worshipers are concerned) Puritan Manichaean contempt of Beauty, Art, Symbolism in our modern worship, weighs me down, God forgive me, Sunday after Sunday . . . and yet I am content. I am content not to galvanize into fictitious life for my own self-will, to please my own taste, that which the Lord of the Church, has taken from the Church for His own purposes . . . when in despite of their unmeaningness to the many, in despite of the repugnance of the many to them, these things are wilfully adopted and forced on the middle and lower classes, because a few of the upper classes benefit from them, they are at best fopperies, and may become deadly sins. . . . All things are lawful for me—crucifixes, images, processions, chantings, incense, flowers, festivals, fasts—but all things are not expedient. And I will eat no meat—and have no daily service while the world standeth, if it cause my brother to offend, as these things do . . . many have, unfortunately, learnt to connect all this with Romanism; the creed which they abhor and despise—sooner than have which, they would remain heathens. And therefore any movement which begins with these external restorations . . . will have no hold on the minds of the People . . . will, and indeed does, loosen their faith in the real *"Gentlemen and Ladies"* (and do not fancy that I do not love those words, I who have had from boyhood to fight against the temptation to the proudest worship of family—as the descendant of men who were gentlemen and landlords before a Norman set foot in England—and that family pride intensified, as it always is by ruin and poverty) . . . I feel how indispensable, how precious a real aristocracy (such as the English is more nearly than any that ever has appeared on God's earth) is, and always will be.

On questions of teetotalism and Sunday amusements also Kingsley took, for the sake of his people, positions highly unconventional in a clergyman. He believed in the Sunday opening of museums and picture galleries and took active part in the agitation for the opening of the Crystal Palace on the Sabbath. "I have often fancied," he wrote to Maurice (July 1856), "I should like to see the great useless naves and aisles of our cathedrals turned into museums and winter gardens, where people might take their Sunday walks, and yet attend service." (I, 484.) In his own parish he encouraged Sunday cricket. It is "better than beer," he used to say to his sons, "and the poor lads don't get a chance to play on week-day: but remember *you* do." (II, 8.) In a Westminster Abbey sermon in 1873 he urged the Sunday afternoon opening of the British Museum as a means of promoting temperance but he had for years distressed many good members of the Temperance Society by refusing to advocate teetotalism. That a man should be a teetotaler, rather than a drunkard, needs, he agreed, no proof; also that a man should go about in a sack rather than be a fop, and waste time and money on dress, but temperance in beer, like temperance in clothes, is at once a more rational and a higher virtue either than sackcloth or water. His own pet remedies against drunkenness were characteristic: proper sanitation of the workingman's dwelling so that he might live in a wholesome atmosphere which did not provoke a craving for drink, and the establishment of small associate home-breweries where he can brew his own pure beer at a low price and free himself from the tyranny of the public house.

On social questions of this kind Kingsley thought in terms of the people yet his social ideal was actually not a democratic but a feudal one. He stated it quite definitely in "My Political Creed," written for the *Christian Socialist* December 14, 1850: I am a monarchist. I prefer despotism to a republic, a rule which will become either, as in America, the puppet of the Press or, as in

England, the slave of the moneyed class. There can be no enfranchisement of the people without monarchy. The crown in England now has too little power; capital, too much. Revolution is on the way though no country is better able to avert it. That the will of the People is the source of power is an atheistic doctrine. There is no authority but God. The earthly authorities which exist are ordained of Him.

This in the 1840's was radicalism: it conceived the landlord as having duties; the poor as having rights. The duties of the clergyman of course under such a God-directed system were heavy and Kingsley's personal practice strode always vigorously ahead of his preaching. For years at Eversley he never dined out during the winter months when cottage lectures in the outlying districts and an adult school held in the rectory dining-room occupied six evenings a week. A Sunday school met there, morning and afternoon, and he established a coal club, a shoe club, a loan fund, a maternal society, a lending library and a singing class, on Hullah's plan, to improve the church music. Mrs. Kingsley, though helping and approving behind the scenes, did not, apparently, take a very active personal part in parish work. Aged parishioners who speak of Kingsley with tireless enthusiasm remember her simply as a very fine lady who admirably kept her home, and there is a possibly revealing sentence in a lecture on "Woman's Work in a Country Parish" which Kingsley delivered in 1855: "It is said that a clergyman's wife ought to consider the parish as *her* flock as well as her husband's. It may be so: I believe the dogma to be much over-stated just now." Kingsley remembered, too, his youthful boredom in Chelsea and never let shop talk spoil the flavour of a family dinner. Before his marriage he drew up a regular rule of life for the household, "not so as to become a law, but a custom":

Family prayers before breakfast; 8:30 to 10, household matters; 10 to 1, studying divinity, or settling parish accounts and business—our doors open for poor parish visitants; between 1 and 5, go out in all weathers, to visit sick and poor, and to teach in the school; in the evening we will draw, and feed the intellect and the fancy. . . . We must devote from 9 to 12 on Monday mornings to casting up our weekly bills and accounts, and make a rule never to mention them, if possible, at any other time; and never to talk of household matters, unless urgent, but between 9 and 10 in the morning; nor of parish business in the evening. (I, 108.)

We will hunt out all the texts in the Bible about masters and servants, to form rules upon them; and our rules we will alter and improve upon in time, as we find out more and more of the true relation in which we ought to stand to those whom God has placed under us. ... I feel more and more that the new principle of considering a servant as a trader, who sells you a certain amount of work for a certain sum of money, is a devil's principle, and that we must have none of it, but return as far as we can to the patriarchial and feudal spirit towards them. (I, 109.)

Mrs. Kingsley records that at the time of her husband's death all the servants in his house had lived with him from seventeen to twenty-six years, and those who had left the rectory previously, had left to marry and go to homes of their own.

The rectory where these rules were practised is an agreeable rambling house with two-story bow windows, enormous rooms and leagues of passage and stairway. Most of it was built in the seventeenth century but Mrs. Kingsley gave it a modern air with sofas, drapes, and watercolours, an engraved Raphael over the chimneypiece—"La Belle Jardinière," the wedding gift of Cowley Powles —, a quantity of little shelves and cupboards and plenty of pretty souvenirs and curiosities. The house faces east onto a lawn with three great fir trees, then a sunk fence and the winding road that runs to Bramshill Park. The Rector's study on the south side of the house is a rectangular room of uninteresting proportions. Its carpet of course was red; so were the chairs and heavy curtains. The tall French window opens onto the garden. The stretch of grass there between the flower beds, Kingsley's special place for pacing up and down, was known as the quarter-deck. It is there, in a soft high-crowned hat, that most photographs show Charles Kingsley. Lowes Dickinson painted him in his red-cushioned chair by the open window, flowers in a vase on the table, a fishing-rod propped in the corner, a pile of books on the floor. An outdoor portrait would have shown also a long clay pipe. His churchwardens Kingsley bought by the barrel and used to secrete all over his parish, behind rose trees in the garden, under whin bushes on the moor, from which, on a round of clerical calls, he would suddenly extract one, swiftly fill and light it and smoke a few soothing puffs.

Few of the photographs show the household pets but they were numerous and beloved. Cats there were always for Kingsley was

Eversley Rectory and Church

MRS. CHARLES KINGSLEY

very fond of them. The stables had a white cat and the house a black or tabby. The Scotch terrier, Dandy, was for thirteen years a parish character, attending cottage lectures and lessons in the village school. Then there was Sweep, the fine black retriever, and Victor, the dachshund, named in honour of the Queen whose gift he was. Kingsley had a great love of fine horses but even in the years when he felt able to keep a hunter he never indulged himself in anything better than an old hack picked up cheap for parish work. Some of his best feats of hard riding were performed on an aged mare appropriately known as Puff. Wild pets were cherished as well as the domestic ones: a family of running toads inhabiting a hole in the garden bank; a pair of sand wasps which returned every spring, and their children's children, to a crack in Kingsley's dressing-room window; a favourite slow-worm in the churchyard; and innumerable birds, the most wonderful, he said, of God's creations. He believed quite firmly that animals, like man, would continue their existence in some blessed future state.

Beyond the garden were the stables, the outhouses and the glebe, in all a not inconsiderable establishment.

To the north of the rectory lies the churchyard, only a hedge between. Kingsley made it into a little arboretum with rare trees and shrubs, so that the parishioners might have something lovely to look at as they gossiped together before the service. The churchyard was admired but it was the fashion then, and seems to be so still, to speak of the Eversley church as ugly because it was not Gothic. As a matter of fact its square red-brick tower and simple classic lines are very good. The builder of the church, John James, was a workman of Wren. An extraordinary tablet in the nave claims that he was architect of the Greenwich Hospital and most of Wren's fifty-seven City churches. His chancel screen at Eversley Kingsley, alas, with a touch of the neo-Gothic weakness which he so often ridiculed in others, had painted in Pre-Raphaelite polychrome, selecting texts to be inscribed upon it in Old English lettering and designing the pots of pseudo-medieval lilies which decorate the altar side. He seems also to have been pleased by the introduction of "a large east window in the perpendicular style . . . in place of a paltry round-headed one which before existed." (Sir William H. Cope, Bart., *History of the Parish of Eversley* reprinted from *Eversley Parish Magazine,* 1886.) Parts of the chancel do actually date from the end of the fifteenth century.

His parish stood always in the centre of Charles Kingsley's imagination but even in those early days his horizons were never narrowed to its boundaries. He was deeply concerned in the '40's over the parlous state of church and nation and, like most men under thirty, dreamed of medicining them with a Review. It was to be a periodical in which everyone should be responsible for his own signed article and in which, instead of all attempting to pose as Macaulays and Lockharts, they should talk of such subjects as honestly concern young men. Its mottoes should be Anti-Manichaeism and Anti-Atheism, and it should concern itself with the Christianizing of democracy, that new element in Church and State which, whether it be good or evil, is now too strong to be stopped. Kingsley firmly wrote himself down as no revolutionary but he believed that true democracy, the rights of man as man, was the very pith and marrow of the New Testament. The Church must, he argued, in the divinest sense, make friends of the Mammon of Unrighteousness, the new commercial aristocracy, the scientific go-aheadism of the day, which must save her as she must save them.

The ideal review never emerged but the letters about it laid the lines for Kingsley's friendship with Anthony Froude. In 1848, March 30, he writes while on a visit to Powles at Oxford: "Froude gets more and more interesting. We had such a conversation this morning—the crust is breaking, and the *man* coming through that cold polished shell." (I, 153.) The friendship was established on an enduring basis a year later by Kingsley's impulsively courageous behaviour when Froude pulled down the University's wrath upon his head with the publication of *The Nemesis of Faith,* that heartbroken cry of a youthful seeker after truth which shrilled to an orthodox generation like wanton blasphemy. Sewell, Senior Tutor of Exeter, burnt the dangerous novel in his lecture hall and Froude was compelled to resign both his fellowship and a prospective headmastership in Australia. His father, the Archdeacon of Totnes, cut off at the same time all parental support. Kingsley, who was in Devonshire with his wife and children, immediately wrote Froude to come to him, and there he stayed for two months quite unconscious that Kingsley was being suspected of heresy because he harboured a heretic and was receiving letters of protest by every post. Kingsley's parents were of course terribly distressed, and he writes to his mother:

A thousand thanks for your letter, because you have honestly and lovingly spoken your whole mind to me.

But you will really break my heart, which has sorrows and perplexities in plenty, if you thus say that I misunderstand you. I honestly believe you one of the most thoroughly liberal-minded persons I ever met with. I owe to you, under God, much of my own liberalism, as well as nineteen-twentieths of the groundwork of my moral and intellectual training: and it seems to me quite dreadful that you should think me ungrateful, or that I impute to you fear of the world; if I did, which I do not, filial reverence would make me silent on the point. All I meant to say was, that I thought your motherly anxiety for my character made you pain yourself more than was needed. I assure you that I meant no more.

I cannot but believe that dangerous as my present position may seem, I am not tempting God; that he has, by a train of circumstances, pointed out the course which I ought to take, and that he will help me through it. Pray for me that whether right or wrong now, I may be taught what is right, and pray for me that I may be kept unspotted. Froude is no atheist, no man less so. He is now writing a work on God, in the most reverent spirit. Neither is he an infidel, not even a mere Unitarian, though he has very wrong views about our blessed Lord's divinity, while he admires and loves his character and the revelation which he believes was made through him. And on this point it is, that I hope to do him good, by shewing him that the doctrines of the Gospel instead of contradicting, confirm all the truths which he reverences most.

But the more I see of him, the more I learn to love the true doctrines of the gospel, because I see more and more that only in faith and love to the incarnate *God,* our Saviour can the cleverest, as well as the simplest, find the peace of God which passes understanding.

The sentiments in Froude's book are *not* his own: they are those of too many men, alas! now. It is a spiritual tragedy, that book, which is most fearfully true; and he wrote it to shew what must be the end of a man, who too weak for action, destroyed his own moral sense by daring and morbid speculation. I think he was most mistaken in writing it, that it is too deep in its plot to be generally understood, and so do good, while the doubts which it states will act poisonously on the minds of those who are already unhealthy, and I think and hope that he is beginning to see that.

But now, having said all this, I must say, that whatever may seem to me to be my duty to Froude there can be no doubt of my duty to *you*. "Honour thy father and thy mother," there is no mistake about *that* at all events. And therefore *I solemnly promise you, either to get rid of Froude, or leave Lynmouth immediately and not to remain in his company one day longer than the common courtesies of life require. Can I say more?* (1849.)

It was during this visit that Froude met Mrs. Kingsley's elder sister, Charlotte. Two years before she had become a Catholic and, despite the distress of her relatives, was determined to enter a convent. Froude asked permission to talk with her and, to the general amazement, succeeded in changing her mind. They were married in October.

During these same early years at Eversley Kingsley began another friendship, perhaps the most important of his life, that with Frederick Dennison Maurice. In the summer of 1844 when their correspondence began Maurice was chaplain of Guy's Hospital and Professor of English Literature and Modern History at King's College. He had rented the Chelsea Rectory for three months from Kingsley's father. Maurice's religious struggle had been the reverse of the usual nineteenth century trial. Brought up by an ardently Unitarian father he found himself more and more attracted by the doctrine of the Trinity and constrained at last to take orders in the Church of England. It was a characteristic action. He had a mind so elaborately and intricately subtle that his response to any situation was usually unpredictable and frequently bewildering to his followers. Lowes Dickinson has painted him with a face full of power and a singularly winning sweetness but so sensitive that it is almost painful to look at him. The affection, adoration even, which he excited in younger men made no impression upon his profound humility. "What shall be done," said Kingsley, "to the prophet who prophesieth into his waistcoat pocket?" for Maurice spoke often with his head buried in his hands. (J. M. Ludlow, "The Christian Socialists of 1848," *Economic Review,* October 1893.) He really considered himself an inferior person although his theological thinking, by those who could follow it, was deemed profound. To many it was hopelessly obscure but, as Kingsley said to Ludlow, "one may not be used to being at the bottom of the sea." To Maurice's *Kingdom of God,* given to Kingsley by Miss

Grenfell, he felt indebted for his view of the word of God and the meaning of the Church of England, and where shall the young priest go for advice but to the elder prophet? On two matters that troubled him he begged the favour of counsel: his want of any philosophical method of reading the Scriptures without seeing in them merely proofs of human systems, and the great prevalence in his parish of the Baptist form of dissent, founded on supralapsarian Calvinistic dogmas received into the heart as the deepest counsels of God.

Maurice's reply was characteristic in its gratitude for Kingsley's kind expressions, its careful discussion of the young man's problems and prompt appointment of a time when they might talk them over further. This was the beginning of a large and very intimate correspondence, lasting until Maurice's death nearly thirty years later. Much of it is in print; more is preserved in manuscript in the British Museum. Kingsley always looked to and addressed Maurice as "Master" and maintained that when he was praised for original theological thinking he was merely preaching Maurice. "N-now, J-j-john T-townsend," Ludlow relates he once said, excusing himself to his visitor when he went to write a sermon, "I am g-going to c-commit p-petty l-larceny; I am g-going to t-take a s-sermon of M-maurice's and t-turn it into l-language understanded of the p-people." (*op. cit.*) Maurice, however, discussed his own affairs with the younger man on a footing of perfect intimacy and had high respect for his opinion in the many good works at which they laboured in common. To Maurice, too, Kingsley owed some of the most interesting of his many friendships, Thomas Hughes and the whole Christian Socialist group, and Tennyson. Maurice stood godfather to Kingsley's eldest son born in 1847.

In the summer of 1847 Kingsley took the Sunday services at Pennington near Lymington and earned thus a six weeks' holiday for his family. They stayed at a little seaside place, Milford, on the edge of the New Forest. He had a horse and rode there constantly. "It was only," Mrs. Kingsley says, "either at a great crisis in his life, or in a time when all his surroundings were in perfect harmony, that he could compose poetry. And now, when in the forest, and in the saddle once more, or alone with his beloved ones on the seashore, with leisure to watch his babies, his heart's spring bubbled up into song, and he composed several ballads" (I, 148): "The Young Knight," "A New Forest Ballad," "The Red King," "The Outlaw." The summer gave him too the idea for a novel, the history of a wise woman in the new forest, which he began years later to work upon but never finished.

CHAPTER VI

"IF IT SHALL DETER ONE YOUNG MAN"

IN 1848 Kingsley published his first book, *The Saint's Tragedy*, his prose Life of St. Elizabeth reworked into a blank verse closet drama. London reviewers were inclined to be complimentary and he became at a bound something of a hero to the young men in the universities, for he dealt frankly with a problem very real to many of them: is marriage as holy a state as celibacy? The "earnest" Oxford tutors of the '40's were nearly all zealous High Churchmen. Their following was large but many of the serious-minded undergraduates revolted against the way of life they preached so ardently and here was a book which showed that there might be poetry in a manly Christian strife *against* asceticism. When in the spring of 1848 Kingsley went up to stay with Cowley Powles he found himself a lion whom undergraduates flocked to see and for whom great meetings were arranged. A few years later Kegan Paul was maintaining in a debate in the Oxford Union that Charles Kingsley was one of the greatest poets of the age.

The theme of *The Saint's Tragedy* is the struggle of Elizabeth of Hungary to reconcile her pure love for her husband, Lewis the Landgrave of Thuringia, with the Church's teaching of asceticism. Her husband dies and, under the guidance of her confessor Conrad, stern and high-souled but, according to Kingsley, mistaken, she is obliged to separate herself from her children, to submit to all sorts of humiliations and at last to renounce even the pleasure of giving to the poor. The facts are in accepted history and legend but the delineation of Elizabeth's state of mind is Kingsley's own interpretation. That he had cause for interest in the theme we already know. The idea of the power and beauty of monogamy bulks large in his whole scheme of life and in all his writings. Man, he was accustomed to argue, is a sexual animal; the notion that marriage was not instituted until after the fall is a private gloss and an erroneous one. In the early ages of Christianity the world was so sunk in lust that, by Christ's wise guidance, his ministers concentrated their efforts upon preaching one great message: "Ye are not beasts but immortal souls." Then, in the fullness of time, God raised up Christian art, chivalry and woman worship as witnesses that the flesh is not merely to be subdued but is the symbol and outward expression of the soul. "In the beginning God created them male and female" can only be taken to mean a woman for each man and a man for each woman. Joined to his "helpmeet" man becomes a higher being than he could ever be alone. The Bible itself set forth the gradual rise of the monogamous law from intermarriage with sisters, concubinage, polygamy, up to our Lord's assertion of the original idea of marriage, the one husband and one wife. Lovers whose minds are high and pure now shrink from second marriages because the married state is spiritual and timeless, an eternal union. For the hardness of our hearts only are we allowed to marry without love and "such shall have trouble in the flesh." The highest state is the married state because in it man can know most of God who reveals himself through family ties and family names. Fully to understand the meaning of "a Father in Heaven" we must be fathers ourselves; to know how Christ loved the Church we must have wives to love, and love them.

These matters Kingsley expounded at length in talk and correspondence. "God has showed me these things," he wrote to one young man, "in an eventful and blissful marriage history, and woe to me if I preach them not." (I, 191.)

The Saint's Tragedy stated also for the first time other themes which were to run through Kingsley's work: the ennobling influence of woman, the necessity for humility before God, the importance of serving the poor in brotherhood and in love. It showed, too, what Kingsley could do in verse and what he cared to do with an historic background. A good historic romance to most of the nineteenth century was one in which the speech and costumes and properties were carefully got up. Kingsley laboured over these details in his historical novels; with St. Elizabeth he was a little less careful. One finds her, for instance, singing to her husband, "Oh! that we two were Maying," that lyric (Act II, Sc. 10) which, set to music by Hullah, was to be sung to every shawl-draped piano in the kingdom. Reviewers cried out against the anachronism of some of the conversation: "Very smart and pointed dialogue, but such as we are familiar with upon the Irish famine." (*Spectator,* January 22, 1848; see also *Fraser's,* March 1848.) Kingsley, however, had not done this unwittingly. He writes John Conington (January 15, 1848): "For anachronisms—they are intentional—in that particular scene the anachronism is in the expressions, and not in the notions embodied in them. But throughout my play I have followed the Shakespearian method of bringing the past up to my readers, and not the modern one of bringing my readers down to the past." (I, 153.)

Kingsley suffered from the historic disability of his century, the conviction that after all hearts do not change very much even with a change in "notions" or with the Pyrenees. He is particularly successful therefore when he draws such a type as the Devon seaman who certainly did not alter greatly between the days of Elizabeth and those of Victoria. He is less happy with his Alexandrian Jews who seem to have just come down from Cambridge or with the Puseyite ladies whom he moves about in the thirteenth century. The fury he roused by his portrayal of medieval Catholics stirred those of the nineteenth century to sound literary criticism. The idea, cried the *Dublin Review* (April 1864), "that there was a 'degrading and agonizing' conflict in the mind of St. Elizabeth, between 'healthy human affection' and a Manichaean idea of the unlawfulness of married life and its relations—is, we need hardly say, a creation of Mr. Kingsley's own brain, and perfectly unjustified by anything to be found in Theodoric." The Tractarian *English Review* in the course of a laudatory article (December 1849) remarked that Conrad's utterances were too horrible for truth and certainly not typical. They might be found as outpourings of extreme ecstasy but not as sober philosophic argument.

   Conrad—   Ah! poor worldlings!
  Little you dream what maddening ecstasies,
  What rich ideals haunt, by day and night,
  Alone, and in the crowd, even to the death,
  The servitors of that celestial court
  Where peerless Mary, sun-enthroned, reigns, . . .

Lewis— Who dare aspire to her? Alas, not I!
To me she is a doctrine, and a picture:—
I cannot live on dreams.

Conrad— She hath her train:—
There thou may'st choose thy love: If world-wide lore
Shall please thee, and the Cherub's glance of fire,
Let Catharine lift thy rapt soul, and with her
Question the mighty dead, until thou float
Tranced on the ethereal ocean of her spirit.
If pity father passion in thee—hang
Above Eulalia's tortured loveliness;
And for her sake, and in her strength, go forth
To do and suffer greatly. Dost thou long
For some rich heart, as deep in love as weakness,
Whose wild simplicity, sweet heaven-born instincts
Alone keep sane?

Lewis— I do, I do, I'd live
And die for each and all the three.

Conrad— Then go—
Entangled in the Magdalen's tresses lie;
Dream hours before her picture, till thy lips
Dare to approach her feet, and thou shalt start
To find the canvas warm with life, and matter
A moment transubstantiate to heaven.
(Act I, Sc. 2.)

The reviewers were not of course aware that Kingsley gives his monks such language because these were the terms in which the ascetic doctrine once presented itself to him, as he had his own conception of mysticism.

He saw, too, in the thirteenth century, the dawn of what had been his own salvation from the dream world, Muscular Christianity—though it must always be remembered that he did not like the term. In the Introduction to *The Saint's Tragedy* he wrote of his favourite character Walter of Varila:

His dislike of priestly sentimentalities, is no anachronism. Even in his day, a noble lay-religion, founded on faith in the divine and universal symbolism of humanity and nature, was gradually arising, and venting itself, from time to time, as I conceive, through many most unsuspected channels, through chivalry, through the minne-singers, through the lay-inventors of pointed architecture, through the German school of painting, through the politics of the free-towns, till it attained complete freedom, in Luther and his associate reformers.

Kingsley was always impatient with the Neo-Gothic conception of the past. The Middle Age, he stated roundly in his Introduction, was coarse, barbarous and profligate. It was that which called forth the apostolic holiness and the Manichaean asceticism of the medieval saints. The world was so bad that to be saints at all they were compelled to go out of the world. There has been too much ignorant abuse and of late too much blind adoration of the period. We must learn to see it as it is, the dawning manhood of Europe, rich with the enthusiasms and dark with the fierce extravagances of youth.

After *The Saint's Tragedy* Kingsley never tried the dramatic form again though his hexameter *Andromeda* has some dramatic qualities. Baron Bunsen thought that he had "dramatic power" and that he ought to continue Shakespeare's historical plays, an opinion which Mrs. Kingsley quotes with pleasure though it does not seem to have been general. Certainly Kingsley cherished at one time some serious thoughts of writing for the stage and he and Tom Taylor planned to collaborate on a comedy. "My practical knowledge of the theatre," Taylor wrote him (June 19, 1852), "would be sure to be of use. I have sufficient command of dialogue to take my share of the actual clothing of the skeleton when put together and in the putting together the practical knowledge alluded to would be called into play, more than in anything else. Then as I have access to the best theatres here our work would be sure of finding a channel through which to reach that goal of all plays—the stage."

There is no indication that this scheme was developed further. Kingsley certainly had none of the skill in concentration necessary for the stage and he seems in his thinking to have confused drama with dialogue. "I can't think, even on scientific subjects," he told Tom Hughes, "except in the dramatic form. It is what Tom said to Harry, and what Harry answered him." (T. Hughes, Prefatory Memoir, *Alton Locke,* 1876.) The sermons fall constantly into this form; so do letters and essays, notably *Phaethon* in which the parts are marked. Kingsley had, however, a real Puritan distrust of the theatre.

J. H. Rigg, head of the Wesleyan Training College in London (he is one of the many instances of warm friendships established by Kingsley with men with whom he fundamentally disagreed) tells of a conversation at a private party in his home in which Kingsley declaimed against the stage stating that, in his judgment, the amusement of charades for young people was injurious and degrading. "Acting was only fit for slaves, not for free, Christian Englishmen." (J. H. Rigg, "Memoir of Canon Kingsley," *Modern Anglican Theology,* London, 1880.) In Kingsley's Commonplace-Book, among the later entries, is written:

"Oh those theatres! Never pass them without a sigh! Noble organs of usefulness! Why is the Devil to reign undisputed in them? How untrue the Puritans were to their own mission when they made over stage plays to Satan."

One of the lectures which Kingsley delivered in America in 1874—and before that (1873) at Harrow—dealt with "The Stage as It Was Once"—in Greece, but his complete dramatic credo is in "Plays and Puritans," written originally for the *North British Review* (May 1856). The British stage declined, is his thesis, with the Stuarts: "the taste of Charles the First's, and of Charles the Second's court, are indistinguishable." The chief subject of comedy was adultery and

... adultery is not a subject for comedy at all. It may be for tragedy; but for comedy never. ...

... as the staple interest of the comedies is dirt, so the staple interest of the tragedies is crime. ...

We should not allow these plays to be acted in our own day, because we know that they would produce their effects. We should call him a madman who allowed his daughters or his servants to see such representations. Why, in all fairness, were the Puritans wrong in condemning that which we now have absolutely forbidden? ...

... there is far less of these elements in Shakespeare than in any of his compeers: but they are there. And what the Puritans hated in him was exactly what we have to expunge before we can now represent his plays. ...

On the matter of the stage, the world has certainly come over to their way of thinking. Few educated men now think it worth while to go to see any play, and that exactly for the same reasons as the Puritans put forward; and still fewer educated men think it worth while to write plays: finding that since the grosser excitements of the imagination have become forbidden themes, there is really very little to write about. (*Miscellanies,* 1859, Vol. II.)

But there is a dramatic ideal and it was that undoubtedly which Kingsley set before him in *The Saint's Tragedy*:

The highest aim of dramatic art is to exhibit the development of the human soul; to construct dramas in which the conclusion shall depend, not on the events, but on the characters; and in which the characters shall not be mere embodiments of a certain passion, or a certain "humour": but persons, each unlike all others; each having a destiny of his own, by virtue of his own peculiarities, of his own will, and each proceeding toward that destiny; unfolding his own strength and weakness before the eyes of the audience; and that in such a way, that after his first introduction, they should be able (in proportion to their knowledge of human nature) to predict his conduct under any given circumstances. This is indeed "high art." (*op. cit.*)

It had not been altogether easy to get *The Saint's Tragedy* into print. Kingsley himself was so uncertain of its value that before he made any attempt at publishing he consulted four friends: the Hon. and Rev. Gerald Wellesley, his father's predecessor at Chelsea, then Rector of Strathfieldsaye and later Dean of Windsor; his old schoolmaster Derwent Coleridge, at that time Principal of St. Mark's College, Chelsea; Maurice and Cowley Powles. They were unanimous in admiration and he took the MS. to London. Maurice promised a Preface and Coleridge gave Kingsley a note to Pickering but he declined to venture and the drama was finally published by the printer of the *Christian Socialist,* John Parker.

The Preface was not really an advantage to the book for Maurice had his enemies as well as his following. The *English Review* (December 1849) cried out that it was a "very gratuitous act of pomposity" which prejudiced one at the outset against a book containing "much which is both beautiful and valuable." The *Athenaeum,* however (April 1, 1848), found the Preface "sound and deep" though confused. It was the fashion to find Maurice obscure and he frequently was, though not particularly here. In most respects the reviewers were kind. Some of them were pleasantly extravagant in their enthusiasm. *Fraser's* (March 1848) had been looking for a successor to Wordsworth, a man to speak for the age, a healthy and efficient school of poetry, and thought *The Saint's Tragedy* an indication of the dawn of a worthier state of things. Kingsley should take a little more care with his verse but "Oh! that we two were Maying" was an admirable lyric. The *Athenaeum* (see above) said, that, considering the times, it was scarcely to be expected that Elizabeth should be displayed in so fit an attitude and fair a light, yet we were never allowed to forget the real significance of her sacrifice. Such a protest against pseudo-medievalism was very valuable now. The *Spectator* (January 22, 1848) found "genuine poetic spirit" and a "condensed, vigorous and manly style." Acutest of all was the anti-Maurice writer in the *English Review* (see above); he felt that the poem had "merits of a high order" and "must secure its author's fame" though it had faults in plenty: exaggeration, an overstrained boldness verging upon coarseness, a tendency to bitterness and occasional bursts of fine talk. (With his first book Kingsley invited the phrases which were to pursue him through his literary life: coarse and manly.) The author had understated the ascetic argument and overstated the ascetic aberration. Elizabeth is so passionate a character that her asceticism seems a natural climax and we do not pity her as the author wished us to. Lewis is self-consistent, "a very nice man." The Nurse is vulgar and likable. Walter will probably be the favourite with most readers. In the verse the reviewer found echoes of Shakespeare and Browning but he thought Charles Kingsley a true poet and he admired of course "Oh! that we two were Maying."

There are Shakespearean echoes, somewhat blurred, in the prose; more of Browning in the verse. Blank verse was not a natural speech to Kingsley. His lines seldom seem wrought by the idea; they are fitted to it artificially. The accent jumps again and again on an unnatural syllable.[1] Yet Kingsley does strike out now and then a vigorous and original phrase:

> Possession's naught;
> A parchment ghost.
> (Act I, Sc. 2.)

> I dare not turn for ever from this hope,
> Though it be dwindled to a thread of mist.
> (Act I, Sc. 3.)

---

[1] A scarecrow to lear wolves. Go ask the churchplate, (Act I, Sc. 2.)
That's the Church secret
For breeding towns, as fast as you breed roe-deer; (Act I, Sc. 2.)
. . . we monks
Can teach you somewhat there too.
Be it so. (Act I, Sc. 2.)

The lyrics in *The Saint's Tragedy* are introduced partly, one feels, for the relief of the author but chiefly with definite intent to give variety or to set the tone of a scene, as prose is used from time to time in the Shakespearean manner. The bridal feast (Act II, Sc. 1), for instance, where the songs of the Minstrel, the Fool and the monks ring against each other, is an admirable idea, though not very effectively realized. The critics preferred the crusaders' scene (Act II, Sc. 11), and everybody preferred "Oh! that we two were Maying!" (Act II, Sc. 10.)

CHAPTER VII

"ESAU HAS A BIRTHRIGHT"

LIKE that of some greater artists Charles Kingsley's writing was a matter not so much of inner as of outer compulsion. On January 26, 1848, he sent a letter to John Parker, the younger.

I am very desirous of getting employment for my pen just now, for the purpose, to speak openly, of paying my Xmas bills which bricklayers and carpenters in an old tumble down house have increased to a terrific size; and also to build and establish schools in my parish. Can you put me in the way of doing "a stroke of work" in the capacity of hack-writer? I do not care what it is, *salva conscientia*. I have a great hatred of anonymousness where it can possibly be avoided—but those who want money "must not look gift horses in the mouth." My reading has been more various than is usual at my age. . . . I have nothing now on hand but 5 or 6 ballads and the beginning of a sort of fanciful half satiric novel intended to exhibit the struggles of a bold hearted young man after a faith, and an art in the midst of bigots (High and Low Church), dilletanti, pantheist free pencils, and the whole spiritual chaos. I think the thing would do very well for Fraser's but my fear is that towards the end of the book the style which I should feel it my duty to adopt would seem too exclusively *Christian* alas! and perhaps visionary for the mass of your readers. Of course I would give my name if you wished. Adv. Poetry can be furnished to order, at a very moderate price per yard, of any pattern. If you could put me in the way of connecting myself with any publication who would treat me well, you would infinitely oblige,
      Yours very truly

The John Parkers, father and son—the son had been a fellow student of Kingsley at King's College—,were publishers not only of books but of *Fraser's Magazine,* the editor of which was a legendary figure never referred to by name and frequently represented by the Parkers, who conducted negotiations with him, as of stern and unyielding disposition. He was in general, however, well disposed towards the young John Parker's friends and in

April Kingsley's first magazine article, "Why Should We Fear the Romish Priests?" appeared in *Fraser's*. *Yeast,* the fanciful half-satiric novel, ran serially from July to December and in the next four years Kingsley poured out not only two other novels but a continuous river of essays and reviews. *Fraser's* printed the majority of these, anonymously of course, though *Yeast,* anonymous too, had so bad an effect upon Parker's business that he declined to publish *Alton Locke.* He hesitated long, indeed, before bringing *Yeast* out in book form.

Can you tell me [Kingsley wrote to Maurice, (?) January 13, 1851] what the law and gospel with regard to publishers is, in such a case as Yeast: here am I wanting to republish it—for which purpose I would alter and improve it, and finish it off: and here is Parker shilly shallying, still letting I dare not wait upon I would . . . now am I bound if he still hangs off and on, to publish it with him, because he publishes the magazine, or in the event of his refusing to refuse, which is as bad, can I take it to whom I like?

Parker made up his mind at last, however, and brought out *Yeast,* "reprinted from *Fraser's Magazine,*" in the spring of 1851. Chapman and Hall had dared *Alton Locke,* without previous serial publication, in 1850, and this led to its being not infrequently referred to as Kingsley's first novel despite its obvious superiority to *Yeast* in technique.

Yeast's chief interest is autobiographical, an interest not only personal but typical, for one mid-century youth after another welcomed it as the record of his struggles after a faith in the midst of bigots, pantheists and the whole spiritual chaos. Kingsley constantly received letters about it.

"I am driven with a spur to tell you," ran one of them written from Weybridge, July [?1851], "the delight and admiration with which I read your last book *Yeast,* and the positive 'Education' I have derived from it. It was the very book I was in want of and likely to do me more good than any that I know." That letter was signed, George Meredith.

Esau liked the book also,

poor rough Esau, who sails Jacob's ships, digs Jacob's mines, founds Jacob's colonies, pours out his blood for him in those wars which Jacob himself has stirred up—while his sleek brother sits at home in his counting-house, enjoying at once "the means of grace" and the produce of Esau's labour—on him Jacob's chaplains have less and less influence; for him they have less and less good news. He is afraid of them, and they of him; the two do not comprehend one another, sympathize with one another; they do not even understand one another's speech. . . .

. . . Esau has a birthright; and this book, like all books which I have ever written, is written to tell him so. (Preface to 4th ed., 1859.)

Esau's speech Kingsley comprehended and knew how to speak. The hunt with which the book opens achieved no little fame among sportsmen. There is a tale of a Crimean officer who read *Yeast* when he was lying dangerously wounded in a hospital at Scutari and resolved that if ever he got back alive he would "go and hear the clergyman preach who could give such a picture of a hunting scene as the one in the opening chapter." (II, 16.) He did and became a regular attendant at the little Eversley church. On the strength of that same first chapter "one of the proudest old Tory Baronets in England," Sir Francis Astley, offered Kingsley the run of his hunting stables.

In this ability of his to speak to the heart of the fast sporting man Kingsley saw the guiding hand of a wise God who had trained him for this peculiar work. "Did He, too, let me become a strong, daring, sporting wild man-of-the-woods for nothing? Surely the education which He has given me, so different from that which authors generally receive, points out to me a peculiar calling to preach on these points, from my own experience, as it did to good old Izaak Walton, as it has done in our day to that truly noble man, Captain Marryat." (I, 180.)

When *Yeast* was done Kingsley felt that for the moment he had no more to say. He had put into it his whole spiritual history so far. Lancelot is the closest self-portrait he ever drew. And Lancelot's relation to the heroine is that which Kingsley found in his own union and knew therefore to be the God-ordained ideal:

Her mind was beside his as the vase of cut flowers by the side of the rugged tree, whose roots are feeding deep in the mother earth. . . .

. . . on all points which touched the heart he looked up to her as infallible and inspired. In questions of morality, of taste, of feeling, he listened not as a lover to his mistress, but rather as a baby to its mother; and thus, half unconsciously to himself, he taught her where her true kingdom lay,—that the heart, and not the brain, enshrines the priceless pearl of womanhood, the oracular jewel, the "Urim and

Thummim," before which gross man can only inquire and adore. (Chap. X.)

In her personal copy of *Yeast* Mrs. Kingsley wrote: "Let this book be buried with me. The one I love best." (Later she directed that it should be given to her eldest son.) The passages which she has marked indicate very clearly that most of the scenes between Lancelot and Argemone are transcripts of her own love story. The novel, however, unlike the Kingsley romance, has no happy ending. Argemone dies—of typhus caught in nursing the poor—but before that a bank failure deprives Lancelot of his fortune and this, added to his radical principles, makes Squire Lavington reject him as an aspirant for his daughter's hand. Lancelot bravely determines to earn his bread by his brush and enlists himself with some artist friends in London. This gives Kingsley opportunity for a discussion of the future of British art, a subject on which he had very definite ideas. The second part of *Yeast,* which was elaborately projected but never written, was to be called *The Artists* and was to develop this theme.

My hero [Kingsley wrote to Ludlow, 1849] . . . and his friend Mellot, and his cousin Luke, who has just turned Romanist, will be typical of the three great schools. Mellot of the mere classic Pagan, and of the Fourierism which seems to me to be its representative in the world of doctrines; Luke of the Puginesque Manichaean, or exclusively spiritual school, and Lancelot who tries historic painting, and finding that there is nothing to paint about, falls back on landscapes and animals, on the simple naturalism of our Landseers and Creswicks, the only living school of art as yet possible in England. He is raised above his mere faith in nature by the simple Christianity of Tregarva [his game-keeper friend], at the same time that he is taught by him that true democracy which considers the beautiful as the heritage of the poor as well as of the rich; and Tregarva in his turn becomes the type of English Art-hating Puritanism, gradually convinced of the divine mission of Art, and of its being the rightful child not of Popery, but of Protestantism alone.

Thus, I think Lancelot, having grafted on his own naturalism, the Christianity of Tregarva, the classicism of Mellot, and the spiritual symbolism of Luke, ought to be in a state to become the mesothetic artist of the future, and beat each of his tutors at their own weapons, as the mesothet will always include a perfect each of the poles connected with it. (I, 219.)

Kingsley makes Luke a Puginesque painter because he believed their gothic elongations of the human frame to be inspired by the same lack of respect for the body, the same desire to overspiritualize it, which he felt in the ascetic teachings of the High Churchmen. He delighted to make hits at the prevailing passion for the medieval and, perhaps because it amused rather than enraged him, his satire of it in *Yeast* is more successful than his usual rather heavy-handed attempts in that vein.

"Well, Lord Vieuxbois," said the host, casually, "my girls are raving about your new school. They say it is a perfect antiquarian gem."

"Yes, tolerable, I believe. But Wales has disappointed me a little. That vile modernist naturalism is creeping back even into our painted glass. I could have wished that the artist's designs for the windows had been a little more Catholic."

"How then?" asked the host, with a puzzled face.

"Oh, he means," said Bracebridge, "that the figures' wrists and ankles were not sufficiently dislocated, and the patron saint did not look quite like a starved rabbit with its neck wrung. Some of the faces, I am sorry to say, were positively like good-looking men and women." (Chap. VI.)

With Pre-Raphaelitism Kingsley was likewise impatient, though when Ruskin endeavoured to convert him he met with some success. In September 1855 Kingsley wrote in *Fraser's* in a review of *Maud* that Millais's "Rescue" had "all the accuracy at which our new 'pre-Raphaelites' aim, without any of the inaccuracies, sheer monstrosities, and vulgar bedizenments, in which they at first so inconsistently indulged." In 1857, however, in *Two Years Ago,* we find Claude Mellot saying as the climax to an irritated dissertation that "the only possible method of fulfilling the pre-Raphaelite ideal would be, to set a petrified Cyclops to paint his petrified brother." (Chap. IX.)[1]

Claude and his wife Sabina are the only characters of Kingsley who reappear in a second novel. Claude, too, carries half the dialogue in the prose idyll "North Devon." (*Miscellanies,* II.) Kingsley had a special affection for the pair which seems to have come in part from their irresponsibility; no one of course would dream of imitating them as models of conduct; they are merely to be

---

[1] The text of quotations from Kingsley's works is taken in each instance from the first edition but when a novel was published first in two or three volumes, the chapter references are given not to the first but to the later one-volume editions. Otherwise only readers in possession of first editions would be able to trace the references.

enjoyed. "I have been playing with them," he wrote George Brimley (1857) "as two dolls, setting them to say and do all the pretty *naïve* things any one else is too respectable to be sent about, till I know them as well as I know you. I have half-a-dozen pet people of that kind whom I make talk and walk with me on the moors, and when I am at my parish work; and charming company they all are." (II, 43.)

To discussion of art *Fraser's* had no objection but another favourite theme of Kingsley was excluded, by space and the unknown editor, from the magazine, though published in the book: the doubts and hesitations of a young man going over to Rome. Luke has no close relation to the plot except that he is Lancelot's cousin and Lancelot's correspondence with him is part of his own groping for a faith. The convert of course represents Kingsley's type of man who succumbs to Catholicism, sincere but selfish, interested primarily in the salvation of his own soul, a little weak, not quite manly, in a word, un-English.

The conclusion to all the problems in which Lancelot and his friends are enmeshed was unsatisfactory to most people, even to those who most admired the book. A curious, imperfectly explained figure, referred to as "the Prophet," appears unexpectedly more than once to guide Lancelot and his gamekeeper companion Tregarva in new spiritual paths, and the tale ends with Argemone dead and Lancelot with the Prophet, after vespers in St. Paul's, talking of the imminence of that kingdom of God in which he desires to believe and suffering himself to be led away toward a mysterious country where he may learn the reality of that faith of which he has dreamed.

The Prophet was the title by which his disciples usually designated Maurice but the figure in *Yeast* resembles much more closely that very different individual, Sidonia in Disraeli's *Coningsby*. Kingsley was of course accused of plagiarism but, as he assured John Conington (December 19, 1848, I, 191), he did not read *Coningsby* until after the charge was made.

The mythic and metaphysical elements in the tale Kingsley was obliged more than once to defend to Parker.

I have corrected the proofs, and altered all that may seem too metaphysical: but both you and the Editor are much mistaken if you think that people do not like "metaphysics" nowadays. Look at Bulwer's novels and Miss Bremer's, and all religious novelettes, however trashy, and the run which they have had, as a proof of your mistake. And believe me people are craving nowadays for a deeper tone of thought than the common light literature gives them. They are longing to have their thoughts about Love and Art, Sporting and Amusement, connected and incorporated with their deepest religious and political yearnings—this is becoming a religious age, and we must write up to it. . . . I cannot consent to any religious or "theological" bits being cut out. They are integral parts of my story—the whole would become without them a purposeless *lie,* like most magazine stories. There is a God, who guides all men, lovers and fox hunters as well as others, and I dare not forget that. . . . After all, if the Editor does not like my view of life, he can simply leave it. My book will be written, whether in Fraser's or not, please God, and you may bring it out, as you want a book from me this year. . . . I tell you fairly that *the* want which people feel in Fraser's is a want of earnest purpose and deep faith of any kind. (June 25, 1848.)

Once only did Kingsley make public defence of *Yeast,* when the High Church *Guardian* (May 7, 1851, the review was written by John Duke Coleridge) proclaimed that: "We are utterly at issue with him in an opinion which is implied throughout the volume, that a certain amount of youthful profligacy does no real and permanent harm to the character: that the existence of passions is a proof that they are to be gratified." Kingsley wrote to the editor of the *Guardian* and gave the reviewer the lie direct.

Most of the other critics found the book coarse in its energy. Many readers, the *Leader* (April 26, 1851) thought, would prefer it to *Alton Locke* because of its exquisite love passages.

But Lancelot spoke no word all the way home, and wandered till dawn in the woods around his cottage, kissing the hand which Argemone's palm had pressed. (Chap. VII.)

"I see—I see it all, Argemone! We love each other! You are mine, never to be parted!"
What was her womanhood, that it could stand against the energy of his manly will? The almost coarse simplicity of his words silenced her with a delicious violence. (Chap. X.)

Mrs. Kingsley marked that passage.

The *Spectator* (March 22, 1851) found in the book too much preaching by the author but thought that as a series of sketches of the ills of society and of the metaphysical broodings of a thoughtful youth it was "powerful, earnest, feeling, and eloquent." They cited for special admiration the chapter (XIII) on "The Village Revel" which in form and content belongs to *Alton Locke,* the rural counterpart of the urban miseries there. It makes one regret that Kingsley did not steadily utilize in this kind of superjournalism his narrative power and the imagination which made him quiver under the real pains of others but was not strong enough to lift him to completely effective invention. The morals he longed to inculcate sink in far deeper from scenes like "The Village Revel" than when he points them with texts or with philosophy. The chapter is written with more passion than the other episodes. Kingsley cared deeply about his themes of Roman Catholicism and holy matrimony but so far as he was concerned they were settled questions; the miseries of the poor and what might be done to relieve them were problems still burning in his mind.

All the novel's purposes, disjointed though their treatment appears, are fused into a kind of unity in the mind of the young man Lancelot Smith, but Kingsley has not yet learned to knit a story together even in the large loose-jointed fashion of the day; he expects the reader to do it for himself, as he indicates in a somewhat belligerent paragraph prefixed to the first instalment in *Fraser's* (July 1848) where the novel appears as: *Yeast; or the Thoughts, Sayings, and Doings of Lancelot Smith, Gentleman*:

N.B. This work is composed according to no rules of art whatsoever, except the cardinal one,—That the artist knowing best what he wants to say, is also likely to know best how to say it. Readers are commanded to believe that it has a spiritual sequence and method, invisible, like other spiritual matters, to all but "the eye of faith," and to be discovered only in its fruits; which, again, depend mainly on the sort of soil with which it may meet in the brain-gardens of a reading public.

The invisibility of the sequence is the product not only of inexperience but of haste. Kingsley was working his difficult parish without a curate, lecturing at Queen's College and writing for *Politics for the People. Yeast* was written late at night when the day's work was over "and the house still." (I, 184.) *Alton Locke,* the next novel, was composed between five in the morning and family prayers at nine. All his life Kingsley wrote too rapidly, sending first drafts off to the press almost without revision; a pity, because whenever he does revise he almost invariably betters. Even the minor corrections in essays republished from periodicals are improvements. There is an interesting example in *Yeast,* the description of the river in Chapter III, a passage written originally for one of his few short stories, "The Nun's Pool," later printed in the *Christian Socialist* (July and August 1851). *Alton Locke,* Mrs. Kingsley tells us, was the only book of which he ever had a fair copy made.

His habit was thoroughly to master his subject, whether book or sermon, always out in the open air, in his garden, on the moor, or by the side of a lonely trout stream, and never to put pen to paper till the ideas were clothed in words; and these, except in the case of poetry which he could not finish too highly, he seldom altered. For many years his writing was all done by his wife from his dictation, while he paced up and down the room. (I, 233.)

The strain of the night writing of *Yeast* was too great; he broke down completely and was ordered to Bournemouth for a month's rest, but that proved insufficient. He was obliged to give up all work, his father provided for his Eversley duty, and he took his family to North Devon for the winter and spring.

CHAPTER VIII

"I AM A CHURCH OF ENGLAND PARSON—AND A CHARTIST"

THE YEAR 1848, in which Charles Kingsley published his first book, was the year of the Chartist Riots, the exciting cause of his best book. Kingsley had long outgrown that youthful terror of the lower classes inspired by the riots at Bristol and was thinking for their welfare in terms far ahead of his time. He knew from first hand experience the terrible conditions of the agricultural and the industrial labourer; they seemed to him to have such provocation to violent remedies that he was in great fear lest they rush to extremes, injuring their cause and bringing misery upon England. When news came in April that hundreds of thousands of workingmen were marching to London with a monster petition to present to Parliament he found it impossible to sit safe and passive at Eversley and dashed up to the city to make himself of use in the struggle somehow. He went at once to Maurice, who, too ill to go out himself, sent him with a note of introduction to John Malcolm Ludlow.

Ludlow was Kingsley's junior by two years but had had far more experience than he in dealing with social problems. He had worked for reform in India, for the abolition of slavery, and as a member of the anti-corn-law league; he had been in Paris during the February revolution. He treated the excited Kingsley with fatherly indulgence but he liked him at once: "I was intimate with Kingsley the very first day that I became acquainted with him . . . a tall young clergyman, with strongly marked features and singularly piercing eyes. . . . The poor fellow meant well, however misguided; it would be horrible if there were bloodshed. He was going to Kennington Common to see what one man could do. Would I go with him?" (J. M. Ludlow, "The Christian Socialists of 1848," *Economic Review,* October 1893.)

They set out together on foot but they did not get to Kennington, for by the time they reached Waterloo Bridge the crowds were leaving, utterly discouraged by the overwhelming preparations of the Duke of Wellington who insured quiet by filling the Bank, Mint and Custom House with troops, provisioning the Houses of Parliament as though for a siege, swearing in 170,000 special constables and so disheartening the demonstrators that they abandoned their attempt to cross Westminster Bridge and hold the forbidden monster procession to the House of Commons. Kingsley and Ludlow went back to Maurice. "We had talked," says Ludlow, "all the way from Chancery Lane; we talked all the way to Queen's Square, and, by the time we were there, we were friends." (*op. cit.*)

The five points of the Charter are law today but on April 10, 1848, the document was something more than a petition for political reform; it was the symbol and focus of a bitter class struggle. There had been riots in Glasgow, in Edinburgh, in Manchester, and London had some reason to be fearful. Certainly it was not pleasant for Mrs. Kingsley to sit alone at Eversley while her husband was in town, though he wrote her sometimes twice a day. He was in no danger, he assured her, but he must stay up a little longer for he was helping in a glorious work. He and Maurice and Ludlow were sitting up till four in the morning getting out posting placards "to speak a word for God with," texts from the Psalms, "any thing which may keep one man from cutting his brother's throat to-morrow or Friday." (I, 155.) They got one placard printed at once by John Parker and began to beg subscriptions for others. Maurice was immensely pleased with Kingsley's appeal and old John Parker, who had been a working printer's boy, read it with tears in his eyes.

Workmen of England! [the placard began] You say that you are wronged. Many of you are wronged; and many besides yourselves know it. Almost all men who have heads and hearts know it—above all, the working clergy know it. They go into your houses, they see the shameful filth and darkness in which you are forced to live crowded together; they see your children growing up in ignorance and temptation, for want of fit education; they see intelligent and well-read men among you, shut out from a Freeman's just right of voting; and they see too the noble patience and self-control with which you have as yet borne these evils. They see it, and God sees it. . . .

"I Am a Church of England Parson—and a Chartist" 61

You think the Charter would make you free—would to God it would! The Charter is not bad; *if the men who use it are not bad*! But will the Charter make you free? Will it free you from slavery to ten-pound bribes? Slavery to beer and gin? Slavery to every spouter who flatters your self-conceit, and stirs up bitterness and headlong rage in you? . . .

. . . there will be no true freedom without virtue, no true science without religion, no true industry without the fear of God, and love to your fellow-citizens.

Workers of England, be wise, and then you *must* be free, for you will be *fit* to be free.

A Working Parson

Valiantly as he strove to restrain them from violence Kingsley had every sympathy with the workers' demands. He boldly called himself a Chartist at a time when respectable people thought the word synonymous with anarchist, murderer and French Revolutionary. Thomas Hughes, in his Prefatory Memoir to the 1876 edition of *Alton Locke,* tells the tale of one of these public declarations of faith in the early summer of 1848 when some of those who felt that the Chartists had not had fair and courteous treatment arranged a meeting with their leaders at the Cranbourn Tavern. Maurice presided. Bitter speeches followed his opening address and an angry attack upon the Church and clergy. The meeting seemed on the edge of dangerous violence when Kingsley rose, folded his arms, threw back his head and began, with that stammer which always came when he was excited: "I am a Church of England parson—and a Chartist." The room fell suddenly still. He went on to express his sympathy for their claims and his thorough disapproval of their methods. "Probably no one who was present," says Hughes, "ever heard a speech which told more at the time," but it took Kingsley many years to live down the effect of that Chartist declaration upon "the best people," and the effect of a sentence ripped without its context from his first "Letter to the Chartists" and quoted against him even after his death: "My only quarrel with the Charter is, that it does not go far enough." What he actually wrote was this:

My only quarrel with the Charter is, that it does not go far enough in reform. I want to see you *free*; but I do not see how what you ask for, will give you what you want. I think you have fallen into just the same mistake as the rich of whom you complain—the very mistake which has been our curse and our nightmare—I mean, the mistake of fancying that *legislative* reform is *social* reform, or that men's hearts can be changed by act of parliament. If any one will tell me of a country where a Charter made the rogues honest, or the idle industrious, I shall alter my opinion of the Charter, but not till then. It disappointed me bitterly when I read it. It seemed a harmless cry enough, but a poor, bald, constitution-mongering cry as I ever heard. That French cry of "Organization of Labour" is worth a thousand of it, and yet that does not go to the bottom of the matter by many a mile. (*Politics for the People,* May 13, 1848.)

These "Letters to the Chartists" were perhaps the most important of Kingsley's contributions to *Politics for the People,* the penny periodical founded during the excited days in April. Maurice and Ludlow were its working editors and the contributors included, beside the voluminous and versatile Kingsley, Archbishop Whateley of Dublin; Bishop Thirlwall of St. David's; Archbishop Trench, then Professor of Divinity at King's College; Arthur Penryhn Stanley, later Dean of Westminster; Dr. William Guy of King's College Hospital; John Conington, later Professor of Latin at Oxford; Daniel Macmillan, the publisher; Alexander Scott, then Professor of English at University College, London, later Principal of the Owens College, Manchester; James Spedding, who edited Bacon; Lord Sydney Godolphin Osborne, Kingsley's brother-in-law, the social reformer; Sir Arthur Helps, essayist and historian; Sir Edward Strachey, scholar and writer; and Charles Mansfield, the chemist.

For the first number, May 6, Ludlow wrote a prospectus to the "Gentlemen of England"; Kingsley, one to the "Workmen of England," explaining that those who have started this paper are not idlers in the land but since they do not work with their hands may not altogether understand the sufferings and needs of the man who does. They want to learn from him what he is thinking and feeling. "You are in contact with the realities of life; you can help to make all our studies and thoughts more real." Their paper they intend to address not, as is so often done, to the self-interest of the workingman but to his sense of duty.

Politics for the People was issued for a little less than three months, May 6 to July 29, when funds ran low and John Parker began to feel that his connection with it was doing harm to his business. During that time Kingsley had written three "Letters to the Chartists," three articles on the National Gallery and British Museum, and four poems, none of which he ever thought worth reprinting. One, "Old and New," was published posthumously. He projected a great many other contributions some of which show that his imagination was already working at the creation of historical fiction.

I want to have some more Whitford Priory tales out ["The Nun's Pool" already written was rejected by Ludlow but printed two years later in the successor to *Politics,* the *Christian Socialist,* July 5 to August 30, 1851], viz., No. 1. A young poet from the working classes; bringing in Shakespeare, Ben Jonson, *Good* Queen Bess (a great favourite of mine), the extravagance, and at the same time the high intellectual tone of her Court, etc. 2. A good jolly Cavalier and Roundhead story, and storming of the Priory by *our fathers.* 3. A Roger de Coverley story, showing the low ebb of town life, etc. 4. A story about the Methodists, and the fury of the Squire Westerns and Parson Trullibers against them. 5. A French war and high-prices story, old Poor-law, etc. 6. What is the matter with the parish? an exposé of things as they are. 7. How to mend the parish, continued.

I will bring you up a Game-law ballad or two, and will work the end of the week at a National Gallery Article, and a Letter to the Chartists. (To Ludlow, May 29, 1848, I, 179.)

Kingsley's verse was printed anonymously. The articles were signed Parson Lot, a pseudonym which he used frequently in the next ten years. It had its origin at one of the meetings of the group of young men who gathered around Maurice when he was Reader of Lincoln's Inn. Since no parochial work attached to the post he undertook to care for a small district in the parish and set a number of his disciples, chiefly students of the Inns of Court, to work there. Once a week on Monday evenings they met at his house for tea, talked over their work and then read and discussed a chapter of the Bible. Friends and old pupils of Maurice's from the country or distant parts of London often came to these gatherings, Kingsley among them. In one of the lively discussions during the winter of 1847-48 Kingsley found himself in a minority of one and announced that he felt as Lot must have done in the Cities of the Plain when he seemed to his sons-in-law as one that mocked. Parson Lot was instantly offered him as a pseudonym.

Parson Lot's "Letters to the Chartists" expanded the ideas in his placard and his address to the Workmen of England: "I must say honestly, whomsoever I may offend, the more I have read of your convention speeches and newspaper articles the more convinced I am that too many of you are trying to do God's work with the devil's tools."

The National Gallery articles were chiefly concerned with the refreshment which the working man can find in beautiful things.

Picture-galleries [they began] should be the workman's paradise, and garden of pleasure, to which he goes to refresh his eyes and heart with beautiful shapes and sweet colouring, when they are wearied with dull bricks and mortar, and the ugly colourless things which fill the workshop and the factory. . . .
God made you love beautiful things only because He intends hereafter to give you your fill of them. That pictured face on the wall is lovely—but lovelier still may be the wife of thy bosom be when she meets thee on the resurrection morn! Those baby cherubs in the old Italian painting—how gracefully they flutter and sport among the soft clouds, full of rich young life and baby joy!—Yes, beautiful, indeed, but just such a one at this very moment is that once pining, deformed child of thine, over whose death-cradle thou wast weeping a month ago; now a child-angel, whom thou shalt meet again never to part! ("The National Gallery," 1, *Politics for the People,* May 6, 1848.)

The second paper talks of Bellini's Doge; the third of museums as promoters of the consciousness of common brotherhood. But brotherhood was not a doctrine which could be preached without reservation in the middle of the nineteenth century. Kingsley's friends and relatives were distressed, those who could help him to professional promotion and those who were interested in his advancement and success. There is little concrete information to be found on the point but Mrs. Kingsley prints one significant outburst, in a letter to her, with this comment: "He had a sore battle to go through at this time with his own heart, and with those friends and relations, religious and worldly, who each and all from their own particular standpoint deprecated the line he took, and urged him to withdraw from this sympathy with the people, which they thought likely to spoil his prospects in life. In reference to this he writes to his wife:

I will not be a liar. I will speak in season and out of season. I will not shun to declare the whole counsel of God. I will not take counsel with flesh and blood, and flatter myself into the dream that while every man on earth, from Maurice back to Abel, who ever tried to testify against the world, has been laughed at, misunderstood, slandered, and that, bitterest of all, by the very people he loved best, and understood best, I alone am to escape. My path is clear, and I will follow in it. He who died for me, and who gave me you, shall I not trust Him through whatsoever new and strange paths He may lead me? (I, 178.)

Years before the strange paths opened Kingsley had made up his mind to be a fighter of abuses. "What is the use," he cried, "of talking to hungry paupers about heaven?" He had seen at first hand enough of the condition of the poor to know that they must be lifted out of the state of beasts before they could begin to think of themselves as immortal souls and he was impatient with the hazy piety of the day which tried to keep its eyes fixed only upon the beautiful. "I will never believe that a man has a real love for the good and beautiful, except he attacks the evil and the disgusting the moment he sees it!" he writes to his wife. (Pimperne, April 21, 1844.) "It is very easy to turn our eyes away from ugly sights, and so consider ourselves refined. The refined man to me is he who cannot rest in peace with a coal mine, or a factory, or a Dorsetshire peasant's house near him, in the state in which they are." (I, 121.)

His Christian Socialist activities undoubtedly militated against Kingsley's appointment to the lectureship for which Maurice, now Professor of Theology at King's College, had been urging him ever since the increasing number of his students made it imperative for him to have assistance.

He did begin, however, on May 13, to lecture weekly at Queen's College which Maurice and other professors at King's had established a year before, primarily for the examining and training of governesses. Kingsley was ready to share in the unpopular task because he believed in the higher education of women. It was one of the many causes whose pioneers counted him among their chief supporters. He was especially interested in promoting the medical education of women and he believed in woman's suffrage though he declined to take an active part in the movement when he thought that its advocates were injuring their cause by indecorous and unwomanly practices. (See Chap. XXI, pp. 180-1.)

Two of his lectures as Professor of English Literature and Composition are included in the volume of *Introductory Lectures delivered at Queen's College* (London, 1849). They greatly disturbed the *Quarterly Review* (March 1850) which inquired whether it were not dangerous to encourage young girls to write poetry and to urge the cultivation of the heart, of personal and concrete sympathies, upon governesses whose first duty is to prevent the rising of personal feelings toward their employers. Kingsley had advocated the practice of verse forms as leading strings to skill in prose, which is "highest," and had italicized to the young ladies his favourite doctrine of woman's rôle in the dual task of life. He advocated, too, boldly, as the first requisite for a modern course of English literature, that it be "a whole course or none. The literary education of woman has too often fallen into the fault of our 'Elegant Extracts,' and 'Beauties of British Poetry.' "

When the breakdown in health which followed the writing of *Yeast* forced him to abandon his lectures in the middle of a course on Early English Literature, he advised his successor, the Rev. Alfred Strettell, "not to cram them with things, but to teach them how to read for themselves. . . . We want to train—not cupboards full of 'information' (vile misnomer), but real informed women." "Don't be afraid," he added, apropos of Chaucer, "of talking about marriage. We must be real and daring at Queen's College, or nowhere." (I, 201.)

Another stage on which he was urged to speak thoughts ahead of his time Kingsley found in *The Christian Socialist, A Journal of Association,* which, in November 1850, rose from the ashes of *Politics for the People* and burned for a year and a half. The Christian Socialists—Maurice had invented the term—wished to make practical trial of their theory that the best way for the workingman to help himself was by means of cooperative associations. They organized one, of tailors, as a model and, as interest grew, formed a Society for the Promotion of Working Men's Associations, on whose council Kingsley sat; and suffered, as Hughes relates, for his ingrained conservatism and sense of decorum were constantly offended by the eccentricities of some of the fanatics attracted by the new social movement. "As if we shall not be abused enough," he used to say, "for what we must say and do without being saddled with mischievous nonsense of this kind." He often suffered, for instance, from finding himself at Association meetings surrounded by bearded men, at a period when to wear a beard was to declare oneself at the very least a French Revolutionary. On one occasion, Hughes says, Kingsley's usual eager voluble discussion of affairs was entirely silenced by the appearance of a bearded member of Council in a straw hat and blue plush gloves. "He did not recover from the depression produced by those gloves for days." Yet despite the blue plush gloves the Society for the Promotion of Associations grew in strength. The gap between its periodicals was bridged by a series of Tracts by Christian Socialists of which the most notable was Kingsley's *Cheap Clothes and Nasty*. Its title was the tailors' own slang for garments made under sweatshop conditions. Its facts came from H. Mayhew's *Morning Chronicle* articles on "London Labour and the London Poor." Kingsley set those concerning the tailors in an excited Carlylean sermon which attracted wide attention. Again he spoke in terms which Esau could understand and the tracts sold well at Eton, lay on the table at the Guards' Club and caused young officers to order coats from the Castle Street cooperative workroom.

The success of the tracts made the Christian Socialists still more eager for a regular periodical and in the early autumn of 1850 Kingsley wrote delightedly to Ludlow: "When 'God sends mouths, He sends meat.' So Lees will lend us the £100 to-morrow. He is *engoué* with the thing; will do anything to help it—seems very much longing to buy up Jacob's Island and build a model lodging-house, etc., etc." Lees, a young Cantabrigian, was reading for holy orders under Kingsley's tuition and Kingsley's enthusiasms were highly contagious. Kingsley's letter went on to lay down a programme for the paper: "1. Politics according to the Kingdom of God. 2. Art and Amusements for the People. 3. Opening the Universities to the People, and Education in general. 4. Attacking Straussism and Infidelity. 5. Sanitary Reform. 6. Association: α. Agitation on Partnership Laws; β. Stores and Distribution; γ. Agricultural Schemes. All the five former subjects *are* connected with Socialism, *i.e.,* with a live and practical Church." (I, 240.)

Parson Lot did three series of articles, two sometimes running at once. The first series was called "Thoughts on the Frimley Murder."

The rector of Frimley, not ten miles from Eversley, had been shot in his own garden by one of the many gangs of thieves and housebreakers whom poverty and unemployment had driven to desperate marauding about the countryside. Kingsley put bolts and bars upon the hospitable doors of Eversley rectory and slept with loaded pistols by his side, which he had occasion to use. His younger pupil, John Martineau (his father was Harriet's cousin) wrote to his mother a boy's delighted account of the excitement:

Eversley, September 6, 1850

There have been plenty more robberies, and a man was stopped between here and Hartford Bridge on the road over the moor. . . . A jeweller's shop at Wokingham, five miles off, was robbed, and a man at Mattingley, near Heckfield. . . .

But I must tell you about our attack. We were well prepared, and had that very day had an extra bar or bolt put on the back door, which is very old and weak, and had a wire tied to a bell close to one of the maid's rooms upstairs, passed across the door on the inside, so that any one shaking the door much would ring the bell; also there was a string going all along near the door, tied to some bells. It was the night Mr. Maurice was here. He slept in my room, and I in Mr. K.'s dressing-room. The six rooms—mine, Lees's, day-nursery, night-nursery, Mr. and Mrs. K.'s room, and Mr. K.'s dressing-room—open into one another, so that we all lock our outer doors . . . and have a communication with one another. Mr. Kingsley had a gun, loaded with slugs, and two pistols, and Lees a rifle and two pistols loaded in his room. Well, at half-past two the bell by the maid's room rang three distinct times, whereupon they foolishly rang it themselves violently instead of coming to wake us. Mr. Kingsley jumped up and ran with pistols straight down to the back door, but was too late to catch them; they had been frightened by hearing the ring, and were gone. Meantime Mrs. K. had waked Lees, who came out, a cocked pistol in each hand, under the impression that they were outside the bedroom doors. He looked immensely absurd with a thin pair of trousers and pair of slippers and nightshirt on, crouching along through the door-way, presenting his pistols, expecting to have to shoot some one the next instant. However, as there was no one to be found in the house, Mr. K. and Lees ran out as they were, over the garden, while I mounted guard with the rifle in the hall and passage. They could find no one, and it was not to be expected that they would, for it was as dark as pitch, so Mr. K., Lees, and Mr. Maurice sat up two or three hours, and the rest of us went to bed. In the morning we found two footmarks side by side . . . close by the wall of the coal place.

September 10, 1850

Having on Saturday seen or heard somebody skulking about the premises for the fourth time in five days, Mr. K. unwillingly took the Speaker's advice and wrote to Odiham for a blue-bottle. He and Lees watched in the stable, while G. Chaplin was at the cottage lecture. About ten o'clock they all three went out to establish G. Chaplin in the stable with the gun for the night. They only had two of the pistols and the gun with them, and they went out carelessly one by one. Mr. K. got out of the back door about a dozen yards before the other two, and the instant he was outside Dandie growled, and a man was heard close by, running away. Dandie dashed forward and Mr. K. fired, and by the light of the pistol he saw the man about fifteen yards off, with leather gaiters, as far as he could make out about the colour of Dandie. They all three pursued him as hard as they could go, but he escaped in the pitch-darkness. Mr. K. fired over Dandie's head, for he could not see the man till the flash. It was exactly in the right place, for D. was, as he supposed, close to his heels, but unfortunately Mr. K. had one of the short little pistols loaded with three slugs and not a bullet, and at fifteen yards such a little pistol would hardly send them into a man far enough to hurt him much, especially through thick clothes. However, it is very possible that he may have been hit, and Mr. K. thinks it as likely as not. (Violet Martineau, *John Martineau the Pupil of Kingsley*, London, 1921, p. 6.)

Kingsley's "Thoughts on the Frimley Murder," however, were not those of an irate property holder who had been kept awake at night. He was aware that economic conditions rather than natural depravity were at the base of the outrages and he met the situation in his own parish by returning to the farmers ten per cent on their tithe payments.

"The Bible throughout is the history of the People's cause," was the theme of Parson Lot's second set of articles, "Bible Politics or God Justified to the People." It protested, too, against the Emerson-Strauss philosophy, which Kingsley defined as every-man-his-own-God, and it showed how all the history of mankind has been guided by a just and merciful ruler. Even what seem to us fearful calamities may be fulfilling His high purposes and will work in the long run for good. Sometimes His instruments may go beyond his commission, as they did in the French Revolution, and will then suffer for it. One of Kingsley's favourite ethnological ideas is introduced here for the first time: the Canaanites because of foul practices and disease were a rotting, dying nation, like the Red Indians in America, like the Romans conquered by the Goths; it was merciful to kill them and put them out of their misery. The articles drew down a rain of argumentative letters as did those on "The Church versus Malthus."

To Volume II of the *Christian Socialist* (July to December 1851) Kingsley's contributions are almost entirely literary, and not nearly so lengthy as those in Volume I. Part of the cause for this he set forth in an intimate letter to Maurice.

A thousand thanks for all your advice and information, which encourages me to say more. I don't know how far I shall be able to write much for the Christian Socialist. Don't fancy that I am either lazy or afraid. But I will tell you the truth. The last Frimley letter, and the one before it also, Ludlow did not like . . . and, I am sorry to say, put in the last one, in spite of his dislike; thereby binding me to continue the series, malgré lui, and not knowing really what to say to please him. Not that there is the least unpleasantness: but he has renewed about the last letter the old theory which he started about the latter part of Yeast, that it was written when I was ill and tired, and therefore unworthy of me. . . . And though I am not thinskinned and nervous, after the manner of poets, yet such a notion does utterly paralyze my pen, when I cannot alter my opinions, and must go on in the same strain or none. I wanted to give up this Frimley series, and go on with the Bible letters. But to that he reasonably enough objects. And indeed, I dare not go on with them, for the next subject which I shall have to face are those exterminations of the Canaanites, on which I must say things which will horrify him, and he will have to protest against them . . . and if he does, I must protest against him and the whole kiss-the-devil school—and there is confusion and discord enough already without that. . . . Altogether I am a very foolish person who has sat down to build a tower without counting the cost.

And moreover if I do not use my pen to the uttermost in earning my daily bread, I shall not get through. I am paying off the loans which I got to meet the expenses of repairing and furnishing; but with an income reduced this year by more than £200, having at last given up, thank God, that sinecure clerkship [in his father's church in Chelsea], and having had to return ten per cent. of my tithes, owing to the agricultural distress, I have also now, for the first time, the opportunity, and therefore the necessity, of supporting a good school. My available income this year is less than £400. I cannot reduce my charities, and I am driven either to give up my curate, or to write for my bread, and either of these alternatives, with the increased parish work, for I have got either lectures or night school every night in the week, and three services on Sunday, will demand my whole time. (January 16, 1851.)

The Frimley letters ceased but Malthus and the Bible Politics went on till June. The more literary contributions—most of them were propaganda too—included "The Nun's Pool," part of which was incorporated in *Yeast*, and a half dozen poems, among them

"*I Am a Church of England Parson—and a Chartist*" 71

"The Three Fishers," all later included in his first volume of collected verse.

In 1854 the Society for the Promotion of Working Men's Associations collapsed and the Christian Socialist movement virtually came to an end. The cooperative enterprise had failed chiefly because the promoters' knowledge of economic conditions and the state of the market was less sound than their enthusiasm. Kingsley continued to believe in the efficacy of the associative idea, though he became convinced that its time was not yet, the working man was not ready for it. It would take a generation or two of training in morality and "drill" to free him from the dangers of anarchy and the tyranny of demagogues and enable him to work a truly democratic institution. To association for distribution Kingsley looked with much higher hopes for immediate success. It would be, he felt certain, the next form of industrial development. In any case "the failure of a hundred schemes would not alter my conviction, that they are attempts in the right direction; and I shall die in hope, not having received the promises, but beholding them afar off, and confessing myself a stranger and a pilgrim in a world of *laissez-faire*. For it is my belief that not self-interest, but self-sacrifice, is the only law upon which human society can be grounded with any hope of prosperity and permanence." (To John Bullar, November 26, 1857, II, 37.)

CHAPTER IX

"TAILOR AND POET"

THE enthusiasms, the excitements, the disappointments and hopes of the Christian Socialist years precipitated a novel, *Alton Locke, Tailor and Poet. An Autobiography*. It has "revealed itself to me," Kingsley wrote to Ludlow in February 1849, "so rapidly and methodically, that I feel it comes down from above, and that only my folly can spoil it—which I pray against daily." (I, 197.) Kingsley would have been a better novelist had he listened more often and with more respect to the dictation of that voice from above. How loud it spoke to him one may hear in his constant dread of becoming only "an artist," his conception of which dreadful fate is set forth at length in *Two Years Ago*. That was seven years later. Alton Locke falls not because he is only a poet but because he denies his poetry and his social principles, cutting out from his *Songs of the Highways* such radical expressions as offend a benevolent patronizing Dean. He had become a poet of the people under the advice of the old Scotch bookseller, Sandy Mackaye, who reproved him for writing verses about the South Sea Islands:

"True poetry, like true charity, my laddie, begins at hame. If ye'll be a poet at a', ye maun be a cockney poet; and while the cockneys be what they be, ye maun write, like Jeremiah of old, o' lamentation and mourning and woe, for the sins o' your people. Gin ye want to learn the spirit o' a people's poet, down wi' your Bible and read thae auld Hebrew prophets; gin ye wad learn the style, read your Burns frae morning till night; and gin ye'd learn the matter, just gang after your nose, and keep your eyes open, and ye'll no miss it. . . .

"No poetry there! Is no the verra idea of the classic tragedy defined to be, man conquered by circumstance? Canna ye see it there? And the verra idea of the modern tragedy, man conquering circumstance?— and I'll show ye that, too—in mony a garret where no eye but the gude God's enters, to see the patience, and the fortitude, and the self-sacrifice and the luve stronger than death, that's shining in thae dark places o' the earth. Come wi' me, and see." (Chap. VIII.)

And Kingsley, because he was writing like Alton of the woes of London which cried aloud to him to be told, dared to let himself go. It is not without significance that his most propagandistic novel should be also his most artistic, that the closer he stays to his model the nearer he comes to truth. An acute observer in the United States once remarked that had Kingsley been an American he would have been a reporter on the *Tribune* under Horace Greeley.

Contemporary critics with one voice and critics ever since have praised Sandy Mackaye as the best character not merely in this but in all Kingsley's novels; his speech is his own and he walks alive out of the pages. Thomas Carlyle wrote of him (Chelsea, October 31, 1850): "My invaluable countryman . . . is nearly perfect; indeed I greatly wonder how you did contrive to manage him—his very dialect is as if a native had done it, and the whole existence of the rugged old hero is a wonderfully splendid and coherent piece of Scotch bravura." (I, 244.) Critics ever since of course have delighted to point out that how Kingsley did contrive to manage Saunders Mackaye was by looking at Thomas Carlyle. Before even he had read the book Carlyle's good offices found it a publisher, recommending to Chapman and Hall this "new explosion, or salvo of red-hot shot against the Devil's Dung-heap." (I, 234.)

A far less definite figure than the Carlylean one is Alton, the hero of the book. He is interesting chiefly for what happens to him and what happens to him is based upon what happened to the shoemaker-poet Thomas Cooper. Professor Louis Cazamian has pointed this out in his very convincing study, *Kingsley et Thomas Cooper, Etude sur une Source d'Alton Locke* (Paris, 1903). Cooper's Autobiography was not published until 1872 but he and Kingsley knew each other intimately and corresponded for years and the history may well have been transmitted by letter and word of mouth. The self-education at the cost of health, the arrest for inciting a riot which he was really trying to suppress, the unjust trial and imprisonment, the traitor cousin, the quarrel with O'Connor, the saving of a man about to jump into the Thames, all run close parallel to experiences of Cooper. Kingsley was a great admirer of *The Purgatory of Suicides* and deliberately sought Cooper's friendship.

Ever since I read your brilliant poem, "The Purgatory of Suicides," and its most affecting preface, I have been possessed by a desire to thrust myself, at all risks, into your acquaintance. The risk which I felt keenly, was the fear that you might distrust me, as a clergyman; having, I am afraid, no great reason to love that body of men. Still, I thought, the poetic spirit ought to be a bond of communion between us. Shall God make us brother-poets, as well as brother men, and we refuse to fraternise? I thought also that you, if you have a poet's heart, as well as the poet's brain which you have manifested, ought to be more able than other men to appreciate and sympathise with my feelings towards "the working classes." (June 19, 1848, I, 183.)

It was an attack by the *Commonwealth* upon some of Parson Lot's papers in *Politics for the People* which brought Kingsley to the point of writing this letter. The *Commonwealth* attacked him on some of the very points on which he most agreed with it and he found it intolerable to be so misunderstood. He had long chafed under the working men's distrust of him merely because he was a clergyman, their instinctive feeling that he must therefore be an "aristocrat." He genuinely wanted to realize his brotherhood with them, to find some one among their number who would give him such an insight into their thoughts and feelings that he could more effectively consecrate his powers to their service. He asked Cooper to be that man, and Cooper accepted the letter in the spirit in which it was written. A friendship was founded which lasted for many years.

In 1849 appeared the first number of *Cooper's Journal* and Kingsley wrote to Ludlow: "Here is a man of immense influence, openly preaching Straussism to the workmen, and in a fair, honest, manly way which *must* tell. Who will answer him? Who will answer Strauss? Who will denounce Strauss as a vile *aristocrat*, robbing the poor man of his Saviour—of the ground of all democracy, all freedom, all association—of the Charter itself?" (I, 234.)

He undertook the task himself and seven years later converted Cooper to orthodox Christianity. Cooper says that when he began to feel doubts of the mythical theory of Strauss which "never made me happy," "I determined to open my mind fully to my large-hearted friend Charles Kingsley. He showed the fervent sympathy of a brother. We began a correspondence [letters of enormous length] which extended over many months: in fact, over more than a year. I told him every doubt and described every hope I had; and he counselled, instructed, and strengthened me to the end." (*The Life of Thomas Cooper,* Written by Himself, London, 1872, pp. 356, 368.)

A few other portraits in *Alton Locke* can be referred to living models: "O'Flynn," editor of the *Weekly Warhoop,* is Feargus O'Connor, the Chartist leader. "The —— ambassador," to whom Alton is presented at the Dean's reception, is Baron Bunsen. The big medical student who takes rowdy tender care of Alton when, late at night, he faints from hunger in the streets is surely Dr. George Kingsley who had taken his degree at Edinburgh in 1847. The scientific, kindly Dean who patronizes Alton bears resemblance, perhaps, to Bishop Marsh of Peterborough, the benevolent friend of Kingsley's father. His wife was a patroness of the peasant poet John Clare whose relationships with the great have several similarities to Alton's, notably the insistence of his aristocratic friends on the omission from his first volume of poems of certain "too outspoken" and "radical" lines denouncing wealth. Kegan Paul says ("Charles Kingsley," *Biographical Sketches,* London, 1883, p. 129) that the Dean "who rationalises miracle for Alton Locke" was intended for Bunsen but this seems unlikely in a book which contains another, and an indubitable, portrait of quite a different character. Kingsley, however, has neatly blocked all surmises:

"Why!" exclaims the reading public, if perchance it ever sees this tale of mine, in its usual prurient longing after anything like personal gossip, or scandalous anecdote—"why, there is no cathedral town which begins with a D! Through the fen, too! He must mean either Ely, Lincoln, or Peterborough; that's certain." Then, at one of those places, they find there is a dean—not of the name of Winnstay, true—"but his name begins with a W; and he has a pretty daughter—no, a niece; well, that's very near it;—it must be him. No; at another place —there is not a dean, true—but a canon, or an archdeacon—something of that kind; and he has a pretty daughter, really; and his name begins—not with W, but with Y; well, that's the last letter of Winnstay, if it is not the first: that must be the poor man! What a shame to have exposed his family secrets in that way!" (Chap. XIV.)

We may fairly suppose, however, that Alton's mother and her friends were animated by that Baptist form of dissent, founded on supra-lapsarian Calvinistic dogmas, which was one of the causes of Kingsley's first letter to Maurice. Dissenters who read the book raised violent objection not so much to the fact that Kingsley made them unlovely characters as to his providing them with doctrines such as, they insisted, they had never held; just as the High Churchmen had taken exception to his interpretation of the ascetic mentality in *The Saint's Tragedy.* Kingsley could be genuinely tolerant of another's point of view but he was frequently incapable of comprehending it. He was convinced, that he knew the logical goal of Calvinist doctrines better than their holders and he fought them accordingly. "As for the Independents," he wrote Ludlow (January 1850), "I knew most of the facts you told me about them, and had no intention to make the preachers Independents, but types of any Calvinist sect. It was with the *ideal* of Calvinism, and its ultimate bearing on the people's cause, that I wished to deal. I believe that there must be internecine war between the People's Church, *i.e.* the future development of Catholic Christianity and Calvinism even its mildest form, whether in the English Establishment or out of it."

Whatever his difficulty with the dissenters Kingsley was able to get the point of view of the working men and to give it, to their often expressed satisfaction. He writes, for instance, in the 1854 Preface to *Alton Locke,* that "the thoughts and feelings of the hero . . . are compounded of right and wrong, and such as I judged (and working men whom I am proud to number among my friends have assured me that I judged rightly) that a working man of genius would feel during the course of his self-education."

Much of *Alton Locke* is a dramatization of *Cheap Clothes and Nasty,* the material coming from the *Morning Chronicle* articles on which that was founded. Kingsley had the ability to assimilate descriptive facts through reading, visualize them and then describe what he had visualized with that very heat with which he writes of immediate impressions.

Morning Chronicle (September 24, 1849), "A Visit to the Cholera District of Bermondsey":

> The water is covered with a scum like a cobweb and prismatic with grease. In it float large masses of green rotting weed, and against the posts of the bridges are swollen carcases of dead animals, almost bursting with the gases of putrefaction. . . . Wooden galleries and

sleeping rooms . . . overhang the dark flood . . . the very stench of death rising through the boards.

Alton Locke, Chap. XIV:

We rushed out on the balcony. The light of the policeman's lantern glared over the ghastly scene—along the double row of miserable house-backs, which lined the sides of the open tidal ditch—over strange rambling jetties, and balconies, and sleeping-sheds, which hung on rotting piles over the black waters, with phosphorescent scraps of rotten fish gleaming and twinkling out of the dark hollows, like devilish grave-lights—over bubbles of poisonous gas, and bloated carcases of dogs, and lumps of offal, floating on the stagnant olive-green hell-broth—over the slow sullen rows of oily ripple which were dying away into the darkness far beyond, sending up, as they stirred, hot breaths of miasma—the only sign that a spark of humanity, after years of foul life, had quenched itself at last in that foul death.

That Kingsley practised this method consciously is evident from a paragraph in his review of "Recent Novels" written for *Fraser's* (April 1849) while *Alton Locke* was on the stocks:

The authors have used *imagination*; they have imaged the scene to themselves, and, describing the pictures which they saw in their own minds, have therefore described well; . . . Mr. Ainsworth's description, on the other hand, is a mere collection of facts and names *about* the place, without order or chiaroscuro, top, or bottom, or middle—a tourist's guide, not a painter's sketch.

As with the Jacob's Island scenes Kingsley knew the tailors' shop, the Chartist newspaper, the sweater's den by a combination of reading and imagining. One feels fact, too, as well as imagination behind that admirable chapter (XI) on "The Yard Where the Gentlemen Live," an account of the effect produced by his first sight of the country upon a youth London born and bred. Alton walks from London to Cambridge and one remembers that Kingsley as an undergraduate once made the reverse journey, some fifty-two miles, on foot in a single day. Alton is on his way to bespeak from his rich Cantabrigian cousin help in finding patronage for his poems. The pictures of university life are the only ones Kingsley ever drew, though his brother Henry made many of Oxford. In 1862, after he had been for a year Professor of Modern History at Cambridge, Kingsley issued a new edition of *Alton Locke* with the university chapters rewritten. It is easy to accuse him of time-serving but the reason he gives in his Preface seems thoroughly sincere.

> Those sketches were drawn from my own recollections of 1838-1842. Whether they were overdrawn is a question between me and men of my own standing.
>
> But the book was published in 1849; and I am assured by men in whom I have the most thorough confidence, that my sketches had by then at least become exaggerated and exceptional, and therefore, as a whole, untrue; that a process of purification was going on rapidly in the University; and that I must alter my words if I meant to give the working man a just picture of her. . . .
>
> I see at Cambridge nothing which does not gain my respect for her present state and hope for her future. Increased sympathy between the old and young, increased intercourse between the teacher and the taught, increased freedom and charity of thought, and a steady purpose of internal self-reform and progress. . . . And among the young men themselves . . . increased earnestness and high-mindedness, increased sobriety and temperance, combined with a manliness not inferior to that of the stalwart lads of twenty years ago. . . .
>
> Much of this improvement seems to me due to the late High-Church movement; much to the influence of Dr. Arnold; much to that of Mr. Maurice; much to the general increase of civilization throughout the country.

While, therefore, in the 1850 version, Alton, following a boat race on the Cam, is ridden over and pushed into the river by an insolent nobleman, and Lord Lynedale (the model aristocrat) apologizes for his friend and offers a tip which is indignantly refused (Chap. XII), in 1862 Lynedale on foot runs into Alton by mistake. The apology and tip take place as before. The somewhat bacchanalian supper party described in Chapter XIII in 1850 is entirely omitted in 1862. Omitted, too, is George Locke's discourse on the wretched state of the university which, grown away from its founders' monastic ideals, yet makes hypocritical pretence of living by monastic laws, afraid to begin reform lest the whole rotten structure fall. (Chap. XIII.) Lynedale's servant, too, is improved; he is no longer insolent and he does not take Alton for a dun. (Chap. XIII.)

Almost every section of *Alton Locke* was disapproved by some group or other and even Kingsley's friends and admirers united in condemnation of the dream chapter (XXXVI) near the end, but

Kingsley, who had had strange visions in his youth, knew his own mind and clung to this as he clung to the conclusion of *Yeast*.

In that dream chapter Alton, delirious with typhus brought on by prison, emotion and exposure, goes through all the stages of evolution from a madrepore without unity or individuality through a crab, remora, ostrich, mylodon and ape to primitive man. His Beatrice at succeeding stages of the dream is the nobler of the cousin heroines. Enlightened by his dream, Alton sees, on awakening, that the lovely Lillian is a shallow creature. His admiration turns to the, now widowed, Lady Ellerton, though there is no remote possibility of her stooping to care for him even were she not dying of tuberculosis. She makes Alton embark upon a recuperative voyage in the course of which he is to write his autobiography and he dies just in sight of the new world. A crude tale, as Carlyle said, yet with fire in it and a picture of the miseries of mind and body of the working man in the 1840's as valuable as that in *Yeast* of the spiritual unrest of the upper middle class. The reviewers of course found it dangerously revolutionary and their methods of expressing disapproval were not always above reproach.

Sir [wrote Kingsley to the Editor of the *Record*], An anonymous person, signing himself "Presbyter E.," has lately, through your columns, increased the publicity of certain works of mine. I beg to be allowed to make a few remarks on his letter.

If you will examine the title-page of *Alton Locke,* a book whose authorship I hereby frankly avow, you will find, I doubt not, to your great astonishment, that your correspondent does not seem even to have looked at it. He states, *in italics,* its title to be "Alton Locke; or, the Autobiography of a Chartist," and then complains that "so morbid and dangerous" a work should have "gone forth under a title so calculated to ensure a large and rapid circulation." It will seem, I doubt not, absolutely incredible to you after this, that the words in the title which he considers so objectionably alluring, are purely of his own invention and insertion; and that the title stands simply, "Alton Locke, Tailor and Poet, an Autobiography." Such a misrepresentation must be the result of gross carelessness, or of wilful dishonesty, either of which renders his opinion, as to the book in question, utterly worthless.

I must also beg leave to inform you, that whosoever says that I "ignore the fall of man and the corruption of human nature," simply states a falsehood; for I firmly believe both. . . .

The passage about Camille Desmoulins, your correspondent has grossly, I will hope, not wilfully, perverted. My words are *not* that

Camille's saying "is an almighty truth;" for it is not that, or even a truth at all; but, that "it is *the distortion of* an almighty truth;" . . .

I beg distinctly to state that I mean hereby no apology or palliation whatsoever for any opinion *really expressed by me as my own,* either in *Alton Locke* or my *Village Sermons,* because I believe that both of them will be found to accord strictly with scriptural and evangelical truth, and to have for their object the preservation of all that is most time-honoured both in Church and State. . . .

It only remains for me to inform the public, through your columns, that I have just withdrawn my name from the Committee of Queen's College, in the proceedings or lectures of which I have been unable to take any part whatsoever in the last two years. I have done this because I do not wish my name to be used as a handle against an establishment which I have every reason to respect, and in reprobating which I believe you will ultimately find yourself to have been mistaken, though I do not doubt that you have done so from the most conscientious motives (*Record,* November 7, 1850.)

The *Edinburgh Review* (January 1851) likewise so misrepresented the ideas of Kingsley and Maurice that Kingsley sent to the *Morning Chronicle* (January 28, 1851) a letter of refutation.

In September (1851) the *Quarterly Review* put *Alton Locke, Yeast, The Message of the Church to Labouring Men, Politics for the People,* and some sermons by Maurice together with a dozen French works historical and propagandic and headed their article "Revolutionary Literature":

"We should not," they explained, "have taken the superfluous trouble of thus establishing the identity of French and English Socialism, but for the strange spectacle of two clergymen of the Church of England coming forth as the apostles of a doctrine fraught with such terrible consequences, and . . . attempting to invest their miserable delusions with the authority of Christianity and the sanction of the Gospel." This article Kingsley deliberately declined to read. "There is no use for a hot-tempered and foul-mouthed man like myself praying not to be led into temptation, and then reading, voluntarily, attacks on himself from the firm of Wagg, Wenham, & Co." (To George Brimley, 1890 ed., p. 109.)

There were plenty of advocates of the book, however; one of the acutest the *Revue des Deux Mondes* in which Emile Montégut pointed out that England does not know what socialism is and never will. ("Le Socialisme et la Littérature Democratique en Angleterre," May 1, 1851.) It is foreign to the genius of a people who think in facts, not in ideas. Their socialist literature in nowise resembles French socialist literature; it has neither sensuality nor the spirit of revolt. Mr. Kingsley is incontestably "un homme de talent," though he has "la trop grande envie de réunir des choses inconciliables, une sorte de charité intellectuelle beaucoup trop large." Mackaye is "tout simplement une des meilleurs et des plus originales créations de la littérature anglaise moderne." There was almost unanimous agreement on that point on both sides of the Channel as there was admiration for the second of the famous drawing-room songs, "The Sands of Dee." (Chap. XXVI.) So popular did this become that a contest was waged for it between the Scotch and English rivers thirty years after Kingsley's death. The palm of inspiration was at last adjudged by Miss Rose Kingsley to Cheshire (*Journal of the Architectural, Archaeological, and Historic Society for the County and City of Chester and North Wales,* Chester, 1908, XIV, 97.) Kingsley stated the locale as Cheshire in the first edition of *Alton Locke,* but not all the singers of the song had read the novel. The drowning incident was Kingsley's own invention.

CHAPTER X

"THE THREE FISHERS"

THE Church of St. John the Evangelist, Charlotte Street, Fitzroy Square, is probably the most complete Norman edifice in England. Building in the early nineteenth century, its well documented architect included every conceivable Norman feature from occulus to cushion capital, and added even a Norman gallery. The total result, however, is not so much massive as grim and very brown, despite the magenta of the east window; a not inappropriate background for the curious scene enacted there on the evening of Sunday, June 22, 1851.

Many working men came to London in that summer of '51 to visit the Prince Consort's Great Exhibition at the Crystal Palace, and it occurred to some London clergymen to arrange courses of lectures for them. The Rev. Mr. G. S. Drew, Rector of St. John the Evangelist, was especially interested in the project because his church stood close to the John Street lecture rooms much frequented by labouring men of atheistic views. He invited the Rev. Frederick Denison Maurice to preach a sermon in his church and also the Rev. Charles Kingsley.

On the evening when Kingsley spoke the church was crowded. There were hundreds of attentive faces under the symmetrical Norman arches, working men most of them, with a scattering of gentry, curious or genuinely sympathetic. When the moment for the sermon came Kingsley, tall and ungainly, mounted the pulpit and began, his voice, as always when he preached, freeing itself at once from the stammer and becoming deep, resonant, compelling. He preached "the acceptable year of the Lord," and so rare are copies of that sermon that it seems worth while to quote it in some detail:

I assert that the business for which God sends a Christian priest in a Christian nation, is to preach and practise liberty, equality, and brotherhood, in the fullest, deepest, widest, simplest meaning of these three great words: . . .

I say those words express the very pith and marrow of a priest's business. I say that they preach liberty, equality, and brotherhood to the poor and rich for ever and ever.

You will all agree, at least, that there is nothing tending to excuse tyranny, pride of class, persecution, or enslavement of the intellect in them. . . .

But if there was one expression of the Lord Jesus on that day which must, above all others, have given hope to the oppressed poor of Judæa, and struck terror into the hearts of those who had been enslaving their countrymen—adding house to house, and field to field, and making a few rich at the expense of many poor—it must have been the last sentence which he quotes from Isaiah:—"The spirit of the Lord hath anointed me to proclaim the acceptable year of the Lord." Now, there would be no doubt in the minds of His hearers as to what He meant, for that year of the Lord, justly called acceptable and pleasant to the many, was one of the wisest of Moses's institutions, by which, at the expiration of a certain period, all debtors and bond-servants were released, and all land which had been sold returned to its original possessor: so that in Judæa there could be no absolute or eternal alienation of the soil, but only, as Moses ordered, a lease of it, according to its value, between the time of sale and the next year of Jubilee. If I wanted one proof above all others of the inspired wisdom of Moses, I should choose this unparalleled contrivance for preventing the accumulation of large estates, and the reduction of the people into the state of serfs and day-labourers. And this acceptable year, the Lord said He was come to preach; and more—that the Spirit of God had anointed Him to proclaim it—that eternal Spirit of eternal justice and eternal righteousness, whose laws cannot change for any consideration of men's expediency, but true once, are true for ever; and, therefore, if those words of the Lord of all the earth mean anything, my friends, they mean this: that all systems of society which favour the accumulation of capital in a few hands—which oust the masses from the soil which their forefathers possessed of old—which reduce them to the level of serfs and day-labourers, living on wages and on alms—which crush them down with debt, or in anywise degrade or enslave them, or deny them a permanent stake in the commonwealth, are contrary to the kingdom of God which Jesus proclaimed—contrary to the eternal justice and righteousness of the Spirit of God—contrary to the constitution of man and the will of his heavenly Father—and contrary to the idea of the Church, which witnesses for God's kingdom upon earth, and calls all men and nations to enter into it and be saved therein in body, soul, and spirit. And, therefore, I hold it the duty of every Christian priest, upon the strength of that one single text—even if the same lesson did not run through the whole of Scripture from beginning to end—to lift up his voice like a trumpet and cry aloud, as I do now, "How hardly shall they that have riches enter into the kingdom of God." "Woe unto you that are full, for ye have received your consolation already." "Woe unto you that add house to house and field to field, that ye may stand alone in the land till there be no room left." Woe unto you that make a few rich to make many poor. Woe unto you that make merchandize out of the needs of your brethren. Woe unto you who on the hustings and on the platform fall down and humble yourselves, that the congregation of the poor may fall into the hands of your leaders. Woe unto you, for God, the Father of all, is against you —God the Son, the poor man of Nazareth, is against you—God the Holy Spirit, who cannot lie, is against you. There is a way which seemeth right unto a man, but the end thereof is Death. . . .

. . . if you wish to know what the message of the Church really is, you must put out of your heads what the clergy of this particular time or of any other particular time may happen to say it is. You must judge of the Church by her idea, and by her essence, and not merely by the accidents or the diseases of part of her. . . .

And what, my friends, is the message of the Lord's supper? What more distinct sign and pledge that all men are equal? Wherever in the world there may be inequality, it ceases there. One table, one reverential posture, one bread, one wine, for high and low, for wise and foolish. . . .

There is one man at least in this church now who has been awakened from the selfish and luxurious dreams of his youth, by that message of the Bible and of the sacraments, to see the dignity of the people's cause—to feel it at once the most peremptory of duties and the most glorious of privileges to proclaim, in the name of Jesus of Nazareth, the message of the Church of Christ—That the will of God is, good news to the poor, deliverance to the captives, healing to the broken-hearted, light to the ignorant, liberty to the crushed, and to the degraded masses the acceptable year of the Lord—a share and a stake, for them and for their children after them, in the soil, the wealth, the civilization, and the government of this English land. (*The Message of the Church to Labouring Men.*)

He ceased amid an applauding silence. Mr. Drew rose in his reading desk. "Christian friends!"[1] he said, "I have a duty to perform—one of the most painful that has ever devolved upon me; but, being placed over this congregation by the Bishop of London, I feel compelled to say, that while much that the preacher has advanced has given me great satisfaction, I must and do protest

[1] J. Stores Smith, Esq., writer of a letter to the *Leader,* June 28, believed this to be verbatim.

against much that he has said as extremely imprudent and untrue. I may say, also, it is altogether different to what I had been led to expect."

A furious murmur ran through the pews. "Thank God, thank Him on your knees," a friend wrote to Mrs. Kingsley, "that Charles did not answer a single word; if he had, I do not know what might not have happened. Robertson and Hansard had severally to quiet knots of working men, who were beginning to hiss or otherwise testify their disapproval. A word from Charles, or, indeed, from any one on his behalf, might have raised such a storm as God only could have quelled." (I, 290.)

Kingsley merely bowed his head and went silently into the vestry but the incident blazed into a *cause célèbre* and for him personally it was a shattering experience. He had made an egregious failure in a cause for which he passionately cared, the attempt to convince the working man that the Church was genuinely concerned with his welfare. If Mr. Drew, instead of merely doing his duty according to his Neo-Norman lights, had been trying to wound Charles Kingsley as exquisitely as possible he could scarcely have arranged a set of circumstances more pertinent to his purpose.

The story got into the papers of course, accurately and inaccurately, with letters pro and con. The mention of Kingsley's name brought cheers at working men's meetings. The Bishop of London, Blomfield, wrote forbidding him to preach again in his diocese but withdrew the prohibition immediately when he had read the sermon and talked with Kingsley himself. The sermon was rushed into print and sold rapidly.

"The readers of this Sermon will be kind enough to remember," ran the Advertisement, "that it has not been corrected by the writer; . . . His friends took the manuscript from him as soon as it had been preached. They were determined that the awful charge, which is implied in the assertion by a fellow-clergyman, that he believed Mr. Kingsley to have uttered false doctrine, should be submitted to fair trial."

The excitement lasted long. The most eloquent testimony to Kingsley's behaviour throughout the whole controversy is born in a letter in which Mr. Drew defended himself against the accusations in the *Spectator* (November 15, 1851) of one T. C. D. who added to his communication, "Mr. Kingsley is quite uncognizant of this letter." "I am sure he was," wrote Mr. Drew (*Spectator* November 29, 1851). "Would that all Mr. Kingsley's friends had acted as honourably, and with as much candour and kindness, as he has done in that most painful affair which connected so unhappily our names together."

Exhausted in body and spirit Kingsley had gone down to Eversley the day after the sermon. Late into that night he paced up and down the green "quarter deck" before his study door and found his rest by composing—he recited the stanzas to his wife next morning—what is perhaps the truest poem he ever wrote. "The Three Fishers" carries no specific "message" and its story is of the simplest ballad sort; only the poet is moved to the depths of his being and cries out in his pain. Deep stirred, his mind brought up the scenes which had wrought on his excited boyhood, the beach at Clovelly after a storm:

>Three corpses lay out on the shining sands
> In the morning gleam as the tide went down,
>And the women are weeping and wringing their hands.

The burthen is the deep cry of weariness which rose often in his heart but which he seldom uttered save to his wife or Maurice:

>For men must work, and women must weep,
>And the sooner it's over, the sooner to sleep.

It was this mood which made him gratefully accept an invitation to accompany his parents and his brother Henry who were just setting out on a trip to Germany. He left his parish to a curate and took the holiday thoroughly. It was the first time he had ever been out of England and he drank up every new experience with eager thirst. The only flaws were the separation from his wife and the irregularities of the post, but he wrote copious constant letters and, since he was having a surfeit of emotions, more poetry than he had done in years.[2] He was at work, too, on his next novel, *Hypatia*. The St. John's Church incident was closed and he had always the temperament which can forget things done. "I am now

---

[2] The poems of this period which were thought worthy of print include: "Margaret to Dolcino," "Dolcino to Margaret," "The Ugly Princess," "The Baby Sings not on its Mother's Breast," and "A Thought from the Rhine," *Poems*, 1858.

sure," he wrote to Ludlow on the eve of departure, "this thing will work for good, and am happy as a bird, but somewhat done up."

His letters home were a succession of enthusiasms, beginning at Cologne with Kaulbach's "grand pictures in painted glass." "At them I did not cry; but at the choir I did, and cried, too, like a child, at the head of the Virgin in that great triptych of Koloff's, the Adoration; that head is the most wonderful female head I ever saw yet from the hand of man." (I, 292.) Then it was the Rhine and its vineyards, the Drachenfels, Rolandseck, Nonnenwerth *and that story.* Germany was, he admitted, a more charming country than England, and he thanked God therefore that he could not often yield to the temptation to escape there from the work he was set to do. "Really," he wrote after hearing from a pot-house keeper an intelligent discussion of modern art, "this Germany is a wonderful country—though its population are not members of the Church of England." (I, 296.)

Charles and his brother Henry left their parents from time to time to tramp, preferably up and down mountains, with proper British energy, apologizing for the fact that with thirty-pound knapsacks they could do no more than fifteen miles a day; collecting "unspeakable" butterflies, red and blue locusts, twenty-five varieties of plants quite new to them and enough geological specimens to fill all their extra socks. They had one adventure of which Charles Kingsley later made literary capital:

Here we are at Treves, having been brought here under arrest, with a gendarme from the Mayor of Bittsburg, and liberated next morning with much laughter and many curses from the police here. However, we had the pleasure of spending a night in prison, among fleas and felons, on the bare floor. It appears the barbarians took our fishing-rods for "todt-instrumenten" and our wide-awakes for Italian hats, and got into their addle pates that we were emissaries of Mazzini and Co. distributing political tracts, for not a word of politics had we talked. Luckily the police-inspector here was a gentleman, and his wife and daughter ladies, and they did all they dare for us, and so about ten next morning we were set free with many apologies, and the gendarme (who, after all, poor fellow, was very civil) sent back to Bittsburg with a reprimand. We are the lions of Treves at present, for the affair has made a considerable fuss. (August 17, 1851, I, 296.)

The gendarmes and the *todt-instrumenten* reappear in the humorous conclusion to the duel scene in *Two Years Ago* and so does much of the scenery, the flora and minaria of the trip. (Chaps. XXIII, XXVII.)

Kingsley came home so much refreshed that he worked his parish all winter without a curate, wrote *Hypatia* and did his utmost to delay the demise of the *Christian Socialist*. "Parker won't want the first No. of Hypatia till January 1st," he wrote Ludlow (October 1851), "and a great deal more than the first no. is done. So I have 2 months to devote utterly to you and you shall have them. Of course I must keep Hypatia going but you can have 1 and I hope generally 2 articles every week, and all the poetry that comes out of me." The Christian Socialists were, Kingsley felt, at a very critical juncture and must labour hard to keep their hold on the working man, to show him that their practical power to get him what he wanted from Government was greater than that of "all the impudent and ignorant jackanapes in the Leader put together." He only begged Ludlow to remember that he had *two* sermons a week, and that to make them good for anything he had to exhaust his brain of all its more serious thought weekly, and would not have enough left for anything but lighter work.

The weekly articles (November 15, 22, 29, 1851) took the form of a series by Parson Lot, "The Long Game or a Few Words to the Workmen of England." It repeated the idea of "The Message of the Church to Labouring Men," that it is God's will that they should have their stake in the land, and it urged Association as a means for preventing revolution.

In January 1852 the *Christian Socialist* contracted itself from sixteen to eight pages and thus struggled on till the end of June. The final issue, June 28, contained "Parson Lot's Last Words" and also an "Epicedium" signed "Charles Kingsley." "It is written in a hurry," he wrote to Ludlow, "so if you like, reject it: but I have tried to get the maximum of terseness and melody." (I, 330.) "So die, thou child of stormy dawn" was republished later as "On the Death of a Certain Journal." (*Poems,* 1858.)

During the final struggle Kingsley also drew pen in remonstrance to an article in *Fraser's* (February 1852). An anonymous writer on "The State and Prospects of England" spoke of the Christian Socialists as being pure in their intentions but sanctioning apparently, in their pursuit of a contingent good, revolutionary and communist doctrines, and Kingsley wrote to Parker:

The editor of Fraser's has put me in a very delicate position, by the last page of the February number, which—with [the exception of] the article on Disraeli, against which I protest utterly, is the best No. I ever saw. But as a man who is before the public, as one of the members [of] a certain clique, I cannot allow that page to go forth in the same magazine with any writings of mine without a very strong and peremptory explanation of my own opinion about it. To do so, would be to fail as a gentleman and a man of honour, and to lose the whole of that influence with the working men for which I have ventured reputation, caste, even my position as a clergyman. I shall send, through you, a formal letter to the Editor of Fraser's, which I shall submit to the opinion of experienced friends first. On the way in which that letter is received, must, I am afraid, depend my future relations with Fraser's magazine. As far as Hypatia is concerned, I am of course, utterly bounden to it, and I need not tell you, that whatever happens will make no difference in my earnest endeavour to make Hypatia the best I can, and to fulfill my engagement. But all beyond that will depend on your editor.

When it is borne in mind that this is a very characteristic letter it becomes easier to comprehend his controversy with Newman.

The editor of *Fraser's* was evidently able to satisfy Kingsley's honour by the explanation that the magazine never gave space to controversial correspondence, for their friendly relations continued and the projected letter appeared in the form of a pamphlet, *Who Are the Friends of Order?*

With the demise of the journal Kingsley's more violent participation in the Christian Socialist movement ceased but his enthusiasm continued and a few years later, 1854, he was one of those who suggested to Maurice the establishment of the Working Men's College, was one of the signers of its articles of incorporation and one of the first of the staff of distinguished teachers in that admirable institution which still endures. Two ideas were conspicuous in the purpose of the College: the education it gave was to be liberal, not vocational, and there was to be real fellowship between teachers and students. For these ideas, education of the labouring man and increased friendliness between the classes, Kingsley went on working in one way or another all his life: lectures to Mechanics' Institutes, encouragement to towns establishing museums, correspondence with working men, interminable labour in writing, speaking and money raising for sanitation and the promotion of public health. His creed about the whole matter he presented in a letter to Hughes in 1852: "I have never swerved from my one idea of the last seven years, that the real battle of the time is . . . the Church, the gentleman, and the workman, against the shopkeepers and the Manchester school." (I, 314.) The battle could not have been waged forty years ago for the Church was a mere idle phantasm, the gentleman too ignorant and the workman too merely animal, while the Tory Manchester cotton-spinners had not yet joined forces with the shopkeepers. If the present Ministry does not comprehend the necessity of forming a coalition with the workers, the result will be such a wretched competitive democracy as we see in the United States. A true democracy is impossible without a Church, a Queen and a gentry.

CHAPTER XI

"EMPLOYMENT FOR MY PEN"

WHILE *Hypatia* was running in *Fraser's*, from January 1852 to April 1853, Kingsley could check for a little the stream of articles and reviews which he had been emitting almost monthly for the last three years. They began again in October and, as his reputation grew and his respectability strengthened, he became a valued contributor not only to *Fraser's* but to the *North British, Good Words, Good Words for the Young,* the *Reader,* and of course, after 1859, *Macmillan's.* He persistently declined, despite "huge offers" from the *Times,* to make a definite connection with any periodical.

The prose idylls and those reviews with some pretentions to the rank of essays were collected in 1859 into two volumes of *Miscellanies* very popular with Kingsley's public. In 1873 there was a second garner, *Prose Idylls* and *Plays and Puritans.* In 1874 a volume on *Health and Education* was made up chiefly of lectures on his darling topic of "sanitation." After his death Macmillan issued half a dozen permutations of these books under various titles.

The selections Kingsley made were judicious. The collected essays have more elegance and body than those which were left in their original anonymity. The sermons on morbid youthful poetry and unreadable society novels are not reprinted, neither is the defence of Bulwer Lytton against Mrs. Grundy nor that of Clough against the world. The enshrined essays comment on the solider writers, Pope, Byron, Tennyson and Mrs. Jameson, or they mix a little "minute philosophy" with one of the admired Kingsley word-pictures of Devon, Hampshire or the Fens.

The bibliography on page 191 includes a large number of reviews which, since the majority of them were published anonymously, have not been previously attributed to Kingsley but which the testimony of manuscript letters or indubitable internal evidence mark as his. The critical ideas which they contain are not numerous and are, of course, primarily moral: Deep, earnest thought and teaching is what we need today; do not waste our time with trivialities. Why fiddle while Rome burns? Polish, polish! Keep your poems nine years. Be objective (unless you are a woman); do not perpetually recount to us your Wertherian emotions. A book drawn straight from the crude realities of life, like *Jane Eyre* and *The Tenant of Wildfell Hall,* may not be pleasant but is often healthy and useful. To give information about the condition of the lower classes, to rouse our concern and pity, is a worthy literary purpose.

The predilection of those lower classes for tales of horror is Nature's craving for her own proper medicine. The navigator cannot work on water gruel; neither can he keep his mind in a state of healthy motion on the delicate literary fare concocted to please refined tastes. Do not forbid the novels of Reynolds[1] until you have something to offer in exchange.

You may not like the manner in which a particular poem or novel is written but the author, knowing what he wants to say, is the best judge of how to say it.

Many of Kingsley's critical judgments were unorthodox. He admired in Bulwer Lytton qualities which it was customary to decry and thought *The Caxtons* absolutely the best novel extant in the English language. He had great respect for Mrs. Gaskell's *Ruth* though he found it difficult to read "for the same reason that I cannot read *Uncle Tom's Cabin,* or *Othello,* or *The Bride of Lammermoor.* It is too painfully good." (I, 370.) *The Life of Charlotte Brontë* would, he thought, "shame literary people into some stronger belief that a simple, virtuous, practical home life is consistent with high imaginative genius; and it will shame, too, the prudery of a not over cleanly, though carefully white-washed age, into believing that purity is now (as in all ages till now) quite compatible with the knowledge of evil." (II, 25.) Clough's *Bothie,* too, he defended against the popular disapproval, and he said what he could for Tennyson's *Maud.* To any young poet who seemed to know what he was about and to be earnest in the doing of it, he

[1] G. W. M. Reynolds, 1814-79, Chartist leader, editor, and author of sensation novels.

extended a hospitable welcome. One finds appreciation of Meredith and Arnold at a date when their names meant nothing to the reading public. These judgments on his more significant contemporaries and the even less guarded outcries which occur in his letters are frequently instructive.

Poetry is the art of representing phenomena in their relation to the All. Therefore the innate subjectivity of woman's mind prevents her from ever becoming a poet. Even when like Miss Bremer she truly comprehends the communion of the spirit with nature, it is only subjectively. (*Commonplace-Book,* February 1846.)

I can read nothing but *Vanity Fair,* over and over again, which fills me with delight, wonder, and *humility*. I would sooner have drawn Rawdon Crawley than all the folks I ever drew. (To his wife, 1850, II, 25.)

I want to talk to you about Carlyle. I was with him the other evening, with Froude and Parker: and never heard I a more foolish outpouring of Devil's doctrines, raving cynicism which made me sick. I kept my temper with him: but when I got out I am afraid I swore with wrath and disgust, at least I left no doubt in my 2 friends' minds of my opinion of such stuff—all the ferocity of the old Pharisee without Isaiah's prophecy of mercy and salvation—the notion of sympathy with sinners denounced as a sign of innate "scoundrelism," a blame I am very glad to bear: I must tell you all viva voce. If I can temperately. I never was so shocked in my life, and you know I have a strong stomach, and am not easily moved to pious horror. Meanwhile his wife is pining, poor creature, for want of sympathy and attention from him, and is very ill. Whatever her faults may be, *he* has no right to neglect her. I am sick of his present phase, moral and intellectual, though I never can forget what he has taught me: but where should I have been, if you had not brought me on *The* step beyond him? (To Maurice [? Septua.] Sunday, 1856.)

I do hope you will not bother your soul about what the Westminster says. The woman who used to insult you there—and who I suppose does so now—is none other than Miss Evans, the infidel esprit fort, (who is now G. H. Lewes's concubine). I met him yesterday and lucky for me that I had not had your letter when I did so; or I certainly should have given him (he probably being the co-sinner for he pretends to know all about the philosophers, and don't) a queer piece of my mind to carry home to his lady. (To Maurice, Saturday, 1857. See Chap. XV, p. 130.)

How goes on the people's college? And how goes on Ruskin? I am glad to hear from Hughes that he is really at work. It will be far better for him, poor wretch, to be doing that, than going about abusing everybody as he does: but the man's heart must be right, to fall into step with you after all your battles: not because *you* have been any use to him, but because he has to you, and would therefore, had he been mean spirited have owed you a grudge. What has become of his hapless ex-wife? (To Maurice, Bideford, December 1854.)

Ruskin, I dare say, I refused to know; though I have been introduced to him since, and letters have passed between us. But physiognomy, which has been a study of mine for years, gave me certain opinions of that man the first day I ever saw him, which said, "That man, unless utterly changed—more changed, perhaps, than he ever will be in this mortal body,—and I never can be friends." God forgive me, if I be wrong, but all I have seen of his writings (which then I delighted in) since that day; and above all the miserable esclandre with his wife (most curiously corroborating my first impression of his physique) have widened the gulf, as far as I am concerned. . . . For aught I know he is a far better man than I. But the man who wrote Notes on Sheepfolds after knowing what he knew, . . . wants taking down. . . . What flesh and blood he is made of I know: what spirit he is made of, not to lay his hand upon his mouth awhile, above all about "Art," I know not. (To John Bullar, June 27, 1857.)

How do you like Macaulay? [*History of England,* Vol. IV.] Better than the last: but what a shallow and limited intellect. One pardons his Atheism: but one don't pardon the recognition of no idea, no purpose, no principle, not even Whig ones, for all he feels for are Whig *Conclusions,* utterly unconscious of the Divine ground from which they sprang. He understands Milton as little as he does George Fox, and his calumny of George Fox I know not whether to call more ribald, or more stupid. If you have not read it, read, and see what an *irredeemable owl* that man is. (To Maurice, Farley Court, Xmas Eve, 1855.)

I have written a sufficiently stupid and bald review of you for the Saturday [October 3, 1857], and indeed had no heart to write one at all from the first: because I had especial orders "not to lay it on too strong." . . . The cantankerous critters hate being genial, and fancy they shew their superior critical powers by picking and paring and bulaming and snubbing, instead of saying here's a jolly book—we'll take it for what it's worth, and let the devil find out the faults. I'm disgusted with them, and shall write no more for them. But don't you mind, old man. The book's in a second edition and will be in a third, and a fourth you'll see. . . . I've been reading it through again, and like it better than ever. I tell you it's a noble book. (To Hughes [? September, ? October] 1857, of *Tom Brown's School Days.*)

As for poor Maud. It is a sad falling off. There are some scraps in it most exquisite: but as a whole the world (and I) view it much as you do. I think there is but one opinion, even among those who admire him most. But that "Brook, an Idyl," is perfect in its way—non sine menda, perhaps, but Theocritus redivivus—still cui bono? I have said all that can be said for Maud in a late no. of Fraser's Mag. [September 1855]. I love and honour the *man,* as a private friend ... and am in no humour to hit him as I would Balders, Baileys and other presumptuous windbags. I am glad you appreciate Browning's plays: but *he* will never be a poet. The iron has entered into his soul. He was born and bred a Dissenter of the trois état, and though he is a good fellow, nothing will take the smell of tallow and brown sugar out of him. He cannot help being coarse and vulgar, and is naively unaware of the fact. However, if he had been born either a gentleman (of course I mean a churchman, for *all gentlemen owe that name to Church influence over themselves or their parents*) or a hard handed working-man, in contact with iron fact, he might have been a fine poet. As it is "plaudite"—but also "exeat." He has done and run. Who comes next? I don't care. I can tell more truths in prose than I ever could have done in verse, and can earn ten times as much money; wherefore Parnassus has seen my retreat—I doubt not with dry eyes. (To A. W. Gurney, October 3, 1855.)

Kingsley's opinion of Swinburne he did not put into writing but Edmund Gosse tells of an anniversary dinner of the Royal Literary Fund, held on May 2, 1866, at which Kingsley and Swinburne were called on to respond to the toast: Historical and Imaginative Literature. Venables, who proposed it, eulogized Swinburne as the representative of the future generation in poetry, and Kingsley endorsed "every word that Mr. Venables has said." (Edmund Gosse, *Life of Algernon Charles Swinburne,* London, 1917, p. 147.)[2]

Allow me to express to you the intense pleasure with which I have read your *Earthly Paradise.* I can enter into no analytic criticism. I am neither in the humour for it or worthy to do it well. But no volume of Poetry which I have seen appear for 25 years past, has so charmed me, both in matter, manner and spirit, by which I mean nobleness and simplicity of human feeling. If I dared to prefer aught, I might say that I like the Alcestis best of all; but everything has been a balm to me just now when I needed something to comfort me, having just parted with my eldest son to go to the New World, and be a man, instead of staying here and being a fine gentleman.

I thank you for writing the book as if you had written it for me. (To William Morris, July 1, 1868.)

[2] Since there is no corroborative evidence for this tale it may be well to regard it as one more of Gosse's curious contributions to the history of letters.

With the more conspicuous figures in American letters Kingsley was fairly familiar. Longfellow of course delighted him but Whitman's poems he thought the product of a coarse and sensual mind. Washington Irving's prose is as graceful and felicitous as poor Elia's own, and certainly more manly. *The Fable for Critics* is worthy of Rabelais. Together with the *Biglow Papers* and *Uncle Tom's Cabin* it shows that the Americans have right healthy power, artistic as well as intellectual, among them, ready, when their present borrowed peacocks' feathers have fallen off, to come forth and prove that the Yankee eagle is a right gallant bird.

The steward to Lord Scoutbush in *Two Years Ago* is described as "one of those English types which Mr. Emerson has so well hit off in his rather confused and contradictory *Traits*," but this is almost the only good word said for Emerson whom Kingsley regarded as the fount of some of the most insidiously poisonous of contemporary errors. He set this forth in *Alton Locke,* elaborated it four years later in *Phaethon* and dramatized it in *Hypatia.*

To the occasional prefaces which he wrote to the work of other men Kingsley was impelled, not as in the essays and reviews, by a laudable desire to increase his income but by the preacher's impulse to bring to the attention of a larger audience a book which had, he felt, power for good. The biographical sketch introducing Charles Mansfield's *Paraguay, Brazil, and the Plate* (1856) was primarily a work of love (see Chap. III, p. 16) as was the Preface to *South by West or Winter in the Rocky Mountains and Spring in Mexico,* letters which his daughter Rose published anonymously in 1874 after her first trip to America.

In 1854 appeared *Theologia Germanica*: "which setteth forth many fair Lineaments of divine Truth, and saith very lofty and lovely things touching a perfect Life, edited by Dr. Pfeiffer from the only complete manuscript yet known, translated from the German by Susanna Winkworth, with a Preface by the Rev. Charles Kingsley, Rector of Eversley, and a Letter to the Translator by the Chevalier Bunsen." Kingsley admired the "noble little book" but hesitated long over the request to write it a preface, fearing lest its not altogether orthodox theology might be attributed to him. Maurice and Bunsen persuaded him and the result was so satisfactory that two years later he cheerfully agreed to Miss Winkworth's request that he write a preface for the translation she was making of Tauler's Sermons, though "I would certainly leave out the Romanist passages; I am sure that they are really only excrescences, which have nothing to do with the real bone and muscle of his or any man's soul." (Bideford, 1854, I, 498.)

When Smith and Elder asked for a preface for their reprinting of Henry Brooke's *Fool of Quality* he agreed because he loved the book in spite of all its faults. It is "a good book and will do good. Its theology is the finest I ever read." (To Parker, 1859.)

That he should write a preface to *The Pilgrim's Progress* was Kingsley's own idea. Its chief purpose—in which it succeeded—was to help a young illustrator to a publisher. Charles H. Bennett, as more than one artist did, had come to Kingsley for advice about his drawings, and Kingsley never managed to take a half-hearted interest in anyone. He showed Bennett's drawings to Longman, composed the preface which made the edition saleable and wrote the young man elaborate letters of general suggestion and specific comment. For model he offered him Kaulbach whose illustrations of Reinecke Fuchs were, he thought, with three or four sixteenth century exceptions, the finest designs the world has ever seen, for Kaulbach combines Greek health and accuracy of form with German freedom of imagination. Kingsley added the concrete advice, which Bennett took, that he should dress his figures in seventeenth century costume. "Truly to illustrate a poem, you must put the visions on paper as they appeared to the mind of the seer himself." (II, 77.) Bennett adopted, too, almost all Kingsley's detailed criticisms: "I think you must have more smirk about Smoothman's face; and should certainly shave him, all but a very neat little imperial" (II, 77), and so on.

A little later Kingsley was writing the same sort of elaborate criticism to Frederic Shields for his edition of *The Pilgrim's Progress* and was urging him to cast out the morbid fear that his devotion to art was frivolous and worldly. "It seems to me that you are about to become one of the first designers in Europe." (January 11, 1862, Ernestine Mills, *The Life and Letters of Frederic Shields,* London, 1912.) "Don't mind what Mr. Ruskin says. He is too apt to 'bind heavy burdens and grievous to be borne, and touch them not himself with one of his fingers.' The plain fact is, God has given you a great talent, whereby you may get an honest livelihood. Take *that* as God's call to you, and follow it out." (February 28, 1862, *op. cit.*)

CHAPTER XII

"HOW TO TRAIN NOT SCHOLARS BUT MEN"

WRITING for the reviews was one means of adding to a never sufficient clerical income; the other was to take pupils. Kingsley was well fitted by temperament for the enterprise but his outspoken radical views, both social and theological, made orthodox parents hesitate to trust him with their sons. Not without reason; Kingsley's enthusiasm for his beliefs was very contagious and any young man who came into intimate contact with him was pretty sure to be converted to something.

The search for pupils began toward the close of 1849. On December 3 of that year Mrs. Kingsley wrote, in the course of a long gossiping letter to her friend Mrs. Augustus Stapleton: "The expenses of this year owing to Charles's illness, our Curate, and the heavy rates on account of the fever, have been so great that unless we get pupils, we shall not be able to do anything that we have planned for the parish." The terms Kingsley set were £5 a week or £250 a year. He hoped, he said, that the work would be a healthy training for his own mind on points necessarily long neglected as well as giving him an opportunity of saving a young heart or two from this untoward generation.

One young heart was attracted by that liberalism which frightened the others. John Martineau was the son of a cousin of Harriet. The family were broad-minded Unitarians and political Liberals who liked *Yeast* and Kingsley's Chartism. They were eventually a little disconcerted when John was converted to the Church of England but, by Kingsley's advice, he was never confirmed, that the divergence of his views from those of his parents might not be accentuated.

"I entered his house [January 21, 1850] as his pupil," wrote John Martineau, "and was for nearly a year and a half his constant companion; indeed, out of doors, almost his only companion, for during the greater part of that time he had no other pupil, and hardly any intimate friends within reach. He was then in his thirty-first year, in the fulness of his strength; I a raw receptive school-boy of fifteen; so that his mind and character left their impression upon mine as a seal does upon wax." (I, 297.) And the Kingsley influence, despite some not unnatural parental jealousy, continued the dominating one in John Martineau's life. When, at thirty-six, ill health obliged him to retire from his legal work he settled as near as possible to Eversley, and when he died, at seventy-six, he was buried, according to his wish, in Eversley churchyard at Charles Kingsley's feet.

Martineau's boyish letters to his mother give a pleasant picture of the Kingsley household.

We have prayers at 8.45, but I intend in future to be down before that and get some work done. Mr. Kingsley reads a chapter or half a one, and then reads a prayer, the servants all being present; then we have a substantial meat breakfast, and then we work till one o'clock, when we have lunch, and after lunch we go out walking till about five, when we dine; then work from seven to nine; at half-past nine prayers, Mr. Kingsley reading only three or four verses, then I go to bed. . . .

Mrs. Kingsley is very delicate, I believe, and has had the influenza for some time, but I should never have found it out if I had not heard Mr. K. say so to different people. She has only been out three times since Christmas Day. She is particularly kind and delicately attentive; she insists on my having my fire lighted when I get up every morning, and again to go to bed by. A broken brace-end that I happened to leave on my table the other day I found ready mended the next time I came into my room; I have a nice large room, writing materials, pens, book-shelves, and everything very complete, but I am not to work (or, as Mr. K. calls it, "grind") in my bedroom at all. (January 1850, Violet Martineau, *John Martineau the Pupil of Kingsley*, London, 1921, p. 4.)

Mrs. Kingsley for her part thought John Martineau a most excellent boy and no trouble.

In August came a second pupil—the only other of whom there is record—a young Cambridge man reading for orders. With him Kingsley went through the *Leben Jesu* which George Eliot had recently (1846) translated into English. Strauss he considered the great false prophet of the day who must be faced and fought against by the clergy and he intended to equip this young man for the conflict. Lees became enlisted too in another of Kingsley's campaigns. It was he who lent £100 for the establishment of the

Christian Socialist. This Kingsley accepted with joy but when in desperate personal need he wrote to Hughes that he would rather "*smash*, than borrow money of a pupil." (March 5, 1851.) A few months earlier (January [?] 25) he had written: "I am literally penniless at the moment, and if I cannot borrow £500 somewhere I shall have not a farthing to live on, having lost a source of income just as the repayment of heavy loans, contracted to furnish and repair this old lanthorn of a house, were becoming due. . . . If I borrow not £500 for 7 or 10 years I must write G. T. T.[1] on the door and go to a better. I am joking about it because there are things in the world which are *too bad to trust oneself to be sad over.* . . . The only security . . . is a policy of Insurance for £1000." Hughes found him a lender.

Kingsley's general educational theories coincided warmly with those of Dr. Arnold, whom he much admired. "The question is not what to teach," he wrote, "but how to educate; how to train not scholars, but men; bold, energetic, methodic, liberal-minded, magnanimous." (I, 198.) The especial danger of the time he felt to be a sentimental eclecticism, an intellectual vagueness which must invariably become the parent of moral vagueness. He saw the age, left without an absolute standard of right or truth, trying like the Neo-Platonists to escape from its own scepticism by plunging deliberately into any fetish-worshiping superstition which offered it the stability of decisions already made. Education for character therefore seemed to him the important task both of the school and of the university. When in 1850 the Commission was appointed to inquire into the state of Oxford and Cambridge, their discipline and studies, Kingsley was among the many who offered them advice through the press. Several warm letters to the *Spectator* were signed "A Cambridge First-Class man and Country Rector." They were chiefly concerned with the religious bewilderment of the undergraduate. Many young men just down from Oxford or Cambridge came to Kingsley begging for spiritual guidance, and he had in consequence evolved a picture of the universities in which "men were . . . going over to Rome by hundreds. The writings of Strauss or of his followers were . . . gaining ground every term in the libraries and the hearts of gownsmen. Young men were . . . crying frantically to every one, orthodox or unorthodox, who

[1] Gone to Texas, *i.e.*, emigrated. Hughes used this phrase as a book title in 1884.

looked, to use their own phrase, like a 'live man,' 'For God's sake tell me what to believe, or if there is anything really worth believing in, beyond five senses, my pocket, and my ambition?' " (*Spectator,* January 25, 1851.)

Kingsley was violently set right in his notions by a Cambridge undergraduate, one "D." (J. Llewellyn Davies, the theologian), who assured the *Spectator* (February 1, 1851), that not half-a-dozen men in the whole student body owned copies of any work of Strauss and that their "prevailing moral characteristic" was not "frantic earnestness" but "an almost indifferent calmness." Kingsley struck back, but after numerous older and quieter men had corroborated the Cambridge youth he yielded.

More elaborately and more carefully formulated than his theories concerning the universities were Kingsley's ideas on the education of the very young. He had reached a conviction, in accord with the deepest tenet of his religious belief and well in advance of that of most parents and educators of his time, that to make the perfect man the body must be cultivated rather than subdued. His conception that a naughty child is usually a sick child was as disconcerting to his contemporaries as his belief in the rights of the poor and the improbability of an everlasting hell. Some of his dicta read like the prospectus of a twentieth century progressive school:

More than half the lying of children is, I believe, the result of fear, and the fear of punishment. (II, 4.)

It is difficult enough to keep the Ten Commandments without making an eleventh in every direction. (II, 5.)

Are you aware . . . that too often from ignorance of signs of approaching disease, a child is punished for what is called idleness, listlessness, wilfulness, sulkiness; and punished, too, in the unwisest way—by an increase of tasks and confinement to the house? ("Thrift," *Health and Education,* 1874.)

For children, she [physical science] has done much, or rather might do, would parents read and perpend such books as Andrew Combe's and those of other writers on physical education. We should not then see the children, even of the rich, done to death piecemeal by improper food, improper clothes, neglect of ventilation and the commonest measures for preserving health. We should not see their intellects stunted by Procrustean attempts to teach them all the same accomplishments, to the neglect, most often, of any sound practical training of their faculties. We should not see slight indigestion, or temporary rushes of blood to the head, condemned and punished as sins against Him who took up little children in His arms and blessed them. ("Science," *op. cit.*)

The three most common causes of ill-filled lungs, in children and in young ladies, are stillness, silence, and stays.

. . . let it be said once and for all, that children and young people cannot make too much noise. The parents who cannot bear the noise of their children have no right to have brought them into the world. ("The Two Breaths," *op. cit.*)

We are shocked to hear of all Mrs. Hughes's sorrows and we both entreat her to keep to the sofa, and do, do, *put* her *stays* into the fire. They are the cause of boundless misery and disease, and 100 years hence, they will be looked back on as more barbarous and silly than Chinese feet and Indian flatheads. My Fanny, thanks to *no stays* goes on getting better and better. (To Hughes.)

Till the better method of education which the great Arnold inaugurated shall have expelled the last remnants of that brutal mediaeval one, unknown to free Greece and Rome, but invented by monks cut off from all the softening influences of family, who looked on self-respect as a sin and on human nature as a foul and savage brute and therefore, accustomed to self-torture and to self-contempt, thought it no sin to degrade and scourge other people's innocent children. (*The Irrationale of Speech*, 1864.)

Kingsley permitted no corporal punishment in his own home though he came eventually to believe that it might be administered to boys in cases of cruelty or bullying.

If I had my way, I would give the same education to the child of the collier and to the child of a peer. I would see that they were taught the same things and by the same method. Let them all begin alike, say I. (Preface, *Town Geology*, 1872.)

This was not mere oratory; Kingsley worked for the principle with tongue, pen and pocketbook, nationally but especially in his own parish. When he came to Eversley in 1844 he found that scarcely one adult in the parish could read and write. The only school was a melancholy affair, a stuffy ten-foot room, where the teacher simultaneously cobbled shoes, beat the children and dispensed bits of learning. In a cottage on the moor Kingsley discovered a club-footed boy with talent and ambition beyond the shoemaking by which he earned his livelihood. He first taught Frederic Marshall himself, then paid his expenses at Winchester Training College and finally set him up as a master, at £35 a year plus lodging and coals, in the plain but comfortable little school-house which he built on Eversley Common.

On his own children Kingsley practised his educational theories wholeheartedly and they, their mother and numerous visitors bear witness to the rectory as a jolly, comfortable, healthy home— healthy in the Victorian sense; it was always damp and badly drained.

Kingsley's children were four: Rose Georgina, 1845-1925; Maurice, named for his godfather, 1847-1910; Mary St. Leger, 1852-1931; and Grenville Arthur, for Sir Richard Grenville from whom Mrs. Kingsley's family claimed descent and for his godfather, Dean Stanley, 1858-98. That Mrs. Kingsley lost other children before their birth is evident even in the usually guarded terms of the letters and she seems to have been in continual ill health though the care she received was certainly more rational than that which fell to the lot of most of her contemporaries. Kingsley really knew something of physiology and welcomed medical innovations with the open-minded enthusiasm with which he met all scientific ideas. Nine days after the birth of his second daughter he was writing to Lord Goderich:

> Let me thank you most cordially for your hint about chloroform. As for "forbidden ground," can there be forbidden ground between husband and husband; or between two human beings who wish to diminish by one atom the amount of human suffering? . . . It is a real delight to my faith, as well as to my pity, to know that that suffering of childbirth can be avoided. It is the one thing which I hate and curse, as the deepest paradox and puzzle upon earth; but when it is proved to me that man can "by obeying nature, conquer her," in that also I am content. . . . The popular superstition that it is the consequence of the fall I cannot but smile at. (June 15, 1852, I, 326.)

Of Kingsley's delight in his children there is abundant evidence. In 1861 he wrote to the Rev. E. P. Campbell, an old Cambridge friend with whom he had been out of touch for many years: "I have a tall lass of 16, a boy of 13 at Wellington College, a perfect beauty who can shoot and fish, and rides like a bird; a little lass of 8 as clever as she can stand; and a boy of two who will be a topper in some line only yet known to the destinies."

Remembering the pains of his own youth Kingsley ordered his household so that his children were never submerged by the incessancy of parish business and he planned a Sabbath which was a day to be looked forward to instead of dreaded. There was always a Sunday walk on the moor and there were the Sunday picture books in each of which the father drew, according to the owner's order, a scene from a Bible story or a bird, beast or flower mentioned in the Scriptures. Kingsley's letters, too, were often illustrated with his lively pen or pencil sketches, better work frequently than the meticulous illustrations for the books. These parental letters, copious like all his writings, he took real pains to make "jolly" and amusing to their recipients. To ten year old Maurice, for instance, at his first school (St. Neot's, under the headship of Cowley Powles), he sent exciting accounts, amusingly illustrated, of hard runs after the fox, of fishing expeditions, of the capture of poachers, of hares that could be hunted on the next holiday. "Boys are sent to school," he comforted him, "and girls are not, just because boys are stronger than girls and are meant to go out into the world, and seek their fortunes, instead of being taken care of at home; and therefore they must learn to rough it early in life, and to stand up for themselves." "Dad is so pleased," he writes on another occasion, "at your defending the weak from the strong, but I advise you not to throw boys *downstairs,* for fear they should arrive at the bottom with their skulls cracked." And again (1860): "Poor grandpapa is dead, and gone to heaven. You must always think of him lovingly, and remember this about him, Maurice, and copy it—that he was *a gentleman,* and never did in his life, or even thought, a mean or false thing, and therefore has left behind him many friends, and not an enemy on earth. Yes, dear boy, if it should please God that you should help to build up the old family again, bear in mind that *honesty* and *modesty,* the two marks of a gentleman, are the only way to do it.

"You must ask Miss Darke to get you a piece of crape, and to put it round your left arm above the elbow. That is the way officers and men in uniform wear mourning, and if any one asks you why, say it is for your grandpapa."

Maurice went from St. Neot's to Wellington College of which Kingsley had a high opinion, and then to Cambridge to read at Trinity Hall for the Indian Civil Service. "But I think," his father wrote his godfather (November 19, 1864), "that the prospect of being on horseback every day, and killing 'guara' and 'sambur' weighs more with him as yet than that of civilizing and humanizing some tract half as big as England." Maurice was no student and the civil service idea was shortly abandoned for emigration. He went down without a degree, took training at the Royal Agricultural College at Cirencester and went out to South America. Later he went to Colorado, prospected for a railroad in Mexico and eventually saw a good deal of the United States in various capacities, chiefly as surveyor and engineer. "Being a strong conservative," his mother wrote of him in 1878, "the institutions of America social and political are naturally repugnant to him though he has made many friends there." He married an American, Marie Yorke of Louisiana, had three sons and died in 1910 in New Rochelle, New York.

Grenville Arthur was a delicate baby and never so good a sportsman as his elder brother. When he was old enough to be sent away from home he went to Winton House, the school established in Winchester by the Rev. A. C. Johns, the master who had encouraged Kingsley's taste for botany when he was a boy at Derwent Coleridge's. Kingsley and Johns were close friends all their lives and the letters they exchanged about Grenville might serve as models for parent-teacher correspondence:

I cannot express my gratitude to you and Mrs. Johns and your dear girl for all your trouble about my little renegade. I am quite sure this is merely the first struggle of a child who has never met his equals, and been much petted and spoilt. But he is perfectly hardy, strong, and bold, not really sly because he has never been bullied—and quite shrewd—not to say clever, as I suspect him to be. My own belief is that if we can only keep right the *liver* which he inherits from *both* parents, he will be a fine frank forward lad, and a credit to us both.

Your kindness meanwhile is very great. You seem to understand that he is a chick only half out of the egg, who needs a little help in self-deliverance. (Aboyne Castle, Aberdeenshire, September 27 [? 1869].)

From Winton House Grenville proceeded to Harrow. He did not attempt Cambridge but went out to Mexico where he died in 1898.

The two girls seem to have had more of their father's qualities. Rose, the eldest, has been described as "Charles Kingsley in petticoats," and from the time that she was able to ride a pony and catch a butterfly she was her father's constant companion. She rode and walked with him over the Hampshire moors, gardened and botanized, collected beetles and madrepores, and accompanied him on the journeys for which Mrs. Kingsley was not sufficiently robust. In 1871 she went out to America to see her elder brother. Her lively sketches of winter in the Rocky Mountains and spring in Mexico, written for a little Colorado paper, were gathered into a book, *South by West,* for which her father wrote a Preface though it was published anonymously as a young lady's work should be. Rose never married but kept a cottage in Eversley where she did good works in the village and wrote books about rose gardening and French art.

Mary St. Leger, the youngest daughter carried further the family literary tradition. Not long after her father's death she married a former curate of his, William Harrison, then rector of Clovelly. It proved an unsuccessful union and they separated. She had studied as a girl at the Slade School but decided rather to develop her literary bent and under her pen-name of Lucas Malet (combining a Kingsley with a Grenfell grandmother) made herself a career as a novelist, admired and successful though looked at a little askance in the '80's because her books spoke quite openly of seduction and illegitimate children. She adopted a daughter of a cousin, became a member of the Roman Catholic Church, lived much abroad, was granted a Civil List pension for her writings, and died at seventy-nine with her appetite for life by no means weary.

CHAPTER XIII

"EMERSONIAN ANYTHINGARIANISM"

THE writing in 1853 of his third novel, *Hypatia,* cost Kingsley an honorary Oxford D.C.L. When, in 1863, the Prince and Princess of Wales consented to honour Commemoration with their presence they sent in, according to custom, the names of those on whom they would be pleased to see the University confer degrees. Kingsley's name was on the Prince's list and he had warm supporters in the University, especially Max Müller and Stanley, then a Canon of Christ Church. Pusey, however, insisted that Kingsley's published works, and especially that "immoral book" *Hypatia,* made him a person unfit for Oxford honour. The fight was keen but Kingsley at last decided to retire. "The Council, and Stanley, behaved excellently well," he wrote to Hughes, "and not at all cowardly. They would have fought the thing through if old P. had not declared his intention to cry Non Placet in the theatre, and have a fracas before the Prince's face, and that had to be avoided at all risks."

When Stanley suggested proposing him the next year he declined both for his honour and that of his University. "I do not deny a great hankering, for years past, after an Oxford D.C.L. Yet it will not do to let the credit of a Cambridge Professor, be decided on by Oxford men, even though they were angels." (June 8, 1863.) On the same point of honour he declined three years later an invitation from Bishop Wilberforce to preach at St. Mary's:

I thank you heartily, my dear Lord Bishop, for your most courteous request. It has touched me, for many reasons very deeply; and it will make me ever your faithful and attached servant.

But I have a nicety about preaching in Oxford, which I am sure that your chivalrous spirit will understand, even though it does not approve.

As a Professor of Cambridge, and still more as a Chaplain of the Queen, and allowed at times to preach in her Private Chapel, and approach her Royal Person, I do not think it stands with my honour to appear publicly in Oxford, till some public retraction or apology has been made for that scandalous imputation, which, though privately made, was allowed to become notorious through the public press. The very book on which that imputation was grounded, had been read, and graciously approved by Her Majesty; therefore it is for her sake, and for that of my University, and not for any paltry pride about myself, that I fear I must, with very great regret, decline at present the honour which you are so very good as to offer me. (July 29, 1866.)

The immorality of *Hypatia* was very like that of *Yeast*; its author comprehended the sins of high-spirited young men and did not think them past remission; he exalted matrimony as a state more holy than celibacy; not all his ecclesiastical portraits were flattering; moreover in *Hypatia* luscious pagan scenes were described with gusto. Pusey may not have approved of sentences like these:

Her little bare feet, as they dimpled the cushions, were more perfect than Aphrodite's, softer than a swan's bosom. (Chap. III.)

She skipped into the palanquin, taking care to show the most lovely white heel and ankle, and, like the Parthian, send a random arrow as she retreated. (Chap. V.)

He would have approved still less had he realized how frequently Kingsley thought of the beauty of the female foot which for him, as for some other Victorians, seems to have become a kind of symbol.

Her long thin hands, and ivory-channelled feet.
("Sappho," 1847, *Poems*, 1858.)

How happy Miss Rose must be with her dear mam. She must say "Thank God for giving her such a lovely mam with beautiful black hair, and bright eyes, and soft lips to kiss Miss Rose, and white hands to cuddle Miss Rose, and darling darling feet for Daddy and Miss Rose to kiss and kiss and say God bless our darling beautiful mam." (To his daughter Rose, aged three, Duxford, Cambridge, 1848.)

Her little bare feet were peeping out from under her dress. He bent down, and kissed them again and again; and then looking up, as if to excuse himself,—
"You have such pretty feet, mother!"
Instantly, with a woman's instinct, she had hidden them. . . .
"Your dear father used to say so, thirty years ago." (*Westward Ho!* 1855, Chap. III.)

"Valencia and I used to run about without shoes and stockings at Kilanbaggan, and you can't think how pretty and white this little foot used to look on a nice soft carpet of green moss."

"I shall write a sonnet to it." (*Two Years Ago,* 1857, Chap. X.)

> And at night the septette of Beethoven,
> And the grandmother by in her chair,
> And the foot of all feet on the sofa
> Beating delicate time to the air.
> ("The Delectable Day," 1872, *Poems,* 1884.)

In point of fact, of course, *Hypatia* was written with the loftiest of moral purposes, an attempt to warn and save the Church. The most dangerous sin of the age, Kingsley felt, was that intellectual arrogance, born of scientific enthusiasm, which believed that it could by seeking find out God, which permitted each man to set up his own intellectual creation in place of the concept hallowed by the Church and time. In a chapter of *Alton Locke* (XXII) he presented at some length "An Emersonian Sermon" by the American Mr. Windrush, once a Calvinist preacher, and a comment by Sandy Mackaye who concludes:

"Oh, ye gowk—ye gowk! Dinna ye see what be the upshot o' siccan doctrine? That every puir fellow as has noa gret brains in his head, will be left to his superstition an' his ignorance, to fulfil the lusts o' his flesh; while the few that are geniuses, or fancy themselves sae, are to ha' the monopoly o' this private still o' philosophy—these carbonari, illuminati, vehmgericht, samothracian mysteries o' bottled moonshine. An' when that comes to pass, I'll just gang back to my schule and my catechism, and begin again wi' 'who was born o' the Virgin Mary, suffered oonder Pontius Pilate!' Hech! lads, there's no subjectives and objectives there, na beggarly, windy abstractions, but just a plain fact, that God cam' down to look for puir bodies, instead o' leaving puir bodies to gang looking for Him."

Phaethon, subtitled *Loose Thoughts for Loose Thinkers,* the long essay published just before *Hypatia* (1852) is an expansion of the theme. It caused George Eliot to write: "Perhaps you may not be as much in love with Kingsley's genius, and as much 'riled' by his faults, as I am." (J. W. Cross, ed., *George Eliot's Life,* 1885, I, 219.) In *Phaethon* Professor Windrush is visiting at an English country house and his "magniloquent unwisdom" incites a dialogue between Kingsley and one of those simple, right-minded, puzzled country gentlemen to whom he was specially called to minister. The refutation of the Professor is attempted by means of a Socratic dialogue, a method of argument in which Kingsley's delight considerably exceeded his power. An acute analysis of his abilities and limitations here was made by James Martineau in the *Prospective Review* (February 1853):

We have few greater teachers than Mr. Kingsley, yet none more certain to go astray the moment he becomes didactic. The truths which move him most he reads off at a glance; and the attempt to exhibit them to others as the result of intellectual elaboration naturally fails. His genius is altogether that of the artist, for the apprehension of concrete reality, not that of the philosopher, for finding in thought the grounds and connexions of what he perceives. With rare qualifications for seeing, feeling, and believing right, were he to abstain from reasoning, he would not often be wrong.

When Kingsley left philosophy and dramatized his theme he produced his most successful novel:

My idea in the romance [he wrote Maurice of *Hypatia* (January 19, 1851)] is to set forth Christianity as the only really democratic creed, and philosophy, above all, spiritualism, as the most exclusively aristocratic creed. . . . Of English subjects I can write no more just now. I have exhausted both my stock and my brain, and really require to rest it, by turning it to some new field, in which there is richer and more picturesque life, and the elements are less confused, or rather, may be handled more in the mass than English ones now. I have long wished to do something antique, and get out my thoughts about the connection of the old world and the new; Schiller's *Gods of Greece* expresses, I think, a tone of feeling very common, and which finds its vent in Emersonian Anythingarianism.

Maurice approved and began to help at once with suggestions for reading. A little later in the year Kingsley was writing to Parker:

As for the Tale, I see no reason why it should not be fit for Fraser's, or any other magazine. Its interest lies exclusively in *pure Art,* in dramatic representation of a very interesting and important era. I have carefully avoided pointing any moral whatsoever much as I have been tempted to make people see what I suppose the wise see without my telling them, that it is an attack on the Emersonian pseudo-spiritualism of the present day, not on metaphysical grounds, but showing *in action* that it has less hold on the human sympathies than even the lowest forms of orthodox Christianity. I am trying to make the interest depend entirely on the plot, as much as in any French novel-about-nothing. I see no reason why you should be afraid of it.

Parker wanted the tale for *Fraser's* and Chapman released Kingsley from his obligations to him that he might take the advantages of serial publication which he thought great. "By bringing it out piecemeal I should get passing criticism on the *plot*, which would help me to weave it better and better as I went on. And that it would be better in a pecuniary point of view is self-evident." (To Parker, 1851.)

In January 1852 *Hypatia,* by the author of *Yeast* and *The Saint's Tragedy,* began to appear in *Fraser's.* The unpointed moral was fairly apparent to most readers who liked it because to them, as to Kingsley, the transcendental philosophy was totally unsatisfying. The Victorian individualist was obliged, for his peace of mind, to believe that he counted personally in the scheme of things. To be of the human race was not enough; he must feel that God had direct concern for his particular welfare. The answer to this for Kingsley was the incarnation, the answer which the Jew finds in *Hypatia*; God the loving Father, a creed to satisfy not only the philosopher but all mankind, who must learn it in the light of that faith which is higher than reason. "I want a faith past arguments; one which, whether I can prove it or not to the satisfaction of the lawyers, I believe to my own satisfaction, and act on it as undoubtingly and unreasoningly as I do upon my newly rediscovered personal identity. I don't want to possess a faith. I want a faith which will possess me." (*Hypatia,* Chap. XVII.)

But though its purpose is transparent enough *Hypatia* is, as Kingsley promised, a thoroughly good story. He had been pondering technique, "those sparkling conversations, that graceful interpenetration of sentiment and action, that wonderful art in inventing plots and situations, which make French novels, with all their faults, perfect studies for the fiction writer" ("Recent Novels," *Fraser's,* April 1849), and *Hypatia* overflows with situations and plots. Sometimes they come straight from the historical source— Gibbon, the Letters of Synesius or the *Ecclesiastical History* of Socrates, Surnamed Scholasticus, sometimes there is a skilful pointing and vivifying or a personifying of historic wholes. Most readers and reviewers admired Kingsley's knowledge of the period with which he dealt but they occasionally questioned the accuracy of his details and not infrequently objected to his modernizing of the past. As he had done with *The Saint's Tragedy,* he defended his colloquial style. It was superior to "the stilted inflated melodramatic tone, making every person and action cold, distant, unreal, which has spoilt every English historical romance." (To Parker, 1852.) When Max Müller objected to the "respectable Benjamin Franklin tone" of the "Gothic saga" in Chapter XII Kingsley declined to alter it but put Müller's criticisms and those of Ludlow into the mouth of one of the listeners, Agilmund. By press criticism Kingsley was not much disturbed. "Will you tell me of any really lasting work which has not been attacked at first?" But when Parker suggested that the appearance of *Hypatia* in its pages was doing harm to *Fraser's* he grew angry.

As for there being any danger to you and Fraser's from me, I can tell you that the very fact of the notice of my work's coming out has procured you fresh subscribers already; and that the bargain will be, as it ought, as good a one for you as for me. As for being in a delicate position, I am so just in this respect, that this book will show whether or not I can be an Artist—and I should tell you that Froude thought it "infinitely better and more artistic" than anything I have written. As for compromising your character or Fraser's by dealing with me—did you compromise it by that really offensive book Yeast? . . . Do not fancy that I am a man tabooed, my dear Parker. On the contrary I find no falling off in the exceedingly good society of all sorts in which I have lived from my youth—but on the contrary, a great deal more kindness and attention than I deserve, from new respectabilities of all classes of opinion, from the Speaker [of the House of Commons] and Sir Charles Wood down to Monro of Harrow Weald, and that dear old ignorant Philistine Doctor Keate late of Eton.—I send you back your letter as I am sure you will wish me to forget that last paragraph. (1852.)

For all his talk of rewriting and of the serial publication as a mere rough draft Kingsley altered scarcely a word when *Hypatia* came to book form. This was partly, doubtless, because of pressure of time and partly because of his constitutional attitude toward criticism, of which his response to Max Müller's strictures on his Gothic saga was typical; he listened patiently and gratefully to advice but, unless it came from Maurice or from Mrs. Kingsley, he seldom took it. He made an error in this instance, for what Müller said of the song was true of the Goths all through the novel; they talk, as the *Church of England Review* (October 1858) observed, "a language which, in spite of the archaic Teuton tint washed over it, sets you thinking of the crew of the winning boat at Cambridge, any time last summer." So, too, is the lovely Pelagia elder sister to the nineteenth century sentimental prostitute, driven to sin in her helpless youth, a true woman still at heart and capable of one great love. Hypatia herself has a touch of Tennyson's Princess. She was a courageous statement on Kingsley's part of the attitude of mind he was attacking—Emersonianism in full beauty, but she strains her intellect beyond its powers and she stands in the last great scene naked before the cross. Still it must have been her queenly qualities, her dominance over the masculine minds about her, which caused Victoria to prefer *Hypatia* to all Kingsley's books. (*The Saint's Tragedy* was the Prince Consort's favourite.) Tennyson, too, bowed to *Hypatia,* though he could not stomach the last scene. "It is very powerful and tragic; but I objected to the word 'naked.' Pelagia's nakedness has nothing which revolts one . . . but I really was hurt at having Hypatia stript." (*Alfred Lord Tennyson,* A Memoir, by His Son, London, 1897, I, 367.)

Kingsley's own favourite character in the book was the Jew Raphael Aben-Ezra who is a rather more fluent Lancelot Smith, with a certain jaunty calm about him which is highly annoying when one regards him as a leading personage and highly revealing when he is looked upon as an embodiment of the kind of young man Kingsley would like to have been. His struggles with "the great world-problem—'Given Self; to find God'" (Chap. XIII) are those of the earnest youth of the day. They were especially suggested to Kingsley by his friendship with A. N. Louis, a Jew who, by his ministrations, was received into the Church of England in the year in which *Hypatia* appeared.

Kingsley, with his natural sympathy for all forms of honest belief found it especially easy to comprehend the Jews because he thought the sanctity of national and family life upon which the Hebrews insisted the essential basis of Christianity. It was the emphasis in *Hypatia* on the sanctity of family life which made Maurice, when he declined to have the book dedicated to him, suggest its subscription to Kingsley's parents.

For the welfare of the book Maurice's disassociation was undoubtedly wise. His Preface to *The Saint's Tragedy* had been a weight about her neck and in the year of *Hypatia's* book appearance his *Theological Essays* caused his dismissal from the Professorship of Divinity at King's College. This was because, as the minutes of a meeting of the College Council stated: "the opinions set forth and the doubts expressed in the said essay . . . as to certain points of belief regarding the future punishment of the wicked and the final issues of the day of judgment, are of dangerous tendency, and calculated to unsettle the minds of the theological students of King's College."

Kingsley flew of course to Maurice's defence. "For if you are condemned for these 'opinions' I shall and must therefore avow them and they will have to squelch me as well as you. And I will not, please God, die unavenged in the true sense." (July 21, 1853.) He wanted the correspondence with Jelf published at once and he wanted to begin a campaign of letters to the journals but his vigorous schemes were subdued by Archdeacon Hare and other calm heads.

Even without immediate expression his friendship for Maurice was sufficiently well known to intensify the fear which *Hypatia* had kindled in many orthodox breasts. When, on a leave granted by the Bishop because of Mrs. Kingsley's ill health, he spent the greater part of the winter and spring of 1854 near Torquay, at Maystowe, Babbacombe, only one member of the local clergy invited him to occupy a pulpit and that was for a Lenten week-day service. The pleasant side of this ostracism was that he had something very like a holiday and could spend much time in delighted collection of marine specimens. "The Wonders of the Shore," published in the *North British Review* in November 1854, grew into *Glaucus,* which went into edition after illustrated edition, cemented a lifelong friendship with Philip Gosse and attracted the notice of the Prince Consort.

The peaceful waters of Torbay were troubled only by the necessity of preparing a series of four lectures on *Alexandria and Her Schools* which Kingsley was invited to deliver before the Philosophical Institute of Edinburgh whose members were impressed rather than alarmed by *Hypatia*. The theme of the lectures was that of the novel, the wretched decline of Neo-Platonism, the aristocratic philosophy, and the lesson of that decline for nineteenth century England.

Kingsley was delighted by his first incursion into Scotland, and the success of the lectures was enormous though he had been painfully nervous about their reception, crying with fear in his room before he delivered the first one. He spoke well, was much cheered and clapped, saw his audience increase at each lecture, was begged to publish, treated with much cordiality and introduced to all sorts of notables, among whom he particularly enjoyed Sir James Maxwell. Altogether it was "one of the most pleasant and successful episodes in my life. . . . I have got my say said without giving offence, and have made friends which I hope will last for life." (I, 419.)

CHAPTER XIV

"A SANGUINARY BOOK"

LIKE *Hypatia, Westward Ho!* was a novel of propaganda, a recruiting novel for the Crimean War. Kingsley began to write it in Devonshire in the spring of 1854 shortly after France and England had entered the hostilities.

I am shut up like any Jeremiah here [he wrote to Maurice from Bideford, October 19, 1854], living on the newspapers and my old Elizabethan books. The novel is more than half done, and a most ruthless bloodthirsty book it is (just what the times want, I think). Ludlow will be horribly scandalised at the reverence which it pays throughout to that "much misunderstood politician," Judge Lynch. I am afraid I have a little of the wolf-vein in me, in spite of fifteen centuries of civilisation, and so, I sometimes suspect, have you, and if you had not you would not be as tender and loving as you are. Sooner one caress from a mastiff than twenty from a spaniel. I wish you were here, I want to ask you a thousand things. I am sometimes very sad; always very puzzled, and long to be rid (I am ashamed to say) of a great deal of which I ought not to be rid. This war would have made me half mad, if I had let it. It seemed so dreadful to hear of those Alma heights being taken and not be there; but God knows best, and I suppose I am not fit for such brave work; but only like Camile Desmoulins, "une pauvre créature, née pour faire des vers." But I can fight with my pen still (I don't mean in controversy—I am sick of that. If one went on at it, it would make one a very Billingsgate fishwife, screaming and scolding, when one knows one is safe, and then running away when one expects to have one's attack returned).—Not in controversy, but in writing books which will make others fight. This one is to be called *Westward Ho!* and its motto is old Demosthenes'.

If you will consider these things, you will vote worthily τῶν ἐν Μαραθῶνι καὶ ἐν Σαλαμῖνι τροπαίων!

I hope to have the MSS. in the printer's hands by Christmas; had I more time I could have made a more finished thing of it; but not perhaps a more popular one, and immediate popularity is what I have aimed at. "Mercenary" you will say: but there are reasons, which you may guess, and I have tried to obey the catechism, and even in a hurry speak the truth always and be honest and kind to all!

The writing of it has done me much good. I have been living in those Elizabethan books, among such grand, beautiful, silent men, that I am learning to be sure of what I all along suspected, that I am a poor queazy, hysterical half-baked sort of a fellow, who would not have been half as good a boy as Alexander Smith, if I had not had ten times his advantages, and so am inclined to sing small, and am by no means hopeful about my book, which seems to me only half as good as I could have written and only one-hundredth as good as ought to be written on the matter; but at least God bless you. (I, 433.)

As for a ballad [he wrote to Hughes, Bideford, December 18, 1854], oh! my dear lad, there is no use fiddling while Rome is burning. I have nothing to sing about those glorious fellows, except, "God save the Queen and them." I tell you the whole thing stuns me, so I cannot sit down to make fiddle rhyme with diddle about it—or blundered with hundred, like Alfred Tennyson. He is no Tyrtæus certainly, though he has a glimpse of what Tyrtæus ought to be. But I have not even that; and am going rabbit-shooting to-morrow instead. Would that the Rabbits were Russians, tin-pot on head and musket in hand!—oh for one hour's skirmishing in those Inkerman ravines, and five minutes butt and bayonet as a bonne-bouche to finish with! But every man has his calling, and my novel is mine, because I am fit for nothing better. The book will be out the middle or end of January, if the printers choose. It is a sanguinary book, but perhaps containing doctrine profitable for these times. My only pain is that I have been forced to sketch poor Paddy as a very worthless fellow then, while just now he is turning out a hero. I have made the deliberate *amende honorable* in a note.

The doctrine of *Westward Ho!* is found in condensed form in *Brave Words for Brave Soldiers and Sailors,* a little tract which Kingsley wrote off excitedly in a few hours in response to a request for something which would touch the heart of the fighting man. Published anonymously to avoid, Mrs. Kingsley tells us, "the prejudice which was attached to the name of its author in all sections of the religious world and press at that period" (I, 439), it was distributed by thousands at Sebastopol in the winter of 1855 and seems to have received an attention quite unlike that bestowed by the soldier upon most of the uplifting documents sent to him. Three years after Kingsley's death it was reprinted, with some of his sermons to soldiers, at the request of an army chaplain and a colonel of artillery. "The Lord Jesus Christ," the *Brave Words* run, "is not only the *Prince of Peace*; He is the *Prince of War* too.

He is the Lord of Hosts, the God of armies, and whosoever fights in a just war, against tyrants and oppressors, he is fighting on Christ's side, and Christ is fighting on his side; Christ is his Captain and his Leader, and he can be in no better service. Be sure of it; for the Bible tells you so."

With the necessity he always felt for erecting a logical scaffolding for his intuitive convictions Kingsley had not only made Christ the Prince of War but had worked out a defence of the taking of human life: You cannot take away *human* life. Animal life is all you take away, and very often the best thing you can do for a poor creature is to put him out of this world, saying, "You are evidently unable to get on here. We render you back into God's hands that He may judge you, and set you to work again somewhere else, giving you a fresh chance as you have spoilt this one." (To Thomas Cooper, Torquay, 1854, I, 380.)

It was on these grounds that Kingsley had defended Rajah Brooke in 1849 when the press was crying out against his excesses in Borneo. The truest benevolence, he argued, is occasional severity. Sacrifice of human life? Prove that it is human life. It was to Rajah Brooke that he dedicated *Westward Ho!*

With this attitude toward war Kingsley even more than most of his contemporaries found in the Crimea a desperate relief, an opportunity to dissipate that mid-century melancholy which produced *Maud* and the Spasmodics. Kingsley, with all his feverish energy and love of life, had his periods of dreadful doubt, though the world would have been amazed to hear it. His lowest point seems to have come after the novel was completed. The writing of *Westward Ho!* was a sort of desperate whistling to keep up thinning courage. It is time that old hysterical mock disease should die. It is better to fight for the good than to rail at the ill. Those who did not see it in that light he was constrained to suspect of insincerity. "Be sure that there is a strong Russian feeling among the Puseyites," he wrote to Augustus Stapleton ([?] August 1855), "just because they hanker after the Greek Church, 'faute de Rome' and mark that the prayers about the war put forth by some of the party . . . avoid praying for its success, or committing themselves as to its justice, some even hinting at our 'sin' in it."

Westward Ho! was written at North Down House, Bideford. Mrs. Kingsley's health was frail even after a winter at Torquay, so the family had settled for twelve months in Devon, the rector still on leave from his parish. There were money difficulties but Kingsley trusted in God. "Have we ever," he wrote to his wife in February 1854 during a brief sojourn at Eversley, "been in any debt by our own sin? Have we ever really wanted *anything* we needed? Have we not had friends, credit, windfalls—in all things, with the temptation, a way to escape?" (I, 420.) It was to pay their debts, he reminded her, that he had thought, written, won a name which, please God, might last among the names of English writers. "Would you give up the books I have written that we might never have been in difficulties?"

The war was the moral motive for *Westward Ho!*, its romantic motive was the library of the Rev. Charles Kingsley, Sr. The novel is a sublimated school-boy's dream, the sort of adventure Charles must often have built for himself on the four-mile walk from Chelsea to King's College after an evening spent in his father's study with Hakluyt and Fuller, Camden or Prince's Worthies. There is scarcely an incident in the book which cannot point to a source or at least a parallel in some sixteenth century document —and not one of those incidents but has its whole texture shot through with warm Victorian light.

Frank Leigh sails half across the globe to rescue a Devon maiden carried off by a Spanish don. Hiding outside her house, in imminent peril of his life, he overhears a conversation in which there is reference to her husband: "Husband!" whispered Frank faintly to Amyas. "Thank God, thank God! I am content. Let us go." (Chap. XIX.)

Raleigh and Spenser are talking with Amyas Leigh on watch by night in the camp at Smerwick. "Wherever is love and loyalty," says Spenser, "great purposes, and lofty souls, even though in a hovel or a mine, there is Fairyland." (Chap. IX.)

Frank Leigh composes a "canzonet" on his hopeless love, sings it to the moon; and it sounds like bad Browning. (Chap. IV.) Kingsley was of course unaware that the rhythms of Elizabethan music were something more subtle than the ripple of smooth melody, nor is his ear better when it comes to prose. Every statement in the letter from Sir Francis Drake to Amyas Leigh may be found in Hakluyt (van Meteran's account of the Armada) but the voice is the voice of a loyal subject of Queen Victoria. (Chap.

XXXI.) Kingsley's was an immature, a boy's imagination. He did not recreate for himself scenes in a past age, he pictured Charles Kingsley moving in those scenes and wrote accordingly. The best parts of the book are, as always, those in which he ceases to imagine and begins to draw from life. One of the most successful characters in *Westward Ho!* is old Martin Cockrem—the name and much of his story are out of Hakluyt—who talks with the captains as they wait at Plymouth for the coming of the Armada. (Chap. XXX.) Assuredly that old man with his tales of past heroics and his pathetic greed for muscovado sugar had babbled to Kingsley on the beach at Torquay or Bideford or Clovelly. More than one of the Worthies also has an authentic Devon quality.

Devon scenery too, Kingsley drew at first hand, to the enchantment of his readers; who were equally pleased with the tropical backgrounds which he skilfully vivified from the pages of Gosse and Humboldt. In none of his books is it easier to study his method of working from sources. "I wrote Westward Ho! without any access to town records, much less to state papers," Kingsley explained in reply to some exceptions to his historical accuracy, "chiefly by the light of my dear old Hakluyt." (To J. Cotton, January 7, 1866, I, 446.) There were other sources too: Camden's *Annales*; Prescott's *Conquest of Peru*; Prince's *Worthies of Devon*; Raleigh's *Discovery of Guiana,* Schomburg's edition; Charlevoix's *Historie du Paraguay*; *The Observations of Sir Richard Hawkins in his Voyage into the South Sea*; Drake's *The World Encompassed*; and for background Gosse's *A Naturalist's Sojourn in Jamaica* and von Humboldt and Bonpland's *Personal Narrative of Travels to the Equinoctial Regions of America*. Above all there was Froude who had published in the *Westminster Review* (July 1852) an article on "England's Forgotten Worthies" and who unquestionably helped Kingsley with any number of "hints" from his wide knowledge. Yet Kingsley was completely unable, however much he might read about a period, to comprehend its real spiritual state. His quality as an historical novelist is his skill in striking among the records of a past century on the elements of any number of exciting stories. The tale of the Armada fight, for example (Chap. XXXI), is put together from Camden and Hakluyt (van Meteran) with a dash or two from Raleigh's *History of the World*. The story is told chronologically with that heightening of suspense and increase of interest that comes from following the fortunes of an individual ship. The facts are for the most part so. The boy who reads it will have a fair picture of the externals at least of the great battle, and he, and the most supercilious of modern readers, will be swept off his feet again and again by the narrative rush of *Westward Ho!* Kingsley wrote it, as he always wrote, too fast, but to that is due much of its virtue as well as many of its faults.

One of the results of speed which seems not to have weighed very heavily upon the conscience of the author is an amazing inaccuracy in quotation. Again and again Kingsley appears to have cited whole passages from memory and to have put them into his book without reference to the original. There are numerous small errors such as Diego de Trees for Frees and Philip Miles for Miles Philips. All through his writing and speaking Kingsley maltreats the poetry of others even more brutally than their prose. The inaccuracy of his copious memory was intensified doubtless by the admiration for its scope expressed by Mrs. Kingsley and his parishioners who were incapable of correcting him. The chief blame, however, lies, I believe, with his ear. No one with a real sense of poetic melody could have set as the heading of the thirty-second chapter of *Westward Ho!*

Full fathom deep thy father lies;

an error which is important chiefly because it indicates why Kingsley's own verse is so void of original cadences.

But its faults, annoying as they are, did not prevent the qualities of *Westward Ho!* from making it the first thoroughly popular novel that Kingsley wrote. It was the first of his novels, too, to be brought out by Macmillan, marking an epoch for the firm who regarded it as their first strikingly successful venture in belles lettres. (C. L. Graves, *Life and Letters of Alexander Macmillan*, London, 1910, p. 58.) Kingsley had made the acquaintance of Alexander and Daniel Macmillan in Cambridge where he admired the influence of their bookshop and it was they who first urged *The Saint's Tragedy* and *Village Sermons* upon the notice of undergraduates. In 1850 Kingsley stood godfather to Alexander's son Malcolm Kingsley Macmillan and the friendship ripened.

Westward Ho! was a propitious start for their business connection. The book received at once the royal cachet of Mudie's approval. He ordered 350 copies, advertising it in the London and Manchester papers, and toward the end of the year Kingsley was consulting Hughes on the propriety of paying income tax on the money from his books and reviews. Hitherto it had been an inconsiderable sum but this year it amounted to £400 and "every one must pay while the war is on."

The critics as a whole were laudatory and when they made strictures they were concerned with the style of the book, not, as in the past, primarily with its coarseness or revolutionary doctrine. The *Athenaeum* (March 31, 1855), to be sure, found the ending "ghastly and unwholesome" and the *Guardian* (May 25, 1855) was of course obliged to view with alarm the possible immoral effects of the novel's teaching but the admirers compared the work with Scott's and Thackeray's and Thackeray himself was enthusiastic. The *Leader* (May 19, 1855) thought *Westward Ho!* inferior to *Esmond* but liked its "manly earnestness, glowing vivacity." "We defy any woman to read without tears that scene where Salterne takes Amyas into Rose's room." (Chap. XIV.) Trying Kingsley by the standard of *Quentin Durward,* the *Times* (August 18, 1855), found "certain shortcomings" yet "he is . . . too accomplished to have missed the truth widely, if he has not the supreme genius which can render it with perfect freedom." *Fraser's* (May 1855) of course glowed with praise: "Almost the best historical novel . . . of the day." "In dramatic effect and accuracy of 'costume' it reminds us of *Kenilworth*—can we pay it a higher compliment?" "The man who wrote the following knows a woman's heart to the very core." That passage in Chapter XII was vastly admired. It concluded:

For none knew better than the Spaniard how much more fond women are, by the very law of their sex, of worshipping than of being worshipped, and of obeying than of being obeyed; how their coyness, often their scorn, is but a mask to hide their consciousness of weakness; and a mask, too, of which they themselves will often be the first to tire.

"A passage," said the *Eclectic Review* (June 1855) "which has been repeatedly cited as a proof of Mr. Kingsley's profound insight into the character and temperament of women."

After the book was finished came the depression which the excitement of writing had warded off for a time. Kingsley was very reticent about his deeper unhappinesses, even with his closest friends. To Maurice, however he opened his heart.

As far as so un-"subjective" a person can judge of himself the period of collapse has come to me. I look back upon earlier years with longing, as on a sort of Eden—I mean the years from 1844-1848, and sigh "I have lost my first love." I suppose it is a dream. I suppose if I tried them over again with my present experience I should be ashamed of them; of my vanity and haste, my reckless laying down the law and fault finding, my conceited dream that I knew every body's business better than they themselves did—And yet—I have not lost that vanity, often it seems ready to take baser and more childish forms than ever —of which I am ashamed to speak even to you—and meanwhile I have lost the good side of my other faults, my hatred of evil, my longing to make everything I came near fulfil itself in its vocation. Only do not fear that ultimately I shall be content with being "an artist." I despise and loathe the notion from the bottom of my heart. I have felt its temptation: but I *will* by God's help, fight against that. Indeed if I write another novel, one of my principal characters is to be a man who wants to be an "artist" like old Goethe, (of whom I think less, if not worse, the longer I live) and finds that he becomes, artist or none, a very confused fellow going rapidly to hell. No—I am going to settle quietly here again, and write my sermons, and books for my children, and leave fame to take care of itself, and fine folk and fine society too.

. . .

No. My torment about that book [a "book on nature." See Frederick Maurice, ed., *The Life of Frederick Denison Maurice,* London, 1885, Vol. II, pp. 260 *ff*., for the other side of this correspondence.] lies in a somewhat different direction from what you fancy. Not that you are wrong about me, only that unfortunately for you, the doctor, in probing after one disease you have found a second. Of course I am ready to worship nature all day long, and in the merest Anacreontic Tommy-Moore style too,—to lie among the roses and sing "let us eat and drink for tomorrow we die"—that is more to my taste than any Gnostic or Vestiges of Creation Nature worship, or even the scientific bug-hunting which I recommend to idlers who can't or won't go and die like men, or dogs—considering how we are officered—before Sebastopol. I am losing a zest for work. Everything seems to me not worth working at—except the simple business of telling poor people, Don't fret, God cares for you, and Christ understands you—and that I can't tell fully, because I daren't say what I think, I daren't preach my own creed, which seems to me as different from what I hear preached and find believed, everywhere, as the modern creeds are from Popery, or from St. Paul—And as St. Paul—horrible thought!—seems to me at moments from the plain simple words of our Lord. I *don't* believe he *does* differ from our Lord: but the dread will arise, and torment me. And when my trust in the Bible as a whole seems falling to pieces it is—you must feel it is —terrible work for a poor soul to know where the destructive process must stop; and one feels alone in the universe, at least alone among mankind, on a cliff which is crumbling beneath one, and falling piecemeal into the dark sea. And it is this, in that book which makes me tremble. The denial of Christ as the ideal and perfect man. If I lose that, I lose all. . . . Did He die to deliver the world from sin?—Oh my God, is the world delivered from sin? Do I not hate history because it is the record of brutality, stupidity, cruelty, murder—to bring us *thus* far, to a nineteenth century in which one can look with complacency on no nation, no form of belief, from pole to pole, in which one looks at one's own nation, really the best most righteous of all, with the dreadful feeling that God's face is turned from it, that perhaps He has given it over to strong delusion, that it should believe a lie, and fall in the snare of its own pride? I cannot escape that wretched fear of a national catastrophe, which haunts me night and day. I live in dark nameless dissatisfaction and dread, which has certainly not diminished during the last few months; and I try to forget it in amusement—for in study I cannot. And then I cry—"It is the devil's voice slandering my countrymen to me, slandering priests, statesmen, rich and poor, and I am a devil myself, who am sinning against the Holy Ghost, and calling good men's works evil. The Nation is going right, the Bishops are right in not denouncing the Governors who allow Crimean tragedies; every one is right in leaving well alone— even in leaving ill alone, where it is so inextricably mixed up with good that you cannot root up the tares without rooting up the wheat also." Is that God's voice, or the devil's? (August 6, 1855.)

The other confidant of Kingsley's dark moods was his wife and she, aware that overwork had much to do with his state of mind, exercised her veto when he was about to comply with the Macmillans' immediate desire for another novel. Her advice in practical matters was invariably taken. Daniel Macmillan acceded at once, expressing only a hope that there might be two or three small books while the two years' rest preparatory to the great one were passing. He was certain of the success of a new novel—Mudie was charging fifteen shillings for second-hand copies of *Westward Ho!* while he sold *Esmond* for only nine shillings. He promised a first edition of the next Kingsley novel large enough to yield its author £1000. (Thomas Hughes, *Memoir of Daniel Macmillan,* London, 1882, p. 287.)

CHAPTER XV

"I SEE ONE WORK TO BE DONE ERE I DIE"

IN his next novel, *Two Years Ago,* published in 1857, Kingsley states, indirectly, his own way out of that state of mind described in the last chapter. His way was science and sanitation. Theological doubts might swirl darkly in his brain, he might find it difficult to speak comfortably to his parishioners when he felt no comfort himself, but he was absolutely certain that their souls could not be saved while their bodies sickened and died and at least he could do something to preserve those bodies. "I see," he wrote John Bullar (November 26, 1857), "one work to be done ere I die, in which (men are beginning to discover) nature must be counteracted, lest she prove a curse and a destroyer, not a blessing and a mother; and that is, Sanitary Reform. Politics and political economy may go their way for me. If I can help to save the lives of a few thousand working people and their children, I may earn the blessing of God." (II, 38.)

So Kingsley began to devote himself more and more to the cause of public health in which his interest had always been strong; the interrelation between soul and body was from the beginning a fundamental part of his creed. In connection with his investigations for *Alton Locke* he had campaigned, unsuccessfully of course, for governmental control of London's water supply. While *Westward Ho!* was on the stocks he was giving evidence on sanitary matters as one of a deputation to Lord Palmerston. He preached sanitation to his parishioners at all seasons, from the pulpit and in their kitchens. Kegan Paul describes his visiting a cottage where a man lay sick in a close stuffy room. Kingsley had provided himself with an auger and before the amazed household sensed what was happening the parson had rushed upstairs and bored three or four large holes in the ceiling of the invalid's room, letting in a little desperately needed fresh air. (Kegan Paul, "Charles Kingsley," *Biographical Sketches,* London, 1883, p. 121.)

Kingsley encouraged the Ladies Sanitary Association founded in 1856 for "the diffusion of Sanitary Knowledge among all classes, by the publication of Tracts, the delivery of Lectures, the establishment of Institutions for Training Nurserymaids, and of Loan Libraries of popular Sanitary books." He helped to raise money for public baths and wash-houses. He worked for greater facilities for women's medical education, believing that women were the best teachers for women in matters of health. He wrote and lectured continually on what he liked to call The Science of Health. One of these lectures, which he delivered in Birmingham in 1872 as President of the Midland Institute, had that kind of direct result with which the crusader is seldom blessed. A member of the audience found in it direction for the concrete embodiment of a philanthropic impulse he had long nursed and presented £2,500 to the Institute for the foundation of classes in physiology and hygiene.

In the cholera epidemics of 1849 and 1854 Kingsley did brave service. He was in Bideford when the disease broke out in 1854 and undertook house-to-house visitation in one of the districts there, an experience which makes his *Two Years Ago* descriptions as vivid as some of the scenes of *Alton Locke.* He pictures the heart-breaking labours of those who tried to protect the inhabitants against their own death-breeding carelessness and filth:

"An' if any committee puts its noz into my backyard, if it doan't get the biggest cod's innards as I can collar hold on, about its ears, my name is not Treluddra! A man's house is his castle, says I, and them as takes up with any o' this open-day burglary, for it's nothing less, has to do wi' me, that's all, and them as knows their interest, knows me!" (Chap. XIV.)

In 1849 Kingsley had preached three sermons on "Who Causes Pestilence?" (*Sermons on National Subjects,* 1852.) He republished them as a tract in 1854 when the country had been scandalized by Lord Palmerston's refusal to grant a fast day for prevention of the cholera. God, Kingsley argued, in his Preface and in an article for *Fraser's* (January 1854, "Lord Palmerston and the Presbytery of Edinburgh"), had heard their prayers in '49 and had shown them the way of escape by cleanliness and disinfectants.

The difficulty now lies in those members of the clergy who conceive their duty to be the saving of souls, not the making of people good in this world, or who find that to look on pestilence as other than an act of God interferes with their religious theories, or who, getting their subsistence from the vested interests, are afraid to advocate doctrines which may be inconvenient to them. The sermons are as outspoken as the Preface; one sees why people were excited by Kingsley's preaching.

Do not let us believe this time, my friends, in the pitiable, insincere way in which all England believed when the cholera was here sixteen years ago. When they saw human beings dying by thousands, they all got frightened, and proclaimed a Fast and confessed their sins and promised repentance in a general way. But did they repent of and confess those sins which had caused the cholera? Did they repent of and confess the covetousness, the tyranny, the carelessness, which in most great towns, and in too many villages also, forces the poor to lodge in undrained stifling hovels, unfit for hogs, amid vapours and smells which send forth on every breath the seeds of rickets and consumption, typhus and scarlet fever, and worse and last of all the cholera? Did they repent of their sin in that? Not they. Did they repent of the carelessness and laziness and covetousness which sends meat and fish up to all our large towns in a half-putrid state; which fills every corner of London and the great cities with slaughter-houses, over-crowded graveyards, undrained sewers? Not they. To confess their sins in a general way cost them a few words; to confess and repent of the real particular sins in themselves, was a very different matter; to amend them would have touched vested interests, would have cost money, the Englishman's god; it would have required self-sacrifice of pocket, as well as of time. ("First Sermon on the Cholera.")

We have had our fair warning here. We have had God's judgment about our cleanliness; His plain spoken opinion about the sanitary state of this parish. We deserve the fever, I am afraid; not a house in which it has appeared but has had some glaring neglect of common cleanliness about it; and if we do not take the warning God will surely some day repeat it. ("Second Sermon on the Cholera.")

The hero of the cholera epidemic in the novel and the hero of the novel itself is Dr. Tom Thurnall, modelled, of course with variations, upon Dr. George Kingsley. He is a very likable character despite his unpleasant habit of self-consciously soliloquizing like Raphael Aben-Ezra of *Hypatia*. (It is quite possible that Kingsley thought to himself in much this form.) Dr. Tom's creator makes one believe in his geniality, his pluck, his adventures (reminiscent of Dr. Kingsley's early life and prophetic of his later), his resourcefulness, his real medical and scientific skill, his desire to mend the human ills he encounters from no motive which he will admit to be noble. His weakness, Charles Kingsley indicates, is his trust in his own strength, his disregard for the necessity of dependence upon divine guidance—which he learns at last through a long sad term in a Russian prison and of course through the love of a good woman.

One of the Doctor's special virtues is his devotion to science, in the nineteenth century sense of the collecting and classifying of specimens. In the years when zoölogy, botany and geology were in their infancy the professional scientist had great use for the assistance of the intelligent amateur and Kingsley not only took vast delight in such work himself but urged it constantly upon everyone from working men in evening classes to languid young ladies at the seaside. The value that he saw in it was chiefly moral, a greater love of God through a closer knowledge of the intricate marvels of his creation. "I am sure," he wrote to Maurice, March 29, 1863, "that science and the creeds will shake hands at last . . . and that by God's grace, I may help them to do so." (II, 181.) There were few callings so satisfactory, he felt, as that of the man of science.

Kingsley did throughout his life work which was of genuine value to such men as Philip Gosse, Huxley and Darwin; his correspondence with scientists was large and happy and the two honours which gave him the purest pleasure were his fellowships in the Linnean and in the Geological Society, conferred in 1857 and in 1863. So in *Two Years Ago* it is not enough to have a doctor using a microscope and wading in Devonshire caves for zoöphytes. Kingsley introduces also a retired military man, a Major Campbell, who has made science, especially the collection of marine specimens, his principal avocation. Kingsley says in a letter to Brimley (1857, II, 39) that the Major is a portrait but unfortunately gives no further clue. Certainly he loved him for he makes him the author—Kingsley had a habit of introducing his poems into his prose works—of

> Be good, sweet maid, and let who will be clever.
>
> ("A Farewell," *Poems,* 1858, *Two Years Ago,* Chap. XX.)

Science and sanitation, however, were merely side issues, not the intentional morals of *Two Years Ago*. Its primary purposes were two: to strike another blow at the doctrine of eternal damnation and to show that if any one is damned it is likely to be the man who is "an artist."

I hope [he wrote to Maurice] you will have Two Years Ago in the course of a couple of days. I have ordered a copy to be sent you. It is another side-stroke at the Tartarus doctrine, which is never out of my mind. I am trying, without openly attacking it, which I intend to do, *Please God,* formally, when I am older and steadier, I am trying, I say, to keep continually tapping on it, by little reductiones ad absurdum, and snubs and sneers; to produce if possible, an uncomfortable feeling on the point in the public mind, and a necessity of reconsidering the matter—as if a doctor, having a stupid patient with an unconfest bad tooth, was steadily and perpetually to tap on said tooth, and torture the patient thereby into a slow suspicion that it must be hollow, or it would not be so tender. Now Tartarus is the public's bad tooth: but as all mortals will endure complicated agonies, and call them face-ache, neuralgia, brow-ague, cold in the anythings—all to escape what they quite well know they cannot escape, viz, *having the tooth out,* so is the public affected toward Tartarus. The priest says—"Take away Tartarus? My occupation is gone!" The layman says, "Take away Tartarus? Why, then I have taken all this trouble to be good, to escape a place which don't exist! I must believe stoutly in there being a Tartarus to be saved from, else I must confess myself a fool for having taken so much trouble to get saved." (Saturday, 1857. See Chap. XI, p. 93.)

All through his life Kingsley continued to tap at the "Tartarus doctrine." In 1872 he accepted membership on the Committee for the Defence of the Athanasian Creed and in a letter "For the Private Consideration of the Committee" set down in detail his solution of the doctrinal problem of hell, that heavy stumbling-block to so many humanitarian individualists in the nineteenth century. He felt that the English mind was ripe for the preaching of the great Catholic doctrine of an intermediate state, though it must be presented of course with prudence lest the people confuse it with the Romish idea of purgatory.

As in *Hypatia,* Kingsley presents in fair form the system he intends to demolish. Grace Harvey, the schoolmistress, is beautiful to look upon and of a genuinely religious, even a mystical, nature but she has, alas, been brought up a Brianite[1] and, following the doctrine of hell through to its bitter end, is driven nearly out of her mind by fear that a beloved brother and his friend drowned in their wild youth are lost past all redemption. This was no mere melodramatic invention. Kingsley had personally brought consolation to more than one sensitive soul in that state of vicarious suffering.

Grace's mother is a poor creature who, though a respected member of her congregation, is easily led into theft and dishonesty. She and the other members of the sect who make brief appearance caused the dissenters to cry again, as they had of *Alton Locke,* that Kingsley's conception of their beliefs was fantastically unfair. Yet he was writing what really seemed to him the truth, just as he honestly saw Roman Catholicism in the guise of Eustace Leigh in *Westward Ho!*

While he is touching the dissenters Kingsley makes a side blow at the extremists of the High Church group in the person of an admirable young curate who is quite unable to reach the hearts of his parishioners because they suspect him of Popery. He learns wisdom from Tom Thurnall, with some help from love and experience, and his story ends happily, as of course does Grace's when she marries the humbled Tom.

There is no reformation in this life, however, for Elsley Vavasour, the man who was "an artist." Kingsley had felt the stupidity of his father's attitude, that fear of enjoying one's own artistic propensities; he was quite ready to admit art as an avocation but he could not untie the moral millstone from her neck and only very hardly could he accept art as the centre of a life. To write his novels without their lessons would have been to him mere self-indulgence. He had his own conception of the artist, as he had of the dissenter and the mystic, and what he fought against was that imaginary figure of his own creation.

Elsley Vavasour is a Spasmodic poet. He was born John Briggs and apprenticed to a country doctor but his mind is above his station and he soon manages to escape to the larger opportunities of London. He affects of course all the poetic trappings, Byronic

---

[1] Usually spelt Bryanite. The popular name for the Arminian Bible Christians, a sect founded in 1816 by William O'Bryan, an expelled Methodist. He preached widely in Cornwall and Devon.

curls, a floating cloak and a romantic name. He fascinates the beautiful young sister of a peer and makes her a peevish, unreasonable husband, ashamed of his poverty but without the remotest thought of alleviating it by any means other than writing verses and wishing for fame. His fundamental fault to Kingsley is that he is first not a man but a poet. He regards experience as a series of subjects for potential poems and he looks at the universe not to see what it is like but to study the way in which it affects him.

All is over. What shall we do now? Go home, and pray that God may have mercy on all drowning souls? Or think what a picturesque and tragical scene it was, and what a beautiful poem it will make, when we have thrown it into an artistic form, and bedizened it with conceits and analogies stolen from all heaven and earth by our own self-willed fancy? (Chap. III.)

Elsley is overdrawn, as Kingsley's villains are likely to be, but he does typify the faults of his school, and from temptation to those faults Kingsley himself found it necessary to flee. He credits to Elsley one of his own poems and disapproves the manner of its composition:

Silly-fellow! Do you think that Nature had time to think of such a far-fetched conceit as that while it was making that rock and peopling it with a million tiny living things, of which not one falleth to the ground without your Father's knowledge, and each more beautiful than any sea-nymph whom you ever fancied? (Chap. X.)

The poet's end is terrible. Goaded by a quite unfounded jealousy of his wife's friendship with Major Campbell he rushes away from a pleasant picnic party in Wales, anywhere, anywhere, up Snowdon, the Glyder Vawr, in night and storm. Then comes wretchedness, something like madness, drugs and death. The lesson told. "Poor dear Brimley," wrote a common friend to Kingsley (1857), "attributed his being convinced of sin, and driven to seek Christ the Lord and Saviour, to your last book, especially that fearful account of Elsley Vavasour's chase across the mountain, and Tom Thurnall's experience in the Russian dungeon. He had always said to me that he never could understand what was meant by the sense of sin as spoken of in the Bible, and by Maurice in his Theological Essays. But one night, about six weeks before his death, when he awoke in pain and darkness in the middle of the night, the remembrance of that terrible isolation which you had described in those passages came upon him in awful horror, and drove him to seek help from God. No one who knew Brimley before that time and after it could fail to see how great the change was that was wrought in him." (II, 31.)

Brimley died only a few months after he had written an enthusiastic review of the novel for the *Spectator* (February 14, 1857) and kindly letters to Kingsley who argued with him at length every point of his criticism. He fought especially against the suggestion that a novel should have shape and limits. (*Two Years Ago* starts a new hare in every chapter.) The idea of self-evolution in a story, Kingsley maintained, is a beautiful one for a Greek tragedy but there has never been anything like it in Christian art. Look at the irrelevant scenes and characters in Shakespeare's plays and in *The Pilgrim's Progress,* the best novel ever written. You must have descriptions, too, of everything which can possibly influence your characters and παραβάσεις like those in the Greek romantic drama where the author throws off his mask and speaks for himself. "Women like them better than any part of a book. They like to be taught a little now and then; to feel that the book is the work of a human person, speaking to them as human persons, and therefore I fear the Athenaeum hateth them—just because they are the parts of the book which have the real practical influence." (II, 40.) These παραβάσεις, what women call "delightful subjective bits," have been one of the secrets of Bulwer's success. The reviewer who disagrees with the doctrine may call it an intrusion of the author's self but it is the author's business to make it not that but the expression of the thoughts of many hearts, the putting into words for his readers of what they would say for themselves if they could; "he will be paid at once in thanks, and correspondence, and having the secrets of sad hearts opened to him: as last night, already, brought me one of the saddest and most interesting letters I ever read, from some one to whom reading *Two Years Ago* had awakened a new view of God." (*op. cit.*)

Kingsley argued also that the storm scene on the Glyder was elaborately careful realism. Cockney reviewers will carp because they have never seen anything like it but "what I wanted to do was boldly to defy criticism on that very point, calling the chapter 'Nature's Melodrama,' and showing, meanwhile, that the 'melodramatic element,' was a false, and morbid, and cowardly one, by bringing in Naylor and Wynd, thinking the very same horrors capital fun. I would not have taken Elsley there if I had not taken them there also, as a wholesome foil to his madness." (II, 43.) It was of this scene that the *Saturday Review* complained (February 21, 1857) that it was "rather a bore to have in a single paragraph, twelve or fourteen hard names of plants, with rapturous epithets interspersed."

The survey of the Snowdon ground which furnished material for the melodrama had been made in the spirit of the wholesome Cambridge boating-men. The expedition to Pen-y-gwrydd which Kingsley made in August 1856 with Tom Hughes and Tom Taylor was one of the most rollicking holidays he ever had.

I wish you would make a vow, and keep it strong; for Mrs. Kingsley says that if you will, I may: and that is not to cross the sea like Sophia, but to go with me to Snowdon next summer for a parson's week, *i.e.* twelve days. For why? I have long promised my children a book to be called "Letters from Snowdon," and I want to rub up old memories, and to get new ones in parts of which I know through my brother Henry, but which I have never seen. You do not know how easy it is. You get second class into the mail at Euston Square at 9 p.m., and breakfast at Aber, under the Carnadds, next morning. An ordnance map, a compass, fishing-tackle, socks, and slippers are all you want—as for shirts, who would wear them? Moreover, I *do* know where to fish, and one of the crackest fishers of the part has promised to *give* me as many flies of his own making as I like, while another can lend us boat or coracle, if we went to fish Gwynant and Dinas. I conceive that, humanly speaking, if we went to work judgmatically, we could live for 15s. a-day at the outside (if we are canny, at 12s.) and kill an amount of fish perfectly frightful, and *all the big ones,* by the simple expedient of sleeping by day, walking evening and morning, and fishing during the short hot nights. Wales is a cheap place, if you avoid show inns; and, save a night at Capel Curig, we need never enter a show inn. We may stay two or three days at Pen-y-Gwyrrryy-nnwwdddelld—there—I can't spell it, but it sounds Pennygorood, which is the divinest pig-sty beneath the canopy, and at Beddgelert old Jones the clerk, and king of fishermen, will take us in—and do for us—if we let him. The parson of Beddgelert is a friend of mine also, but we must depend on our own legs, and on stomachs, which can face braxy mutton, young taters, Welsh porter, which is the identical drainings of Noah's flood turned sour, and brandy of more strength than legality. Bread horrid. Fleas MCCCC ad infinitum. Bugs a sprinkling, ditto a worse complaint if you sleep in cottages; inns are safe. For baths, the mountain brook; for towel, a wisp of any endogen save Scirpus triqueter, or Juncus squarrosus; and for cure of all ills, and supplement of all defects, baccy. Do come—you have no notion of the grandeur of the scenery, small as it is compared with the Alps. (To Hughes, Farley Court, December 26, 1855, I, 464.)

Kingsley came back from this holiday with his youth like the eagle's. He did not wait for the expiration of the year of repose but went at his waiting novel with such terrific energy that he had it finished and in type by Christmas time.

While the book was in the writing he had become fired for a new crusade, and two visits made to him in the autumn must have supplied him with some of the materials for the American sub-plot although it had been partly sketched out at least some months before. Kingsley had hoped in fact that his anti-slavery propaganda might make the American edition of the book of use in the Fremont election (November 1856) and this accounts for the political talk in the introductory chapter which the critics found irrelevant. W. H. Hurlbert, the American journalist, who was in England in the autumn of 1856 and was trying to present the abolitionist case in English periodicals, corresponded with Kingsley and made a visit to Eversley. He apparently furnished some "hints" for the part of Stangrave. Kingsley described him to Hughes as "a most admirable Yankee, about your own age . . . a great friend of Lowell's, and one of us to the back bone."

Stangrave is in part an intensification of the Elsley Vavasour lesson, an accomplished man of the world who wraps his talents in a napkin until he is fired by love of the beautiful actress Marie Cordifiamma. Marie is a noble savage more romantic even than Mrs. Stowe's beautiful quadroons from whom she derives. Tom Thurnall, at the dying request of a friend, has helped her to escape to Canada, where, passing as an Italian, she makes an international success on the stage. In London she is adored by the young bloods, including the Poet's brother-in-law, Lord Scoutbush, a right-minded but untaught little guardsman, one of those Esaus to whom Kingsley was especially called to minister. Even the revelation of Marie's race does not console the rejected viscount who tries, fortunately without success, to get himself shot at Scutari. Marie loves Stangrave and he is proud to marry her when she at last consents after she has driven him to engage his latent energies in the cause of her people's liberty. Their marriage is superlatively happy and before the book ends they have two children. For his conception of negro psychology Kingsley was indebted to Harriet Beecher Stowe who stayed at Eversley Rectory on her second visit to England in the autumn of 1856. "How we did talk and go on," she wrote her husband, "for three days! I guess he is tired. I'm sure we were." (Annie Fields, *Life and Letters of Harriet Beecher Stowe,* Cambridge, Mass., 1897, p. 227.)

CHAPTER XVI

"ALL OF ME WHICH WILL LAST"

YOU ARE not wise in rating my work high. I feel in myself a deficiency of discursive fancy, which will prevent my ever being a great poet. I know I can put into singing words the plain things I see and feel; but that faculty which Alexander Smith has (and nothing else)—and which Shakespeare had more than any man—the power of metaphor and analogue—the instructive vision of connections between all things in heaven and earth, which poets *must* have, is very weak in me; and therefore I shall never be a great poet. And what matter? I will do what I can; but I believe you are quite right in saying that my poetry is all of me which will last. Except, perhaps, *Hypatia*. (To ?, 1858, II, 54.)

This—with some modification of the last two sentences—is probably the most accurate estimate of Kingsley's poetical qualities which was made in his lifetime. He was not usually so perspicuous a critic. Emotional, intuitive, spontaneous, "temperamental," he diagnosed himself, according to nineteenth century psychology, as a poet and the conviction was strengthened by his knack of versifying. His too fluent utterance needed external restraint; he thought most effectively, therefore, within the imposed barriers of verse. "There is no denying it:" he wrote Ludlow (June 1852), "I do feel a different being when I get into metre—I feel like an otter in the water, instead of an otter ashore." (I, 338.) To write good prose demanded a self-discipline which his exuberance found very irksome.

For the same reason Kingsley had no skill in inventing metres. He worked best within a set simple form. A melody heard or imagined would set his invention going and his invention was always fertile in the production of tales, pathetic, exciting or lurid. As a poet he succeeds best with the ballad and the passage in *Alton Locke* about the inspiration of "The Sands of Dee" may fairly be taken, I think, as descriptive of a typical creative experience.

Suddenly, after singing two or three songs, she began fingering the keys, and struck into an old air, wild and plaintive, rising and falling like the swell of an Æolian harp upon a distant breeze.

"Ah! now," she said, "if I could get words for that! What an exquisite lament somebody might write to it, if they could only thoroughly take in the feeling and meaning of it."

"Perhaps," I said, humbly, "that is the only way to write songs—to let some air get possession of one's whole soul, and gradually inspire the words for itself; as the old Hebrew prophets had music played before them, to wake up the prophetic spirit within them." . . .

. . . my attention was caught by hearing two gentlemen close to me discuss a beautiful sketch, by Copley Fielding, if I recollect rightly, which hung on the wall—a wild waste of tidal sands, with here and there a line of stake-nets fluttering in the wind—a grey shroud of rain sweeping up from the westward, through which low red cliffs glowed dimly in the rays of the setting sun—a train of horses and cattle splashing slowly through shallow desolate pools and creeks, their wet red and black hides glittering in one long line of level light. . . .

One of them had seen the spot represented at the mouth of the Dee, and began telling wild stories of salmon-fishing, and wild-fowl shooting—and then a tale of a girl who, in bringing her father's cattle home across the sands, had been caught by a sudden flow of the tide, and found next day a corpse hanging among the stake-nets far below. . . .

I . . . went home that night . . . to lie sleepless. . . . As I lay castle-building, Lillian's wild air rang still in my ears, and combined itself somehow with that picture of the Cheshire Sands, and the story of the drowned girl, till it shaped itself into a song. (Chap. XXVI.)

To whatever melodies, heard or imagined, Kingsley composed them, the songs when written cried out for music and any number of people rushed to make it, with more or less indifferent success. It was John Hullah whose settings pleased the poet most, who seemed to strike in his music the exact "tone" that Kingsley had imagined. Their combined creations completely satisfied the contemporary yearning to express emotion in sentimental ennobling platitude, and there was scarcely a well brought up young lady in the kingdom who did not adore Charles Kingsley as the writer of the songs from *The Water-Babies* and "Oh! that we two were Maying."

With a very few exceptions even the ballads and songs have a touch at least of the didacticism which was one of the major qualities of the other verse. Kingsley believed that poetry had a mission. "Without faith there can be no real art, for art is the outward expression of firm, coherent belief. And a poetry of doubt, even a sceptical poetry, in its true sense, can never possess clear and sound form, even organic form at all." ("Alexander Smith and Alexander Pope," *Miscellanies*, I.) A firm coherent belief in a minor poet too often sounds the album note. "Be good, sweet maid," Kingsley's supreme example, and several other admired lyrics were actually composed for albums.

The earnestness of Kingsley's blank verse was even higher than that of the lyrics. Metrically it is undistinguished; he seems to have composed by rule rather than by ear.[1] He was aware that it was not his *forte* and after *The Saint's Tragedy* he tried it only occasionally. "Blank verse is very bold in my hands, because I won't write 'poetic diction,' but only plain English—and so I can't get mythic grandeur enough." (To Ludlow, June 1852, I, 338.) With hexameters he made some experiments, notably his long poem *Andromeda*, and he wrote elaborate letters on his theories. "English hexameters are an awful responsibility, and mine are, I suspect, a last attempt. If they don't do, I despair of the whole hopes of introducing that king of metres into our tongue." (To A. Macmillan, January 8, 1858, C. L. Graves, *Life and Letters of Alexander Macmillan*, London, 1910, p. 116.)

Over his poetry Kingsley worked as he never took time to work over his prose. He rewrote continually. The published form of the poems is very different from that in which they appear in the commonplace-books. "I don't agree with you," he said to Ludlow (1852) "about not polishing too much. If you are a verse-maker, you will, of course, rub off the edges and the silvering; but if you are a poet, and have an idea and one keynote running through the whole, which you can't for the life define to yourself, but which is there out of the abysses, defining you; then every polishing is a bringing the thing nearer to that idea." (I, 340.)

It was partly this desire for perfection which made Kingsley slow to publish, partly his fear of being only an artist, a person

---

[1] This is apparent from the criticism he levels against the carelessness and clumsiness of one Marks of Barhamville whose *Poems* he reviewed for *Fraser's*. ("Readables and Unreadables," June 1850.) He scans a few of Marks's offending lines, insisting on an absolutely regular iambic metre:
> Thé felucca there
> With laten-sail, seen ín th' horizon skirt
> Shaping its course t'ward thé Egyptian shore,
> Gives tó the moon the silv'ry foam, which breaks.

whom the world might confuse with his own Elsley Vavasour. "I have deserted poetry as rats do a sinking ship," he wrote to Archer Gurney in 1855 (October 3). But anonymous poems with a purpose he had given to the Christian Socialist publications when they needed them, and after 1850 verse signed C. K. appeared from time to time, more remuneratively, in *Fraser's*. In 1852 Kingsley began to think about the profits from a volume of collected verse and wrote to Parker:

You spoke to me some time ago about bringing out a volume of poems, and I have no doubt such a thing would have a large sale. I have now enough to make a 12mo of 70 pages, including, 4 or 5 songs and ballads which have appeared in Fraser's, on which of course you have some sort of lien. We could arrange about that—and I think, the simplest plan is for me to publish at my own expense and take the risk of the market. But you know best, and must advise me, whether this is too small a volume (I presume it would be a 2/6 one) to bring out.

This is to be said. That there is *no* trash in it, that everything is of my best, and has been polished over and over till I hate the very sight of them. Also that among them is a quite new poem of 250 lines of blank verse, "Saint Maura," which I am anxious, and I think Maurice is too, to get published as soon as possible, "to prove" as he said "that I am not the mere Pantagruelist some men take me for." Just ask him about that poem when you next see him, and tell me freely your mind about everything. I *could* sit down and swell the volume considerably. But that is a base dodge; nothing should be published till long after it is written and my present list contains a complete cycle of songs about all forms of human passion and a ballad or small poem of each age, from the present time to that of the early martyrs. There are altogether 20 of these minor things, and 9 of the historic ones, in all 29 pieces.

Parker evidently advised against the publication of so small a volume for the *Poems* did not appear till 1858 and then in a volume of more than twice seventy pages. In the meantime an American edition had appeared in Boston (1856). Messrs. Ticknor and Fields gathered from periodicals most of the verses which later appeared in English editions, plus one or two which Kingsley preferred to forget. Since they did not have "Andromeda," they added *The Saint's Tragedy,* as Macmillan did when he made a collected edition in 1872.

The critics of the 1858 volume were inclined to be fulsome. They liked Kingsley's hexameters; they liked his healthy tone; they were only occasionally disturbed by the radicalism of some of the ballads; they quoted at length. "Andromeda" was a general favourite. The poem on the crucifixion of Saint Maura, for which Kingsley himself cared so much, many of them found too painful. "Nothing which I ever wrote," he had said to Maurice, "came so out of the depths of my soul as that, or caused me during writing (it was all done in a day and a night), a poetic fervour such as I never felt before or since. It seemed to me a sort of inspiration which I could not resist; and the way to do it came before me clearly and instantly, as nothing else has ever done." (II, 52.) *Fraser's* (June 1858), however, found "Saint Maura" the only unhealthy poem in the book of "a good man, and a good sportsman." The *Saturday Review* (June 5, 1858) thought it too horrible, though it had undeniable power. They were especially delighted with "Andromeda," "a glowing Etty picture of the best kind, but with a romance which Etty wants." "Tell Mr. Kingsley to leave novels and write nothing but lyrics, said one of our greatest living writers to us the other day," reported *Chambers's Journal* (June 16, 1855), "when we shewed him some of these songs. Bunsen urged him to become a Poet of the People. We know no man at present so fitted for that high office."

The ink, however, was scarcely dry upon the poems before Kingsley was plotting another novel. He was to return again this time to the historic vein. The theme, suggested by Froude, was the Pilgrimage of Grace, the North of England rising against Henry VIII's dissolution of the monasteries. In July Kingsley made a journey to Yorkshire to get up names and places but he had been driving his creative powers beyond the bounds of reason. They collapsed flatly and not for five years did he write another novel. He was, he said, like a spider who has spun all his silk and must sit still and secrete more.

There really is very little the matter with me [he wrote to Bullar, November 19, 1859], except what is called in country fellows "idleness." I never call it so. If they say to me, "Jem is a slack hand, he won't do no work; and if he tries, he haint no heart, but gies out at mowing or pitching like any chicken," then I answer, "Very well; you leave Jem alone: he won't live long if you hurry him!" Whereon they ask "And what's wrong wi' he, then?" To which I answer solemnly, "Deficient vitality."—which shuts them up; and is also a true and correct answer. *I* am a slack hand now. I can't think; I can't write; I can't run; I can't ride—I have neither wit, nerve, nor strength for anything; and if I try I get a hot head, and my arms and legs begin to ache. I was so ten years ago: worse than now. I have learnt by that last attack, and have, thank God, pulled up in time. Do not fancy that I am going to fret myself about anything. I have infinite power left of doing two things, which are generally necessary to earthly salvation, viz., eating and sleeping, and to them I am paying great attention. When I tried to work, and yet could not, I had over and above a nasty craving for alcohol—for more wine than I have usually found necessary to digest my food. Since I have left my brain alone, that craving is going off. (II, 93.)

The failure of his creative imagination in no wise affected Kingsley's fluency. He could always write, no matter what his state of exhaustion, and during the five years of respite from novel composing, sermons, essays and books for children flowed from him in a continuous stream.

CHAPTER XVII

CHAPLAIN TO THE QUEEN AND TO THE PRINCE OF WALES

May 7, 1859

I HAVE the honour to inform you, that I have received the Queen's command to offer you the appointment of Chaplain-in-Ordinary to Her Majesty. . . . I will add, that the duties are confined to the Preaching of one Sermon at the Chapel Royal at St. James's in the course of the year, for which there is a salary of £30 per an.

On the arrival of that letter the British sun broke through the clouds and beamed upon Charles Kingsley. His principles had altered not a jot: he remained to his death a Broad Churchman and he would not believe in eternal damnation; he loved the working man and he continued to cry aloud in the cause of sanitary reform; but no one could shout "heretic" at a man who preached at St. James's or suggest that Her Majesty had chosen as Chaplain one who was conspiring to overthrow the State. Kingsley had always had a knot of staunch friends and a wide circle of inconspicuous admirers; now the timid dared to present their garlands in public and the hostile were obliged to offer dissent, if at all, with politeness. Life became smoother socially and before long financially also.

For Kingsley himself the appointment was not only an honour but a very real pleasure. He was a genuine royalist. He admired the Queen as a pattern wife and mother and a wise administrator but he admired her also as something a little higher than human. He found in his excursions into royal society a refreshment as actual as that which came from ascending into the rarer air of Snowdon. He reverenced, but he bore himself with the same naturalness and simplicity with which he went into Parker's publishing house or an Eversley cottage.

Kingsley and Queen Victoria had many traits in common. Their power lay largely in the fact that they were people of their epoch and genuinely believed its fundamental creeds. Each of them too, had made an ideal marriage and felt that in such a union was summed the best of earthly joy. And Kingsley possessed the crowning virtue of admiring Prince Albert almost as much as the Queen did.

It would appear to have been Prince Albert who called the Queen's attention to Charles Kingsley. The first indication of royal favour came with the publication of *Glaucus* which "pierced the 'august abodes' of Windsor" and elicited the present of a handsome book from His Royal Highness. (To A. Macmillan, May 19, 1856, C. L. Graves, *Life and Letters of Alexander Macmillan,* London, 1910, p. 89.) Kingsley's desire to make science serve God was the Prince's own ideal. In the month of November 1858 *Two Years Ago* was the only book he found time to read and he wrote to his daughter in Berlin that it had given him great pleasure by its profound knowledge of human nature and insight into the relations between man, his actions, his destiny and God. (Theodore Martin, *The Life of H.R.H. the Prince Consort,* New York, 1879, IV, 282.)

Queen Victoria, when she began to read Kingsley's books, was undoubtedly attracted by his theology. She was never reconciled to the doctrine of endless punishment; her humanitarian feeling about it was much like his. She liked a Low Church service, one of her household has recorded, and a discourse of about twenty minutes, unwritten, a plain exposition of practical truths arising from a subject of the day. (*The Private Life of the Queen,* by A Member of the Royal Household, New York, 1897.) She enjoyed Scotch Presbyterian sermons rather more than those of the average Church of England divine and Kingsley's had the forthright Scotch quality, though—contrary to the Queen's idea of fine preaching—he did read them. He took care always to adapt his references and illustrations to his audience but the heart of what he preached was the same at Eversley or at Windsor.

Sermons were a favourite form of reading of the day and Kingsley began to publish his as early as 1849. *Twenty-Five Village Sermons* impressed the university undergraduates who had been excited by *The Saint's Tragedy.* Book after book followed: *Sermons on National Subjects,* 1852; 2nd series, 1854; *Sermons for the Times,* 1855; *The Good News of God,* 1859; *Town and Coun-*

try Sermons, 1861; *The Gospel of the Pentateuch,* 1863; *David: Four Sermons Preached before the University of Cambridge,* 1865; *The Water of Life,* 1867; *Discipline,* 1868; *Westminster Sermons,* 1874; and of course many preached on special occasions and published in pamphlet form. They were a very definite source of profit. It was not even necessary to garner a sheaf for book publication; periodicals were glad to have them singly. Mrs. Kingsley was astute enough to see this. A letter to her (November 12, 1868) from the editor of *Good Words* accepting with gratitude a village sermon on "The Self-Education of Young Men" (published February 1869) has a note on the second sheet in Kingsley's hand: "So! you have been sending my sermon to press without consulting me, you thoroughly delicious sly puss. Well, be it so."

A good deal of the vitality of Kingsley's preaching rises even from the printed page. The sermons are direct, fearless, simple, colloquial—a little too colloquial was the only adverse comment made by the Bishop of Winchester at the time of his ordination. (I, 126.) Kingsley never conceived his clerical function as divided from the rest of his life. He made the transition from one rôle to the other with an ease which frequently disconcerted good people accustomed to the conventional formal behaviour of the clergy. On one occasion when a heath fire began on a Sunday morning and a messenger posted down to the church to call out the men, Kingsley, leaving the curate to finish the service, rushed to the scene of action, taking a flying leap, in surplice, hood, and stole, over the churchyard palings.

William Harrison, the curate who became his son-in-law, tells of another Sunday morning when, in passing from the altar to the pulpit, the rector suddenly disappeared. Finally the congregation saw that he had dropped to his knees and was searching on the floor for something which he picked up carefully and carried into the vestry. After the service it was discovered that he had been assisting a lame butterfly whose beauty had attracted his attention.

While he officiated or preached Kingsley's manner was always deeply reverent, often to the surprise of visitors who supposed that his unconventionality and his radical thinking must imply disrespect for divine authority. His earnestness and his complete sincerity were always impressive and he thought it important to take great pains with the preparation of his sermons. The Sunday services which wore him out physically had the effect at the same time of spiritual stimulation. Late on a Sunday evening he usually began to talk over with his wife the subject for next week's sermon. On Monday he rested but on Tuesday the text was chosen, an outline sketched and at least a part of the sermon written or dictated. Then it was allowed to simmer for a day or two but was always finished before Saturday.

There is much contemporary testimony to the effectiveness of Kingsley's preaching. He was "eloquent beyond any man I ever heard," said John Martineau. "For he had the two essential constituents of eloquence, a strong man's intensity and clearness of conviction, and a command of words, not easy or rapid, but sure and unhesitating, an unfailing instinct for the one word, the most concrete and pictorial, the strongest and the simplest, which expressed his thought exactly." (I, 303.) Kegan Paul was impressed by his care for the individual cases in his congregation, the sins or difficulties known only to himself. "When he was most impressive and pathetic it was generally because his sermon touched the sorrow of some *one* in the congregation, though the words seemed general." (I, 229.) E. W. Benson tells how the gipsies on Hartford-bridge flats said that wherever they wandered they thought of Eversley as their parish church. (II, 158.)

Kingsley tried to preach, Mrs. Kingsley says, quietly and without gesticulation, but as the intensity of his emotion mounted he had to grip the cushion on which his papers rested in order to restrain his hands and before the sermon was over they would be involuntarily lifted up, the fingers of the right working with a peculiar hovering motion of which he was quite unconscious while his eyes flashed and his whole frame quivered and vibrated. (I, 360.)

The stammer which came with hurry or excitement seemed to many of his friends an agreeable part of his personality but when Alexander Macmillan once said so Kingsley rejoined that when he heard that he felt inclined to blow out his own brains and then the other man's. "I think stammering as bad as ge-ge-ge-getting drunk." (*Selected Letters of Malcolm Kingsley Macmillan,* London, 1893, Appendix I.)

Chaplain to the Queen and to the Prince of Wales 147

The fact that the stammer vanished in the pulpit, on the lecture platform or in the saddle when his lungs were full of air made it evident that it was a nervous affection. Kingsley was well aware of this himself and sought the best means then available for its cure. "The true method of cure, or at least its elements, had suggested itself to a hard-headed gentleman of Dorsetshire, a Mr. Hunt, the father of a man to whom this writer is under deep obligations, which he here most publically confesses." (*The Irrationale of Speech,* 1864.) Hampered by his own ignorance of anatomy Hunt had his son James trained as a physician and it was he who taught Kingsley the control of lips, tongue, jaw and breath which was of so much service to him. He saw Hunt at various times in London and once spent twelve days with him in his home at Swanage "and came away cured. I don't say I have not hesitated since, and too often, when I am amused and *begin to speak fast.* But I can always instantly stop it, while the *stammering* is absolutely gone." (To ?, November 10, 1858.)

But it was not for his eloquent preaching alone that Kingsley was made a Queen's Chaplain. The honour was a first step toward a higher responsibility. Albert had marked him as a man who might exert a beneficial influence upon the Prince of Wales and the Prince of Wales was shortly to keep terms at Cambridge. On May 9, 1860, therefore, Palmerston offered Kingsley the Regius Professorship of Modern History which had been vacant since the resignation of Sir James Stephen. He accepted it, of course, and entered upon his duties with deep seriousness. "I will do my best at Cambridge," he wrote to Dean Wellesley (May 10, 1860), "to teach young men what I hold right views of history: above all, that great truth (as I consider it) which has been my loadstar for several years past, that the cause of loyalty and the cause of progress, instead of being antagonistic are identical."

In the autumn he went into residence, with his family, in a house on St. Peter's Terrace, leaving his parish in charge of his curate, Frederic Stapleton, son of his good friends at Eversley. By 1863, however, he had found too heavy the expense of keeping two houses and of moving his family back and forth between so he arranged to go up alone twice a year, for his twelve or sixteen lectures and again for the examinations for the degree.

From the point of view of scholarship Kingsley was neither prepared nor adapted for the post which he attempted to fill but his influence upon young men was strong and admirable. He had a reputation among them already from his books. They crowded his first lecture and came in increasing numbers to those that succeeded. They went from the lecture room, Max Müller records (Preface, *The Roman and the Teuton*, 1875) to the University libraries and asked for books for which undergraduates had never asked before.

We crowded him out of room after room [wrote one of his students years later] till he had to have the largest of all the schools, and we crowded that—crammed it. For undergraduates are an affectionate race, and every one of us who wished to live as a man ought to live, felt that the Professor of Modern History was a friend indeed. Tutors and fellows and lecturers came too, and sat on the same benches with undergraduates. And often and often, as he told a story of heroism, of evil conquered by good, or uttered one of his noble sayings that rang through us like trumpet-calls, loud and sudden cheers would break out irresistibly—spontaneously; and wild young fellows' eyes would be full of manly, noble tears. . . .
He was so modest and humble he could not *bear* our cheers. He would beckon for quiet; and then in a broken voice and with dreadful stammering say, "Gentlemen, you must not do it. I cannot lecture to you if you do." But it was no good—we did not mean to cheer—we could not *help* it. (1890 ed., p. 240.)

Kingsley had a theory of history very grateful to the youth bewildered in the cloud of doubts that beset the Victorian undergraduate if he had about him the smallest touch of earnestness. History, Kingsley taught, is God educating man. Grasp that idea and the confused mass of facts reveals a plan; the apparent horrors of war, massacre, pestilence declare themselves wisely and deeply benevolent; it becomes possible to believe more firmly in God the more science and history you know.

The undergraduate was eager to talk with this heartening professor and Kingsley delighted to know personally the men in his classes. His simplicity and hospitality were warmly appreciated by young men accustomed to being brought up short against the artificial barriers that rose then between don and student. They flocked to his house and their enthusiasm together with the warmth with which he was received by all ranks in the University caused Kingsley to think that his alma mater had had a real change of heart since his own student days and to regret the harsh things he had said of her in *Alton Locke*. He rewrote those chapters and made a new Preface "To the Undergraduates of Cambridge." His opinion of the prevailing Cambridge tone is interestingly set forth, too, in a letter to Stanley who had written to inquire how the University had been moved by the publication of *Essays and Reviews*. The book Kingsley himself "deeply deplored" but he wrote:

Cambridge lies in magnificent repose, and shaking lazy ears stares at her more nervous elder sister and asks what it is all about.

She will not persecute the authors of the Essays; and what is more, any scraps of the Simeonite party, now moribund here, who try to get up a persecution, will be let alone—and left to persecute on their own hook. That is the Cambridge danger. Cool indifferentism: not to the doctrines, but to the means of fighting for them.

The atmosphere is the most liberal (save "Bohemia") which I ever lived in. And it is a liberality (not like that of Bohemia, of want of principle or creed), but of real scholarly largeness and lovingness between men who disagree. We "live and let live" here, I find, to my delight. (Cambridge, February 19, 1861, II, 129.)

The Professor made his inaugural address on "The Limits of Exact Science as Applied to History." "Not upon mind, gentlemen, not upon mind, but upon morals, is human welfare founded. The true subjective history of man is the history not of his thought, but of his conscience; the true objective history of man is not that of his inventions, but of his vices and his virtues."

The inaugural lecture was published at once, 1860. In 1864 Macmillan brought out the first year's lectures on *The Roman and the Teuton* and the opponents of Kingsley's appointment instantly seized their opportunity. The *Athenaeum* (April 2, 1864) damned them with faint praise as *impressions de voyage* and was distressed by the Professor's "feminine admiration" for the giant-baby strength of the Teuton and his lack of reverence for Rome. The *Westminster* (April 1864) was more violent: a "feeble, confused, and pretentious performance" by a man with no qualifications for his post other than the possession of some scenery, dresses and properties belonging to an Alexandrian and an Elizabethan drama. "Even those who share his opinions must admit that they have but little reason for feeling proud of their champion; and however laudable they may think his spirit, however sound his principles, they will view with some apprehension his confirmed habit of publishing." As a matter of fact no other lectures were published during the whole course of the professorship except a few in *Good Words* for 1868. The series which one would most like to have had preserved is the one on the United States delivered in 1862. Something of its trend it is possible to deduce from letters. Kingsley had altered the violent abolitionist sentiments with which he wrote *Two Years Ago*. "I could not help finding out, when I came to read up," he wrote to Hughes (July 13, 1863), "that the Northerners had exaggerated the case against the South infamously; and since then they have proved themselves such a set of contemptible blackguards, that I, on the whole, respect the South one-millionth of a grain more than I do the North." Lincoln he thought a poor, cute honest fellow risen to a post he was unfit to fill. His proclamation was detestable, so utter a violation of the Constitution and his own oaths, that nothing but secession remains possible. (To Henry Kingsley, Cambridge, [?] 1862.) Yet despite its iniquity the war was likely to prove "a blessing for the whole world by breaking up an insolent and aggressive republic of rogues, and a blessing to the poor niggers, because the South once seceded, will be amenable to the public opinion of England, and also will, from very fear, be forced to treat its niggers better." (To Hughes, *op. cit., supra.*)

Right or wrong, America, Kingsley felt, was significant to Englishmen; they must attempt to learn its history and to comprehend its present. He was a warm supporter, in 1866, of the proposal to establish an American lectureship at Cambridge, the holder of the chair to be selected by the authorities of Harvard College. Those who feared that this would mean the Americanizing or democratizing of the ancient university he urged to remember that the proposal came from the representatives of that class in the United States which regards England with most love and respect, which feels itself in increasing danger of being swamped by the lower elements of a vast democracy, which has been withdrawing more and more from public life in order to preserve its own purity and self-respect. It is morally impossible that such men should go out of their way to become propagandists of those very revolutionary principles against which they are honourably struggling at home.

Whether Kingsley lectured on America or any other subject the undergraduates remained enthusiastic but criticism of his scholarly deficiencies increased and he decided to resign. "I feel the truth," he wrote to Maurice (November 12, 1867), "of all you say about the Press—who more? and if it were really for the good of the University, I would hold on. But I feel more and more my own unfitness for the post. My memory grows worse and worse, and I am only fit for a preacher or a poet-author: not for a student of facts (moral and historical at least). I feel so strongly that what the press urges against me is, on the whole, true: that I am very much inclined to accept its decision. But I shall do nothing rashly." His friends urged against his resignation and he held on for two years more.

The high point of the professorship had been the period of residence of the Prince of Wales. He came up in February 1861 and Kingsley was asked to arrange for him a special class in Modern History. At Oxford he had gone as far as the reign of William III. The eleven undergraduates who made up the class were selected by the Master and the Senior Tutor of Trinity. The Prince, who lived at Madingley, rode in twice a week to Kingsley's house for lectures with the class and again on Saturdays to go through a résumé of the week's work with the Professor alone. Kingsley carried the course up to the reign of George IV and at the end of each term set questions for the Prince which were satisfactorily answered.

Like most young men the Prince of Wales took a great liking to Kingsley, talked freely with him at Cambridge, corresponded with him after he left,[1] had him appointed one of his Chaplains in Ordinary and after his marriage often desired him to spend a week-end at Sandringham, occasions in which Kingsley took much delight. He found the young Prince "very interesting, putting me in mind of his mother in voice, manner, face, and everything." (To Frederick Stapleton, Cambridge, February 8, 1861.)

I shall be content [he wrote to Hughes, Cambridge, November 22, 1861], at least for this year, to help train up that jolly boy in the way he should go.

1. By preaching to him thorough and sound Liberal doctrine.

[1] A number of these letters written by the Prince to Kingsley are still extant. They are now, I have reason to believe, in the possession of the Royal Family.

2. By trying to make him admire and respect all great and good men of the English nation. He is ready enough to take in both lessons and if I can teach even a little of them to him I shall not have lived in vain. Nothing can exceed the generous confidence toward me of those who have the right to say what opinions he shall be taught; and God give me grace to deserve it.

CHAPTER XVIII

"THE ONLY COURSE FIT FOR A GENTLEMAN"

THE conventional thing to say about Kingsley in the Newman controversy[1] is that he crossed swords with an opponent too strong for him, that his slashing blows were no match for his adversary's subtle skill; or one says that in the *Apologia* Kingsley inspired a book greater than any he was able to write himself. These things are true but there is another feature of the unequal duel which is important to social history, the domain where Kingsley's chief significance lies. The Kingsley-Newman *rencontre* displays, more completely perhaps than any single incident on record, the limitations of that conception of the gentleman which was so important a Victorian axiom. To Kingsley, as to most of his contemporaries, and to a large fraction of the British race today, the concept of the gentleman was the fundamental philosophy of life—and a gentleman for Kingsley, it will be remembered, was of necessity a member of the Church of England. Throughout his combat with the Roman priest he was totally unable to conceive that Newman was concerned with issues so large that gentlemanliness melted into air.

For Newman himself Kingsley had had at first profound admiration. He had come under the spell of his preaching and had heard much of him from Froude who had been his devoted admirer. *Yeast* (Chap. XIV) contains a winning brief portrait and "The Irrationale of Speech" (*Fraser's*, July 1859) has a description of his preaching concluding with a deeply moved exhortation:

[1] Mrs. Kingsley in her Memoir passes over the Newman controversy in two brief pages, saying that it is before the world. All the documents in the case have been recently published by the Oxford Press: *Newman's Apologia Pro Vita Sua. The Two Versions of 1864 and 1865, preceded by Newman's and Kingsley's Pamphlets*, with an Introduction by Wilfrid Ward, 1931. I have also drawn largely upon Wilfrid Ward's *Life of John Henry Cardinal Newman*, London, 1912, Vol. II, Chap. 20.

"Oh thou great and terrible—sophist, shall I call thee? or prophet? Why art thou worse than dead to Englishmen? Why is thy once sweet voice all jarred, thy once pure taste all fouled, by bitter spite and insult to thy native land? Why hast thou taken thyself in the net of thine own words, and bewildered thy subtle brain with thy more subtle tongue?"

In 1864 "The Irrationale of Speech" was reprinted in a small pamphlet. It is not improbable that Kingsley was reading proof on this at the time when he was writing for *Macmillan's Magazine* (January 1864) a review of "Froude's History of England" and that it was Newman's preaching fresh in his mind which caused him to use that name when he wanted a specific example of Catholicism:

> The Roman religion had, for some time past, been making men not better men, but worse. We must face, we must conceive honestly for ourselves, the deep demoralization which had been brought on in Europe by the dogma that the Pope of Rome had the power of creating right and wrong; that not only truth and falsehood, but morality and immorality, depended on his setting his seal to a bit of parchment.
> . . .
> Truth, for its own sake, had never been a virtue with the Roman clergy. Father Newman informs us that it need not, and on the whole ought not to be; that cunning is the weapon which Heaven has given to the saints wherewith to withstand the brute male force of the wicked world which marries and is given in marriage. Whether his notion be doctrinally correct or not, it is at least historically so.

Kingsley was mentally incapable of comprehending Newman's movement to Rome. He himself could not have made the transfer unless he had lulled his Protestant logic with lying subtleties and he was constrained to believe that a similar weakening had necessarily taken place in Newman's mind. He felt the apostasy more bitterly because he had once so reverenced and loved.

The article was brought at once to Newman's attention. The review was signed merely C. K. and so unaccustomed was Newman to concern himself with periodical literature that it never occurred to him to look on the cover of the magazine for the author's name. He wrote (December 30, 1863) to the Messrs. Macmillan a letter concluding:

> I should not dream of expostulating with the writer of such a passage, nor with the editor who could insert it without appending evi-

dence in proof of its allegations. Nor do I want any reparation from either of them. I neither complain of them for their act, nor should I thank them if they reversed it. Nor do I even write to you with any desire of troubling you to send me an answer. I do but wish to draw the attention of yourselves, as gentlemen, to a grave and gratuitous slander, with which I feel confident you will be sorry to find associated a name so eminent as yours.

The letter was of course shown to Kingsley, "and he," wrote Alexander Macmillan to Maurice (January 8, 1864), "is going to write to Dr. Newman as kindly as he can. Old passages about Froude and others have left a bitter flavour in his thoughts and feelings about the great pervert."

Kingsley's letter was dated January 6:

I have seen a letter of yours to Mr. Macmillan, in which you complain of some expressions of mine in an article in the January number of Macmillan's Magazine.

That my words were just, I believed from many passages of your writings; but the document to which I expressly referred was one of your Sermons on "Subjects of the Day," No. XX, in the volume published in 1844, and entitled "Wisdom and Innocence."

It was in consequence of that Sermon, that I finally shook off the strong influence which your writings exerted on me; and for much of which I still owe you a deep debt of gratitude.

I am most happy to hear from you that I mistook (as I understand from your letter) your meaning; and I shall be most happy, on your showing me that I have wronged you, to retract my accusation as publicly as I have made it.

On January 14 he wrote further:

The course which you demand of me, is the only course fit for a gentleman; and, as the tone of your letters (even more than their language) makes me feel, to my very deep pleasure, that my opinion of the meaning of your words was a mistaken one, I shall send at once to Macmillan's Magazine the few lines which I enclose.

The ingenuous letter which Kingsley suggested sending to the Editor of *Macmillan's Magazine* ran:

In your last number I made certain allegations against the teaching of the Rev. Dr. Newman, which were founded on a Sermon of his, entitled "Wisdom and Innocence." . . .

Dr. Newman has, by letter, expressed in the strongest terms, his denial of the meaning which I have put upon his words.

No man knows the use of words better than Dr. Newman; no man, therefore, has a better right to define what he does, or does not, mean by them.

It only remains, therefore, for me to express my hearty regret at having so seriously mistaken him; and my hearty pleasure at finding him on the side of Truth, in this, or any other, matter.

When Newman took exception to this Kingsley responded (January 18):

I do not think it probable that the good sense and honesty of the British Public will misinterpret my apology, in the way in which you expect.

Two passages in it, which I put in in good faith and good feeling, may, however, be open to such a bad use, and I have written to Messrs. Macmillan to omit them. . . .

. . . it seems to me, that, by referring publicly to the Sermon on which my allegations are founded, I have given, not only you, but every one an opportunity of judging of their injustice. Having done this, and having frankly accepted your assertion that I was mistaken, I have done as much as one English gentleman can expect from another.

The letter finally appeared in the February number of *Macmillan's* thus:

In your last number I made certain allegations against the teaching of Dr. John Henry Newman, which I thought were justified by a Sermon of his, entitled "Wisdom and Innocence" (Sermon 20 of "Sermons bearing on Subjects of the Day"). Dr. Newman has by letter expressed, in the strongest terms, his denial of the meaning which I have put upon his words. It only remains, therefore, for me to express my hearty regret at having so seriously mistaken him.

Newman saw then that there was no hope of bringing Kingsley to comprehend his offence but he felt it essential to clear before the world his character and that of the Roman priesthood. He struck, without malice but without mercy. He published the whole correspondence in a shilling pamphlet, *Mr. Kingsley and Dr. Newman: A Correspondence on the Question Whether Dr. Newman Teaches that Truth is No Virtue?* One comment only he made, "Reflections" at the conclusion. They indicate very clearly the difference between Kingsley's way of thought and his own:

I shall attempt a brief analysis of the foregoing correspondence; and I trust that the wording which I shall adopt will not offend against the gravity due both to myself and to the occasion. It is impossible to do justice to the course of thought evolved in it without some familiarity of expression.

Mr. Kingsley begins then by exclaiming,—"O the chicanery, the wholesale fraud, the vile hyprocrisy, the conscience-killing tyranny of Rome! We have not far to seek for an evidence of it. There's Father Newman to wit: one living specimen is worth a hundred dead ones. He, a Priest writing of Priests, tells us that lying is never any harm."

I interpose: "You are taking a most extraordinary liberty with my name. If I have said this, tell me when and where."

Mr. Kingsley replies: "You said it, Reverend Sir, in a Sermon which you preached, when a Protestant, as Vicar of St. Mary's, and published in 1844; and I could read you a very salutary lecture on the effects which that Sermon had at the time on my own opinion of you."

I make answer: "Oh . . . *Not*, it seems, as a Priest speaking of Priests;—but let us have the passage."

Mr. Kingsley relaxes: "Do you know, I like your *tone*. From your *tone* I rejoice, greatly rejoice, to be able to believe that you did not mean what you said."

I rejoin: "*Mean* it! I maintain I never *said* it, whether as a Protestant or as a Catholic."

Mr. Kingsley replies: "I waive that point."

I object: "Is it possible! What? waive the main question! I either said it or I didn't. You have made a monstrous charge against me; direct, distinct, public. You are bound to prove it as directly, as distinctly, as publicly;—or to own you can't."

"Well," says Mr. Kingsley, "if you are quite sure you did not say it, I'll take your word for it; I really will."

My *word*! I am dumb. Somehow I thought that it was my *word* that happened to be on trial. The *word* of a Professor of lying, that he does not lie!

But Mr. Kingsley re-assures me: "We are both gentlemen," he says: "I have done as much as one English gentleman can expect from another."

I begin to see: he thought me a gentleman at the very time that he said I taught lying on a system. After all, it is not I, but it is Mr. Kingsley who did not mean what he said. "Habemus confitentem reum."

By this rejection of his high-minded apology Kingsley was completely bewildered. His code went no further. "Not upon mind, gentlemen, not upon mind, but upon morals, is human welfare founded." He could believe only that he was dealing with pure unprincipled wickedness. He fought it with all the spirit of his ancestors. Urged on by Froude, though Macmillan at first counselled silence, he published a pamphlet in reply, *What, Then, Does*

Dr. Newman Mean? "I am answering Newman now," he wrote concerning this, "and though of course I give up the charge of conscious dishonesty, I trust to make him and his admirers sorry that they did not leave me alone. I have a score of more than twenty years to pay, and this is an instalment of it." (Quoted by Ward, II, 8, from the "Recollections of Father Ignatius Dudley Ryder.)

It is not necessary to follow Kingsley through the bad logic and hot-hearted obtuseness of the pamphlet. It is unfortunate for his fame that it must go down in history as "the embedded fly in the clear amber of his antagonist's apology" (*Quarterly Review,* October 1864), for the *Apologia* contains all of John Henry Newman and the pamphlet only the worst of Charles Kingsley.

Many friends, of course, rallied to Kingsley's defence; many letters of sympathy came to him from strangers; some of the critics upheld him; but England as a whole admired Newman. It was impossible to read the *Apologia* clear-sightedly and believe that that man lied. That Protestant England did read clear-sightedly is the work, says Wilfrid Ward, of Richard Holt Hutton, editor of the *Spectator,* a known admirer of Kingsley and a sympathizer with the theology of Maurice. It was his high sense of justice which brought him to Newman's defence. He feared the prejudices of the English public in questions where Popery was concerned. Kingsley's method of attack, with its appeal to that prejudice, he thought unfair. He did not realize, perhaps, the honesty with which Kingsley took his prejudices for cogent arguments, but he described Kingsley's manner of thought with severe truth:

Mr. Kingsley, in the ordinary steeple-chase fashion in which he chooses not so much to think as to *splash up* thought, dregs and all,—often very healthy and sometimes very noble, but always very loose thought,—in one's face, had made a random charge against Father Newman in *Macmillan's Magazine.* . . . The sermon in question, which we have carefully read, certainly contains no proposition of the kind to which Mr. Kingsley alludes, and no language even so like it as the text taken from our Lord's own words, "Be ye wise as serpents and harmless as doves." (*Spectator,* February 20, 1864.)

Mr. Kingsley evidently holds it quite innocent and even praiseworthy to blurt out raw general impressions, however inadequately supported, which are injurious and painful to other men, on condition only that they are his own sincere impressions. He has no mercy for the man who will define his thought and choose his language so subtly that the mass of his hearers may fail to perceive his distinctions, and be misled into a dangerous error,—because he cannot endure making a fine art of speech. Yet he permits himself a perfect licence of insinuation, so long as these insinuations are suggested by the vague sort of animal scent by which he chooses to judge of other men's drift and meaning. (*Spectator,* March 26, 1864.)

Shortly after the publication of his pamphlet Kingsley, in a state of highly nervous fatigue induced by the strain and wear of the Cambridge professorship and augmented by the controversy, grasped at the chance for a brief holiday with Froude who was going to examine MSS. in Spanish archives. It was his first sight of France and he overflowed with curiosity and enthusiasms, botanic and economic. "The splendour of this city," he wrote his wife from Paris (March 25, 1864), "is beyond all I could have conceived, and the beautiful neatness and completeness of everything delight my eyes. Verily these French are a civilised people." (II, 193.) But to Frederick Stapleton, his curate, he said, "When I get back, I will tell you further volumes as to what I have seen of the Mari-idolatry of France. I could not have conceived such things possible in the 19th century. But I have seen enough to enable me to give Newman such a revanche as will make him wince, if any English common sense is left in him, which I doubt." (Fontainebleau, 1864.)

At Biarritz Kingsley was taken ill so he stayed there with "Tulk who is an M.D." and never went over the border into Spain, though many excursions were made in the country round about and the French trip eventually became an article for *Good Words.* ("From the Ocean to the Sea," July 1866.)

The *Apologia* began to appear in weekly pamphlets while Kingsley was in France. He was striving to hold his mind away from the painful affair, however, and even after his return Mrs. Kingsley would not let him read the document until it was complete. "My own idea," Alexander Macmillan wrote him (May 19, 1864), "is that you should read every word of Newman's Apologia. Nothing could possibly be more soothing, I should think. But Mrs. Kingsley should judge. As I understand matters, the second number put the battle substantially into your hands. He is however neither a knave nor a fool—he is John Henry Newman."

On June 8 Kingsley wrote to Macmillan:

Here is my ultimatum on the Newman question, which please shew (privately) to any one and every one you like, including Mr. Hutton.

I have determined to take no notice whatever of Dr. Newman's apology.

1. I have nothing to retract, apologize for, explain. Deliberately, after 20 years of thought, I struck as hard as I could. Deliberately I shall strike again, if it so pleases me, though not one literary man in England approved. I know too well of what I am talking.

2. I cannot trust—I can only smile at—the autobiography of a man who (beginning with Newman's light, learning, and genius) ends in believing that he believes in the Infallibility of the Church, and in the Immaculate Conception. If I am to bandy words, it must be with sane persons.

3. I cannot be [?] weak enough to put myself a second time, by any fresh act of courtesy, into the power of one who, like a treacherous ape, lifts to you meek and suppliant eyes, till he thinks he has you within his reach, and then springs, gibbering and biting, at your face. Newman's conduct has so much disgusted Catholics themselves, that I have no wish to [?] remove their just condemnation of his doings.

The world seems inclined to patronize Dr. Newman and the Cafards just now, because having no faith of its own, it is awed by the seeming strength of fanaticism. I know them too well either to patronize or to fear them.

I wish poor dear Thackeray had been alive. He knew what I know, and would have taken a tone about this matter, which would have astonished too many literary men. He was too true a liberal to pat lies and bigotry on the back.

Give my really kind regards to Mr. Hutton, for whom I have a sincere respect.

Newman having more than made his case, withdrew from the 1865 and all subsequent editions of the *Apologia* the first two sections ("Mr. Kingsley's Method of Disputation" and the "True Mode of meeting Mr. Kingsley") and the devastating "Answer in Detail" with its "Blot one . . . Blot two . . . Blot thirty-nine." On Kingsley's death he wrote to Sir William Cope (February 13, 1875):

The death of Mr. Kingsley,—so premature—shocked me. I never from the first have felt any anger towards him. As I have said in the first pages of my "Apologia," it is very difficult to be angry with a man one has never seen. . . .

. . . much less could I feel any resentment against him when he was accidentally the instrument, in the good Providence of God, by whom

I had an opportunity given me, which otherwise I should not have had, of vindicating my character and conduct in my "Apologia." I heard, too, a few years back from a friend that she chanced to go into Chester Cathedral and found Mr. K. preaching about me, kindly though, of course, with criticisms on me. And it has rejoiced me to observe lately that he was defending the Athanasian Creed, and, as it seemed to me, in his views generally nearing the Catholic view of things. I have always hoped that by good luck I might meet him, feeling sure that there would be no embarrassment on my part, and I said Mass for his soul as soon as I heard of his death. (Ward, II, 45.)

CHAPTER XIX

"AS GREAT A TALKER AS ANY MAN IN ENGLAND"

IF one knew nothing else of Charles Kingsley the mere list of his friends would excite inquiry. The range and quality of his relationships was very great. With all his inability to comprehend certain types of delicate mental activity he had wide sympathy with beliefs fundamentally different from his own if only they were founded upon honest, and preferably passionate, conviction. He had a theory that many men walked straight in the way of God without being aware who it was that led them, and he cherished a warm hope that in another life, if not this, their eyes would be unbound and they would see that divine guide of whose direction in the most trivial actions of his own life he was daily more conscious. Kingsley could talk, then, freely and gladly with Jews, with atheists, with Methodists, with Socialists and revolutionaries, and talk with them not only on neutral subjects but on the very points on which they vitally differed. He had, too, a never slaked curiosity about all things in God's universe and loved nothing so much as to find a man who would enlighten him on any fraction of it. Without being an expert in any field, except that of parish priest, he knew the technical jargon of a dozen professions and had read so rapidly and discursively that he could at any moment talk agreeably and with eager fluency on zoöphytes, flax culture, watercolours, liquid sewage, national schools or Mary Queen of Scots.

It is quite evident from the enormous enthusiasm with which contemporary letter writers speak of him, that only about one-third of Charles Kingsley got into his written works and that in that third the proportions are all wrong. The exuberance in which his acquaintances loved to refresh themselves is perceptible on the printed page only in the headlong rush of his narrative and in some of his more unguarded letters. Less attractively it manifests itself in the too great fluency, the redundancy of almost everything he wrote. Those are traits less annoying, perhaps, in conversation than in print, if the speaker be agreeable and the topic interesting. The nineteenth century also seems never to have had too much of anything; they found abundance synonymous with richness. It is of Kingsley's talk which everyone who knew him writes with enthusiasm. The recollections of persons now alive who saw him in their childhood always begin: "I remember a drive, or walk, from —— to ——, Kingsley talking all the way." Young men were excited by the range and variety of his conversation and the deference with which he listened to *their* ideas. Women marvelled at his talk. His contemporaries delighted in it. The dissenting voice is very rare. Miss Mitford, who lived not far from Eversley, records that "between his stammering and his discursiveness there is no getting on with him: we have not met yet, but I hear this on all hands." (Elizabeth Lee, ed., *Mary Russell Mitford, Correspondence with Charles Boner and John Ruskin,* London, 1914, p. 197.) Yet when they did meet she promptly fell a victim to his "extraordinary fascination," his "charming admixture of softness and gentleness, with spirit, manliness, and frankness—a frankness quite transparent—and a cordiality and courtesy that would win any heart." (R. Brimley Johnson, ed., *The Letters of Mary Russell Mitford,* London, 1925, p. 225.) "I could be as great a talker as any man in England," Kingsley said once to Hughes, "but for my stammering. I know it well; but it's a blessed thing for me. You must know, by this time, that I'm a very shy man, and shyness and vanity always go together. And so I think of what every fool will say of me, and can't help it. When a man's first thought is not whether a thing is right or wrong, but what will Lady A., or Mr. B. say about it, depend upon it he wants a thorn in the flesh like my stammer. When I am speaking for God, in the pulpit, or praying by bedsides, I never stammer." (T. Hughes, Prefatory Memoir, *Alton Locke,* 1876.)

Hughes speaks also of "the sort of . . . Rabelaisian fit (except that it had no taint of Rabelaisian filth) which used to come upon him frequently . . . in the company of his intimates, when he reminded one of a great fullgrown Newfoundland yearling dog out for an airing, plunging in and out of the water, and rushing against and shaking himself over ladies' silks and velvets, dandies' polished boots, or schoolboys' rough jackets; and all with a rollicking good humour which disarmed anger, and carried away the most precise persons into momentary enjoyment of the tumbling. But even when mirth was most fast and furious, he could 'come to heel' (as he would have said) in a moment, and turn at a hint from Mr. Maurice, or any one whom he respected, to serious and earnest discussion and work." (*Macmillan's Magazine,* March 1877.)

This incapacity for self-discipline, the readiness to let himself be directed by the people whom he respected, was very characteristic. It accounts for a great part of his admiration for his wife. She not only attended for him to all practical details of life, large and small—for years he never addressed a letter for himself—she decided what he should write and when, she prescribed rest, made household, business and even professional decisions. There is a significant little story of a Sunday morning adventure, told by John Martineau.

With pain and care Kingsley had prepared a sermon setting forth his interpretation of the much discussed Athanasian Creed and planned to preach it on the next day appointed for the Creed to be read. But when the Sunday came he forgot the Athanasian Creed and read the Apostles' Creed as usual. This was in the days before he had introduced singing into the Eversley services so that when, before the sermon, the rector went to the vestry to change his surplice for a gown the congregation sat in silence until his return. Minute after minute went by on that Sunday morning and still the rector did not reappear. At last the worried clerk came from the vestry, approached the rectory pew and whispered to Mrs. Kingsley who went hurriedly out into the churchyard. She found her husband sitting on a tombstone the picture of despair. "Fanny, what shall I do?" was all he could say. Promptly she decided that another sermon must be preached, but Kingsley never preached extempore and to get another MS. was no simple matter; all the rectory household were in church, the door locked and the key in the pocket of one of the servants. Mrs. Kingsley efficiently organized the relief expedition, the rector returned to his pulpit and the substitute sermon was preached to the edification of the patient though bewildered congregation.

This was that direction in matters of "morality, of taste, of feeling" which Kingsley felt to be so peculiarly the woman's part.

Intellectual decisions he made for both and she accepted with admiration, which is not surprising; Kingsley was very persuasive about his opinions. The number of conversions, most notably that of Thomas Cooper, which he made by his personal influence is striking. He had the power, too, to establish friendship where he could not carry conviction. He wrote to Thomas Huxley, when he heard of the death of his son, a long letter on the immortality of the soul, and Huxley in reply expressed his own opinions "more openly and distinctly . . . than I ever have to any human being except my wife." (September 23, 1860.) "The way in which you received my heathen letters," he wrote later (May 5, 1863), "set up a free masonry between us, at any rate on my side; and if they make you a bishop I advise you not to let your private secretary open any letters with my name in the corner, for they are as likely as not to contain matters which will make the clerical hair stand on end." (Leonard Huxley, *Life and Letters of Thomas Henry Huxley,* London, 1900.)

Kingsley's clerical hair never stood on end for scientific cause. He was convinced that the truth of science was God's truth and he stepped therefore always straight on boldly wherever it seemed to lead. "I have found time to read *Omphalos* carefully," he wrote to Philip Gosse (May 4, 1858), "and will now write you my whole heart about it. For twenty-five years I have read no book which has so staggered and puzzled me. . . . It will not make me throw away my Bible. I trust and hope . . . but . . . I would not for a thousand pounds put your book into my children's hands. . . . Pray take all I say in good part, as the speech of one earnest man to another. All I want is God's truth, and if I can get that I will welcome it, however much it upsets my pride and my theories." (Edmund Gosse, *The Life of Philip Henry Gosse,* London, 1890.)

In the same spirit Kingsley met the *Origin of Species,* delighting to see the spread of a doctrine which terrified so many of his colleagues. He wrote Darwin (January 31, 1862) of the shooting in Lord Ashburton's park of a pair of "blue rocks" and the scientific sportsmen's discussion of the species. "My own view is—and I coolly stated it, fearless of consequences—that the specimen before us was only to be explained on your theory, and that cushat, stock dove, and blue rock, had been once all one species; and I found—to show how your views are steadily spreading—that of five or six men, only one regarded such a notion as absurd." (II, 135.) "I find, in Cambridge," he wrote five years later (December 15, 1867), "that the younger M.A.'s are not only willing, but greedy, to hear what you have to say; and that the elder (who have, of course, more old notions to overcome) are facing the whole question in quite a different tone from what they did three years ago. . . . I trust you will find the old university (which has always held to physical science and free thought, and allows, as she always has done, anybody to believe anything reasonable, *provided he don't quarrel with his neighbours*) to be your firmest standing ground in these isles." (II, 249.)

This was probably Kingsley's greatest strength with his generation, his ability to reconcile science and revealed religion. It endeared him, of course, to scientists like Gosse, whose son speaks of him as his father's "friend from the outer world whom he preserved longest" (Edmund Gosse, *The Life of Philip Henry Gosse*, London, 1890, p. 333), and it is a tribute both to Kingsley's powers and to those of the Church of England that such thinkers as Darwin, Huxley and Sir Charles Lyell, valued his support and found it worth while to carry on discussion with him. Small wonder that to men and women less definitely in advance of their time Kingsley seemed a profound thinker.

Because of the message in his books many distinguished visitors to England took a great deal of trouble to meet him. He seems to have had a special attraction for literary ladies. Harriet Beecher Stowe went out of her way to visit Eversley. So did Frederika Bremer, who thought him the embodiment of her dream of the brother she lost in youth. So did a royal lady, Queen Emma of the Sandwich Islands, who sent him her picture and her husband's Hawaiian translation of the Book of Common Prayer. Kingsley carried on, too, a little nearer home, a lively correspondence with Harriet Martineau, an earnest one with Mrs. Gaskell. Miss Mitford found him "the *beau ideal* of a young poet."

With literary men Kingsley foregathered in London at Parker's and at the Macmillans, both those publishing houses being far more than business offices. He knew, as has been indicated, many of the distinguished writers of his day, most notably perhaps Tennyson, Thackeray and Matthew Arnold. One letter to Arnold exists (II, 338) and one from him, written at the time of Kingsley's death, in which he puts his finger upon a trait that had much to do with the strength and integrity of Kingsley's friendships: "I think he was the most generous man I have ever known; the most forward to praise what he thought good, the most willing to admire, the most free from all thought of himself in praising and in admiring, and the most incapable of being made ill-natured, or even indifferent, by having to support ill-natured attacks himself. Among men of letters I know nothing so rare as this." (II, 471.) Sir Arthur Helps wrote (March 7, 1858) of Kingsley's opinion of Lewes' *Seaside Studies*: "That man must be very distasteful to you for many reasons (I like him very much); and for you to recognize amply and liberally all the merits in any work of his shows a largeness of mind and a fairness which I love beyond everything to see in my friends." (E. A. Helps, ed., *Correspondence of Sir Arthur Helps,* London, 1917.)

This generosity and largeness of mind made it possible for Kingsley to found more than one of his friendships upon a controversy. That with Thomas Cooper, whom he converted, was precipitated by an attack on Kingsley in the *Commonwealth*; that with J. H. Rigg, head of the Wesleyan Training College in London, began with Kingsley's objection to an article on his doctrine which Rigg wrote for the *London Quarterly Review* (April 1857). The friendship with Llewellyn Davies, the theologian, rose from the controversy on the reform of the Universities. "You and I," Kingsley wrote the young man (February 28, 1851), "have been hammering away at each other lately through the medium of the Spectator: and if what our mutual friends tell me be true, we both are on the same side at heart, and are using the strength which might assist each other to do good, in counteracting each other's forces . . . if you are of my opinion, it will be much wiser for us both to pull together, or at least try if we cannot do so. And therefore I tender on paper the right hand of full reconciliation, which you may accept or not, as you will; only as I tender it honestly and utterly, do you accept it so, or not at all." (I, 266.)

Again to George Jacob Holyoake, who vigorously fought attempts to combine Christianity with Socialism, we find Kingsley writing: "Much as we disagree, and must, I fear, on many very important and solemn matters, your conduct in this had made me sincerely respect you, independently of, and indeed long before, the kind expressions, etc., from you in your letter about a book of mine with much of which you must utterly disagree." (Joseph McCabe, *Life and Letters of George Jacob Holyoake,* London, 1908, I, 340.)

With E. A. Freeman, who had vigorously belaboured him for the inaccuracies of *The Roman and the Teuton,* Kingsley formed a cordial relationship. They met at the home of Alexander Macmillan and Freeman was much embarrassed at the encounter until relieved by Kingsley's extreme courtesy and the discovery of a common cause in their admiration for Germany—it was the time of the Franco-Prussian War. Kingsley, it may be seen, was an exciting, a delightful but never a very restful friend.

It is because of this continual motion of mind and body that the caricatures of him are rather more satisfying likenesses than the formal portraits. Some of his own pen and ink sketches in letters to his children give a very lively idea of him, so does the violent *Vanity Fair* caricature (March 30, 1872; original is in the National Portrait Gallery). The Lowes Dickinson portrait (National Portrait Gallery), painted for the Macmillans, has great charm and truth but it is a portrait of Kingsley weary. Set it beside the Lowes Dickinson etching of Kingsley lecturing in his academic robes, add the *Vanity Fair* watercolour drawing and one has a very good idea of the qualities of the man. Somewhat too formal are most of the photographs and engravings which make the frontispieces in his books. They give the flashing eye, the hooked nose and the side-whiskers but they are more than a trifle forbidding. So is the excellent Woolner bust in the Baptistry of Westminster Abbey, near the memorials to Maurice, Keble and Wordsworth. Since the sculptor felt that whiskers, as a passing fashion, should not be represented in marble, the face seems at first unlike any of the portraits to which one is accustomed but to those who knew Kingsley, and especially to his wife and children, it was a likeness highly pleasing.

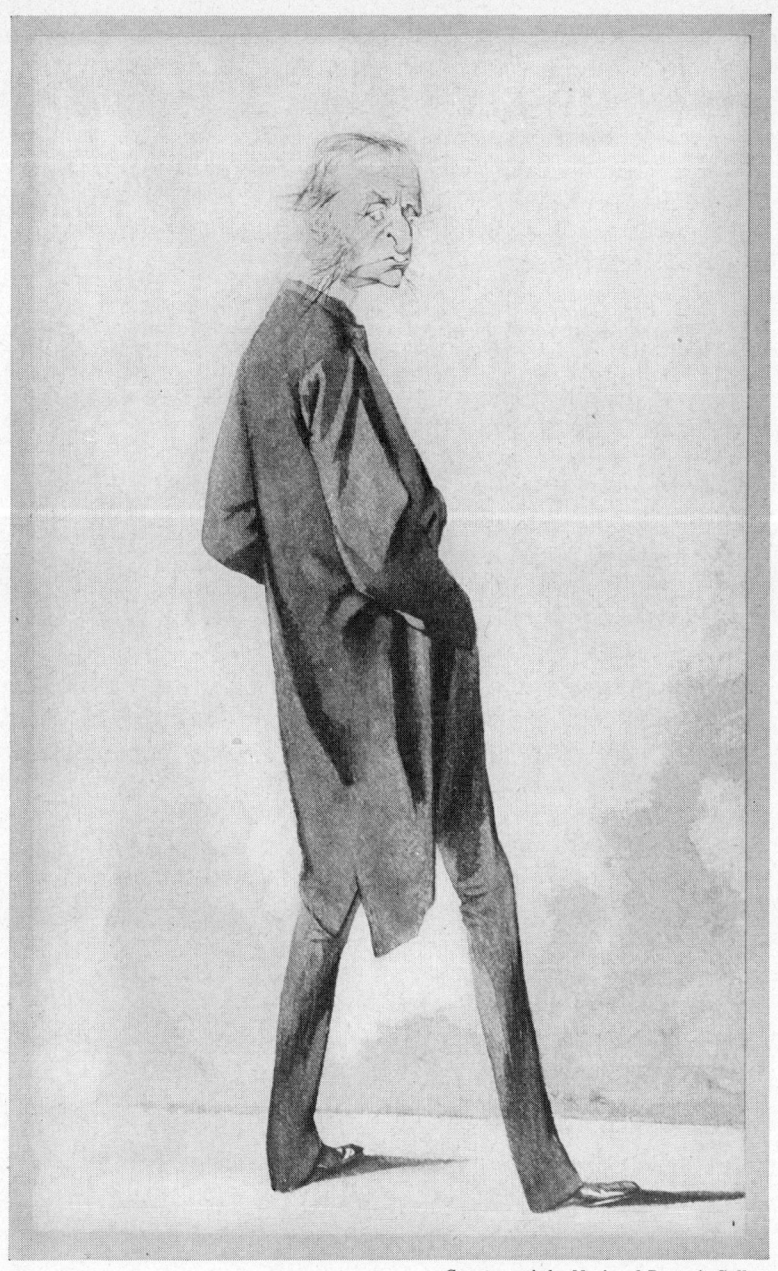

Courtesy of the National Portrait Gallery
"Rev. Canon Kingsley, 'The Apostle of the Flesh,'" drawn for *Vanity Fair*, March 30, 1872, by T. Gibson Bowles ("Jehu Junior")

Courtesy of the British Museum

CHARLES KINGSLEY AS HE SAW HIMSELF
"I was just going at the place when he fell."
To his son Maurice, [?] 1858

Climbing in Wales, a page from a letter to his daughter
Mary, 1856

CHAPTER XX

"MUSCULAR CHRISTIANITY, A CLEVER EXPRESSION"

THRICE after the success of *Two Years Ago* Kingsley tried to write a novel and thrice his overstrained creative energy sagged and he relinquished the attempt. His daughter Mary Harrison ("Lucas Malet") found the abortive MSS. among his papers long after his death. One of them, *Darling, the History of a Wise Woman,* a tale of the New Forest, there is no means of dating precisely. The material for word-pictures was gathered during a holiday in 1847 but the story, which was to deal with a group of French refugees after the Terror, was probably undertaken ten years later. The Yorkshire journey made in 1858 to secure materials for *The Pilgrimage of Grace* furnished background also for the novel, projected in 1859, which Mrs. Harrison completed and published in 1916 as *The Tutor's Story*. This seems to have been the *Alcibiades* of which Malcolm Kingsley Macmillan wrote to his friend Cecil Standish:

> Twenty years ago or so Kingsley told my father of a scheme he had for a novel to be called *Alcibiades*. The idea was, of course, to be a young, well-born nature, which, after being imbued with philosophy (at an English university, presumably), and shown itself apt to learn, is corrupted by wealth, fashionable society, powers of persuading men, etc. Alcibiades's career, in fact, translated into modern times. . . .
> But when once in my hearing my father asked Kingsley about this, he said, "The truth is, Macmillan, that I now *know* too much ever to write the book. I have been too much behind the scenes (*i.e.* of court, fashionable, diplomatic, etc., life), and should inevitably do what is most wrong for a novelist, introduce personal portraits, paint real calamities." (February 13, 1879, C. L. Graves, *Life and Letters of Alexander Macmillan,* London, 1910, p. 350.)

Mrs. Harrison's novel does not follow the Alcibiades motive but she leaves the tale on the Yorkshire moors where Kingsley set it. Intimate knowledge of his locale was essential to him in his novel writing. In 1856 he abandoned the idea of a story of the Vaudois massacres because he could not then get his friend Alfred Strettell, consular chaplain at Genoa, to guide him through the Swiss valleys. (*op. cit.*, p. 88.) The scenario was in Macmillan hands but *Two Years Ago* was written instead.

The Yorkshire scenery was not wasted, despite the ill success of the two novels; it flourished greenly in *The Water-Babies,* which Mrs. Kingsley persuaded him to write in 1862. She had been delighted with *The Heroes* which Kingsley wrote for his children (1855) because he thought Hawthorne's versions of the Greek myths distressingly vulgar. Kingsley's versions are slightly bowlderized and perhaps a little overinsistent on their moral ("Do right, and God will help you") but they are engaging narrative, written in Biblical rhythms, and definitely superior to Hawthorne. The popularity of *The Heroes* was great. They were published with illustrations in colour; and were translated into various languages, including modern Greek. The eight pictures for the book Kingsley made himself and they were much admired though they are so carefully done, so conscientiously worked over that they give small evidence of the real life and vigour with which he could draw.

When *The Heroes* was published Grenville Arthur was not quite two so that only the three elder children's names appear in the dedication. One spring morning, however, when Grenville was six years old, so Mrs. Kingsley recounts, his father sitting at breakfast was reminded of an old promise:

" 'Rose, Maurice, and Mary have got their book, and baby must have his.' He made no answer, but got up at once and went into his study, locking the door. In half an hour he returned with the story of little Tom. This was the first chapter of 'The Water-Babies,' written off without a correction." (II, 137.)

The first chapter is very much superior to the others in freshness and coherence but Kingsley enjoyed the Rabelaisian fun (without taint of Rabelaisian filth) which he introduced into the later chapters and so apparently did thousands of Victorian children and their elders. The story was published serially in *Macmillan's,* August 1862 to March 1863, and then brought out as a book. It is probably the most widely known of Kingsley's writings; it has been published in innumerable editions and translated into unexpected languages. The contemporary chorus of praise was loud. Only an occasional voice found fault. The *London Review* (January 13, 1864) saw it as yet another manifestation of that Muscular Christianity with which Kingsley's name had become inextricably associated, not always with admiration. "What is there in intellect, Mr. Kingsley appears always to be gratuitously remarking, comparable to children and ladies, and Cambridge undergraduates and working men?" But they added: "In fun, in humour, and in innocent imagination as a child's book, we do not know its equal."

Kingsley himself thoroughly enjoyed the fun, the humour and the innocent imagination but he wore his fun with a purpose. "When you read it," he wrote Maurice, "I hope you will see that I have not been idling my time away. I have tried, in all sorts of queer ways, to make children and grown folks understand that there is a quite miraculous and divine element underlying all physical nature; and that nobody knows anything about anything, in the sense in which they may know God in Christ, and right and wrong. And if I have wrapped up my parable in seeming Tom-fooleries, it is because so only could I get the pill swallowed by a generation who are not believing with anything like their whole heart, in the Living God." (II, 137.)

The fooleries of the *Water-Babies* ranged wide. Kingsley's daughter says that "a delightful under-current runs all through the book of allusions to Eversley and Eversley people" (Rose Kingsley, Introduction, *The Water-Babies and Glaucus,* Everyman ed.), which can have been apparent only to a small circle. There were scientific and educational, political and literary hits. Some of those which struck at America were carefully removed from the second edition lest they should give offence—but the Americans had already published the first edition and seemed happily unmoved by the remark that sperm whales "butt each other with their ugly noses, day and night from year's end to year's end. And if they think that sport—why, so do their American cousins." (Chap. VII.) A little more severe are the strictures upon the work of those estimable ladies, Miss Maria Cumins and Miss Susan Warner (Chap. VIII) whose books for children Kingsley could not abide because of "their execrable goody-goody-ness,—the insipid respectability (utterly untrue to life) of their personages, who make up for want of character and want of action by endless analysis of little dirty commonplace motives." (C. L. Graves, *Life and Letters of Alexander Macmillan,* London, 1910, p. 93.)

His own unquestionable ability to please children he exercised again a few years later in *The Hermits* which he wrote for Macmillan's *Sunday Library* (1868) and *Madam How and Lady Why, or First Lessons in Earth Lore,* which ran in *Good Words for the Young* before its book publication in 1870. The *Boys' History of England* which Kingsley undertook for Macmillan was never completed.

Another novel was finally accomplished. "Hereward, the Last of the English" ran in *Good Words* through 1865 and became a book the following year. Though most carefully documented and supervised, though full of vigorous fighting and rich in word pictures of the fen country it was less successful than its predecessors. That it was written with effort is a little too apparent. The lessons preached in the other novels reappear, of course. This time the theme uppermost in Kingsley's mind seems to have been that Muscular Christianity which he urged steadily although he disliked the phrase. In the year of *Hereward's* serial appearance he was invited to be one of the University preachers at Cambridge and chose David as the theme of his four discourses. In the introductory sermon on "David's Weakness" he gave his own interpretation of the phrase so often fathered upon him. "Its first and better meaning may be simply a healthful and manful Christianity; one which does not exalt the feminine virtues to the exclusion of the masculine."

The similarity between those muscular Christians Hereward and David is very close. Both were mighty fighters; both sweet singers to the harp; both rulers and leaders of their people. Hereward, like David, sinned with a woman. It must have distressed Kingsley to make his hero unfaithful to his wife. The early wildness of Hereward was of the sort which, because it indicated vigour and a high heart, Kingsley could forgive—to the horror of the Oxford Professor of Hebrew; but that a man should leave for a beautiful temptress the noble woman who had tamed him and guided him through years of stress and darkness was clean contrary to the Kingsley code. There it stood, however, in his principal source, the *Gesta Herewardi Saxonis,* and Kingsley met it manfully, upholding his principles by dating Hereward's downfall from that abandonment of Torfrida. He had authority for his point of view; the chronicler says, in a sentence which Kingsley quotes, that after the abandonment: "Many troubles came to Hereward: because Torfrida was most wise, and of great counsel in need. For afterwards, as he himself confessed, things went not so well with him as they did in her time." (Chap. XXXVII.)

To historic detail Kingsley was likewise conscientiously faithful. All the proof of the novel was read by the antiquary Thomas Wright who had edited various Hereward documents, and his corrections were almost invariably accepted. "Proofs yesterday," he would write. "I am sorry to say you have gone wrong in money matters . . . no gold coinage from the time of the Romans to that of Henry III . . . only known Anglo-Saxon coin . . . the penny of silver. . . . I rather dislike Martin Lightfoot's putting the Lady Godiva's letter in his cap." (November 24, 1864.) And accordingly in Chapter I Hereward robs the monk of sixteen silver pennies and Martin places the letter respectfully in the pouch at his girdle. On one point only Kingsley refused to yield. Hereward had, according to the chronicler, an incredibly swift horse named Swallow. Kingsley calls her Mare Swallow and endows her with a definite personality. Wright objected, insisting that knights of that period never used mares as chargers, but Kingsley knew his own wisdom in matters of horseflesh and a mare Swallow remained. Macmillan was somewhat tried by Kingsley's deference to Wright, "a man I have no liking for or belief in," but Wright, despite his notorious inaccuracy, was a learned man and his assistance with *Hereward* seems to have been genuinely useful.

No other letters of Kingsley's about the book have survived. He appears not to have written it with much joy. It has, however, those romantic and exciting narrative qualities which still endear his historical novels to the young who, delighted with their rapid movement and elaborate properties, are undismayed by the Victorian sentiments of Saxon heroes or by the didacticism which they are quite accustomed to bear all day long anyway in forms often much less pleasant.[1]

The year after the appearance of *Hereward* Kingsley had a fresh literary experience. For several months in the spring he took over the editorship of *Fraser's* that Froude might bury himself undisturbed in the archives of Spain. Kingsley seized the chance to point the magazine in a direction in which he much desired to see it move. "I want," he wrote to Professor Alfred Newton (April 1867), "to make it gradually a vehicle for advanced natural science, and have written to several leading men in that sense. Could you give me anything, however short?" (II, 246.)

Once again at least Kingsley planned a novel: "The autobiography of a poor English Scholar from about 1490—and going on to about 1530-40 who should see the outburst of the Reformation, know Erasmus, Rabelais, etc. be at the sack of Rome in 1526, at Marguerite of Navarre's court at Pau, and generally about the world. . . . The man would be a simple miller's son from my own parish, and come back to end his days here." (To Alexander Macmillan, January 25, 1868.) This is the only record of the tale. Kingsley never finished another novel.

[1] The impression made by *Hereward* upon one youthful mind is recorded by John Davidson in the Prologue to his play *Godfrida*, London, 1898, p. 5: "When I was a boy [Davidson was born in 1857] I knew by heart Kingsley's 'Hereward the Wake,' having read it every Sunday for several years in a bound volume of *Good Words*. As I developed my play a memory of Hereward, which I did not recognize at first, besieged my fancy. Becoming conscious of its source, and being quite unable to get away from it, I obtained the kind permission of Kingsley's representatives to use it. The matter I have taken occupies a few paragraphs of the novel; but it is important in the play."

CHAPTER XXI

"AT THE SERVICE OF THE GOOD CITIZENS OF CHESTER"

ANY country rector so constantly in public sight as Charles Kingsley was bound to be mentioned again and again for ecclesiastical preferment. After he had been sealed with the royal approval that mention of course increased. Kingsley was not ambitious for power. He found recognition pleasant but he desired advancement chiefly for the financial peace and security it would bring, the relief from writing for bread. His disinclination to a bishopric—there were rumours about Rochester and Manchester—was sincere, and he was not very sorry when he failed to become Dean of Winchester. "You were never more right," he wrote to Raikes Currie (August 20, 1869), "than when you said that I should not like to be a Bishop. I have been too much behind the scenes in bishops' palaces, their intrigue, vulgarity, toadyisms, and pretension; and for my children's sake, far more than my own, I should dread being a bishop. And even a Deanery I shrink from: because it would take me away from home." But a canonry Kingsley ardently desired and tried more than once to obtain. It would permit him to live most of the year at Eversley while opening at the same time a wider sphere of labour and adding to his income the extra hundreds of pounds which his large household sadly needed.

Not until he was over fifty was his wish granted. (The canonry he held from 1845 to 1856 at the Collegiate Church of Middleham in Yorkshire was a purely honorary affair accepted for the pleasant sentiment of being associated with his college friend the Rev. Peter Wood and his father the Dean.) In 1868 the Queen had suggested him for a canonry at Worcester but her Prime Minister courteously replied that "the preferment of Mr. Kingsley, just now, would be seriously prejudicial to Mr. Disraeli." (George Earle Buckle, ed.,

Letters of Queen Victoria, Second Series, New York, 1926, I, 519, 520.) It was a year later, August 13, 1869, that Gladstone wrote to Kingsley offering him the Canonry of Chester, made vacant by Moberly's appointment to the see of Salisbury, and stating that he knew his act would be very agreeable to Her Majesty.

Kingsley accepted with joy and flung himself into the life of the cathedral and of the city of Chester with the same energy and devotion with which he worked his Eversley parish. Whatever else he hurried or slighted he never neglected his parish labours: the careful preparation of sermons and conduct of services; the devoted ministry, physical and spiritual, to the sick; the organization—in a day when such enterprises were rare—of coal clubs and penny readings, night schools and popular concerts; the intimate personal knowledge of every soul within his cure. A parson who talked with women at their washtubs and men mowing in the fields was a new phenomenon on the Hampshire moors. Archbishop Benson tells of Kingsley striding across a field to ask a young ploughman why he had not been at church on Sunday, and ending his talk with "Now, you know, John, your wife don't want you lounging in bed half a Sunday morning. You get up and come to church, and let her get your Sunday dinner and make the house tidy, and then you mind your child in the afternoon while *she* comes to church." (II, 158.)

Kingsley never stood upon clerical formality and could rapidly establish friendly relations with almost anyone. Even the gipsies who camped on the moors called him their "Patrico-rai," their Priest-King, and permitted him, many of them, to baptize or marry them. This devoted ministry was part of Kingsley's favourite principle that one should do eagerly whatever work lay ready to one's hand. Wherever he saw a need in his parish he called what skill he had to meet it, trying some curious experiments. In his Commonplace-Book (July 17, [?] 1847) he has recorded the mesmerizing of a boy for fits and he wrote a long letter (February 27, 1856) about the curing of a temporary madman among his parishioners who walked up and down in melancholy silence, declaring from time to time that the devil had hold of him and would not let him sleep. "I went to the patient and agreed with him fully, that the devil *was* in him; and I said, 'I will tell you why he is in you; because, my dear man, you have been a thief, and a cheat, and a liar' (as all the world knew), 'and have sold yourself to the father of lies. But if you will pray to God to forgive you' (and then I set forth those precious promises in Christ, which the *Record* thinks I don't believe), and 'will lead a new and honest life, you may snap your fingers at the devil.' And after a while the man got well, and has had no return for seven years." (I, 466.)

Demoniac possession Kingsley himself believed in as firmly as his madman. "I am perfectly certain," he says in the same letter, "that the accesses of mingled pride, rage, suspicion, and hatred of everybody and everything, accompanied by the most unspeakable sense of loneliness and *'darkness'* (St. John's metaphor for it is the only one), which were common to me in youth, and are now, by God's grace, very rare (though I am just as capable of them as ever, when I am at *unawares* and give place to the devil by harsh judgments or bitter words) were and are nothing less than temporary possession by a devil. I am sure that the way in which those fits pass off in a few minutes, as soon as I get ashamed of myself, is not to be explained by *'habit,'* either physical or moral (though *'moral* habits' I don't believe in), but by the actual intervention of an unseen personage, I believe our Lord Jesus Christ Himself, driving away that devil."

This sense of imminent divinity made it possible for Kingsley to combine easily occupations which would have seemed to most people hopelessly incongruous. "Up at five," he writes to Hughes (?1851) "to see a dying man . . . was from 5-30 to 6-30 with the most dreadful case of agony—insensible to me, but not to his pain. Came home, got a wash and a pipe, and away again to him at eight. . . . Prayed the commendatory prayers over him, and started for the river with West. Fished all the morning in a roaring N.E. gale, with the dreadful agonized face between me and the river, pondering on *the* mystery. Killed eight on 'March brown,' . . . Came off the water at 3-30. Found my man alive, and, thank God, quiet. Sat with him. . . . Then had to go to Hartley Row for an Archdeacon's Sunday-school meeting—three hours useless (*I* fear) speechifying and shop; . . . Got back at 10-30, and sit writing to you. So goes one's day. All manner of incongruous things to do, and the very incongruity keeps one beany and jolly." (I, 277.)

This same pleasure in doing a different thing every hour, this same interest in all phases of the lives of the people to whom he ministered Kingsley extended to Chester during his months of residence and indeed during the whole year. He would have found reason for liking almost any community in which his lot had fallen but it was particularly easy for him to identify himself, sentimentally and practically, with Cheshire for the Kingsley family came originally from that county and J. S. Howson, the energetic Dean of Chester Cathedral was a superior after his own heart.

Twenty years before Kingsley had written in *Yeast* a description of St. Paul's:

The afternoon service was proceeding. The organ droned sadly in its iron cage to a few musical amateurs. Some nursery-maids and foreign sailors stared about within the spiked felons' dock which shut off the body of the cathedral, and tried in vain to hear what was going on inside the choir. As a wise author—a Protestant, too—has lately said, "the scanty service rattled in the vast building, like a dried kernel too small for its shell." The place breathed imbecility, and unreality, and sleepy life-in-death, while the whole nineteenth century went roaring on its way outside. (Chap. XVII.)

It is not altogether surprising that Dean Howson, as he confessed later, was a trifle alarmed when he heard of Charles Kingsley's appointment to his Chapter. He fancied that there was "no natural affinity between the author of *Alton Locke* and cathedral life," but he found himself delighted with Kingsley's enthusiasm and also with "his old-fashioned courtesy, loyalty, and respect for official position. . . . I believe that to have caused inconvenience to me, to have done what I did not like, to have impeded me in my efforts to be useful, would have given him the utmost pain. That he was far my superior in ability and knowledge made no difference. I happened to be Dean, and he happened to be Canon; and this was quite enough." (II, 410.)

Dean Howson was full of determination to make his cathedral a vital factor in all the life of the diocese. He made a point, too, of having a good choir and Sunday evening nave services which attracted great throngs. Canon Kingsley's preaching made them more popular than ever.

Kingsley went into residence in May 1870. The stall was not a rich one but the £500 per annum was very welcome. The four non-resident canons of Chester occupied by turns a house in Abbey Square, an arrangement perhaps not wholly satisfactory to their wives but having its compensations.

A few days after his arrival Kingsley took the chair at a meeting of the Chester Archaeological Society where he expressed his desire to put himself "at the service of the good citizens of Chester" and those good citizens took him to their hearts at once. From that day until the end of his canonry the local weeklies, the *Courant* and *Guardian,* seldom published an issue in which Canon Kingsley did not furnish the subject for at least one column of news and frequently a leader to boot: Canon Kingsley preaches in the cathedral to an unusually large congregation. Canon Kingsley speaks at the annual dinner of the Old King's Scholars—the boxes of fruit at each place are inscribed with lines from *The Water-Babies*— and the *Courant* wishes that his address could be "printed in letters of gold and circulated in every middle-class household in England." Canon Kingsley speaks in Liverpool at a meeting to raise funds for the restoration of Chester Cathedral; he "rose amid cheers." Canon Kingsley distributes prizes at the King's School, presenting one himself "For Good Conduct and Attention to Studies." Canon Kingsley seconds a motion at a meeting to form a society to prevent the pollution of the River Dee; he talks of the moral influence of pure water. Canon Kingsley lectures on Primaeval Man to the Chester Archaeological Society. Canon Kingsley speaks to a "highly respectable audience" for the benefit of the City Library and Reading Room, his topic, "The Study of Physical Science." Canon Kingsley writes "To the Young Men of Chester" on betting, part of a crusade against the evils of race week. Canon Kingsley organizes a botany class.

That class began with some twenty young shopmen and clerks gathering weekly in a small room in the city library. Two years later the Chester Natural Science Society had 350 members; botanical, geological and zoölogical divisions; such honorary members as Lyell, Huxley, Tyndall and Hooker; an annual Converzatione and exhibition of specimens which was one of the social events of the year; and field trips conducted by Canon Kingsley in which as many as a hundred men and women from all ranks of Chester society "rambled" happily in search of "the beautiful and the pure in nature." A very popular series of lectures given by Canon Kingsley in 1871 was published (1872) as *Town Geology*.

There was only one Chester duty which Kingsley did not accept gladly, that of being a lion. "My husband," Mrs. Kingsley wrote to Edward Stapleton, "likes his cathedral services, especially daily the 8 o'clock A.M. and 5 P.M. He feels his soul at anchor at those hours day by day, and he can take refuge in the Chapter room and Library . . . when we are likely to be invaded in the Residence. There he is safe from every one except parties of *Americans*. . . . The old Verger . . . a great hero worshiper invariably tells them who the Canon in Residence is and asks if they would not like to see him too! and they are all paraded into the Chapter room too suddenly for Mr. Kingsley to make his exit. We get shoals of invitations in consequence to Cincinnati, Milwaukee, New York, etc."

Despite his personal happiness during the Chester years Kingsley was stirred by the war of 1870 only less than he had been by the Crimea. He thought it the most important event since the Revolution of 1793 and that it would work good for generations to come though at an awful price. "Accept my loving congratulations," he wrote Max Müller on August 8, "to you and your people. The day which dear Bunsen used to pray, with tears in his eyes, might not come till the German people were ready, has come, and the German people are ready." (II, 332.) "Were I a German," he said to Sir Charles Bunbury (August 31, 1870), "I should feel it my duty to my country to send my last son, my last shilling, and after all, my own self to the war, to get that done which must be done, done so that it will never need doing again." (II, 334.)

From an English struggle taking place at this time Kingsley felt it necessary to disassociate himself though he deeply believed in the cause. He seriously disapproved of the methods which were being used for the winning of Women's Rights, and saw great injury to the cause in the type of advocates it was attracting. "I think women ought to speak in public, in any ideal, or even truly civilized society. . . . My fear is, not so much that women should speak, as *who* the women are who speak." He was afraid of the foolish, hysterical women, often of questionable morals, whom the cause attracted. "I am aware of the physical and psychical significance of this fact." He objected to the question of women's right to vote or labour being mixed up with "social, *i.e.*, sexual questions." "Meanwhile, I shall do that which I have been doing for years past. Try to teach a noble freedom, to those whom I see most willing, faithful, conscientious in their slavery. . . . To show . . . that wherever man and wife are really happy together, it is by ignoring and despising, not by asserting, the subordination of woman to man, . . . To set forth in every book I write (as I have done for twenty-five years) woman as the teacher, the natural and therefore divine, guide, purifier, inspirer of the man. And so, perhaps, I may be as useful to the cause of chivalry . . . as if I attended many meetings, and spoke, or caused to be spoken, many speeches." (To John Stuart Mill, Chester, 1870, II, 327.)

But though he withdrew from direct participation in the Woman's Rights movement Kingsley continued to labour openly and vigorously for the right of women to be physicians. One of the last acts of his life was to promise Dr. Elizabeth Blackwell, who considered him an invaluable aid in her battle, to serve as chairman of a committee working to secure medical degrees for women.

CHAPTER XXII

"AT LAST"

THE years 1870 to 1875 were years for Charles Kingsley of fulfilment of hopes long nursed. Just after his installation in the Chester canonry, before his first period of residence, he realized a dream which he had dreamed ever since he was a little boy; he made a voyage to the West Indies. He went as the guest of his friend Sir Arthur Gordon, Governor of Trinidad, and, since Mrs. Kingsley's health was not equal to so adventurous a journey, his companion was his daughter Rose.

No weariness or ill health could damp Kingsley's curiosity about almost everything in heaven and earth. A new prospect refreshed him like a cordial. His extraordinary vitality surged up again to meet it. So delighted was he always with widened horizons that he was charmed on first encounter with any country to which chance took him. The West Indies for him combined the delights of novelty with the joys of going home. Few travellers can have visited them so well documented in advance. He knew stories of every bay and island, adventures which had befallen Elizabethan voyagers, and his own grandfather, adventures which he had invented for the personages of *Westward Ho!* He had studied for years the flora, the fish, the fauna and was so excited at actually seeing them at last that he collected specimens enough for a dozen museums and was sadly downcast when he found it impossible to preserve more than a small portion against the rigours of heat, damp and travel. He had theories, too, on the dark races and primitive peoples and was fascinated by the opportunity for a little first-hand observation. Experiences and impressions crowded upon him so thickly that the sentences in his letters tumble over each other in their eagerness to get it all down. An account of his journey had been bespoken in advance by *Good Words* and "Letters from the Tropics" began to appear in March 1870, not a month after his return. They were his family letters, retouched only slightly, and they delighted his huge circle of readers, for they were full of his famous word pictures lit by the most eager personal enthusiasm. Enriched with certain historic and economic data which there had not been time to gather for the magazine, Macmillan brought them out in two volumes in 1871, *At Last: a Christmas in the West Indies,* and found it worth while to make a new one-volume edition the next year.

To the West Indian enchantments succeeded the heartening labours and releases of the Chester canonry and then, in March 1873, came another letter from Gladstone: "I have to propose to you, with the sanction of Her Majesty, that in lieu of your canonry at Chester, you should accept the vacant stall at Westminster Abbey." (II, 406.) Kingsley had no desire to sever his happy connection with Chester but this was the very relief and opportunity for which he had longed for years. A Westminster canonry was worth £1000 a year and that meant complete freedom from the pressure of writing for bread; it meant opportunity for the intellectual, especially the scientific, delights of London, and the honour of preaching to the nation from England's loftiest pulpit. "So far from looking on it," Kingsley wrote Sir Charles Bunbury (April 1, 1873), "as an earnest of future preferment, I acquiesce in it as all I want, and more than I deserve. What better fate than to spend one's old age under the shadow of that Abbey, and close to the highest mental activities of England, with leisure to cultivate myself, and write, if I will, deliberately, but not for daily bread?" (II, 415.)

The period appointed for Kingsley's residence was September and November, when London was bare of fashion but when he preached, to his pleasure, to vast congregations "chiefly of men of the middle and lower class." (II, 417.)

But the welcome relief of Chester and London had come late. His constant lassitude and a numbness in his left side made Kingsley apprehensive of approaching paralysis and his eldest son, when he returned from America for a short visit in the spring of 1873, was horrified to find his father looking like an old man. He urged him to take a complete rest and change before entering upon his new duties and suggested a voyage to America. Kingsley declined to go at once but made plans for the early months of 1874 when he should have completed his first period of residence at Westminster and when repairs necessary for the Eversley house and that in the Abbey cloisters would really oblige him to leave home.

Again his companion was Rose. She had all her father's enthusiasm for travel, scientific, historic, romantic, adventurous, and, a year after the West Indian expedition, had made a journey to America with Dean Howson and his family, spending the winter with her brother in Colorado, the spring in California and Mexico. She was delighted at the opportunity of going again, and with her father. For Kingsley the journey was a glorious holiday but certainly not a rest, even though he found American railway travel luxurious, safe and reposeful. He covered the continent from Washington to Montreal, from New York to California; he was heaped with American hospitality, taken to see everything and entreated again and again to preach and lecture. His lectures were agreeably crowded and this helped to defray the expenses of the trip. For the rest he was presented everywhere with railway passes, private cars and public dinners.

The travellers embarked January 29, 1874, on the *Oceanic* which made an excellent run, reaching New York February 11. Kingsley was met at the dock by a deputation from the Lotos Club which had power to pass his luggage through the customs unopened. He stayed on Staten Island with F. G. Shaw, going to New York for sightseeing and a great dinner and reception tendered him by the Lotos Club. "This air," he wrote his wife (February 12, 1874), "is like champagne. Sea-air . . . and mountain air combined, days already an hour longer than in England, and a blazing hot sun and blue sky. It is a glorious country, and I don't wonder at the people being proud of it." (II, 423.)

February 15 he went on to Boston—Cambridge, Salem, Andover, Georgetown; staying with James T. Fields; delighting in the Agassiz Museum and the Harvard undergraduate; lecturing in Horticultural Hall, under the auspices of the Redpath Lyceum, on "Westminster Abbey," "Ancient Civilization" and "Cyrus, the Servant of the Lord." "Here is a little haven of rest," he wrote (February 19) from Dr. Wharton's in Cambridge, "where we arrived last night. Longfellow came to dinner, and we dine with him to-night. Yesterday, in Boston, dear old Whittier called on me and we had a most loving and like-minded talk about the other world. He is an old saint. This morning I have spent chiefly with Asa Gray and his plants, so that we are in good company." (II, 424.)

In Springfield, on the way back to New York, Kingsley spent the night with Samuel Bowles of the *Republican*. In New York there was a meeting with William Cullen Bryant whose poetry had delighted him from his boyhood, and he assisted Bishop Potter at an ordination. "The old man was very cordial, especially when he found I was of the respectful and orthodox class." (March 1, 1874, II, 425.)

Philadelphia, and an audience of 4,000 packed the Opera House, sitting on the stairs and standing in the aisles to hear the lecture on "Ancient Civilization."

Washington, March 7. Kingsley is received by President Grant, warmly welcomed by the Smithsonian and the Geological Survey, invited to open the House of Representatives with prayer.

New York again; Poughkeepsie; Troy; Hartford, March 14, for a long promised visit to Mark Twain; Boston once more; and New Haven where he stayed with his distant kinsman, Dr. William Kingsley of Yale. "We are housed and feasted everywhere," he wrote on March 23, "I do not tire in the least. . . . This is a marvellous climate. The Americans make themselves ill by hot-air, and foul air, and want of exercise; I who sleep with my window open and get all fresh air I can by day, am always well." (II, 427.)

Montreal and then Quebec where Kingsley lectured (March 28) on "The First Discoverers of America" and impressed *Le Journal* by his "tact infini" and his "profonde sympathie pour les Canadiens Français et pour la France." He himself was impressed by the falls of Montmorency and the kindness of everyone. From Quebec he went to Ottawa to spend a quiet Easter with Lord and Lady Dufferin, then back again to Washington, "500 miles in thirty hours. . . . The long journeys do not in the least tire me, so have no fears for me. The safety of these rails is wonderful, as is their comfort. . . . We have a dinner-party to-night; we are staying with Senator Potter, and to-morrow a dinner-party with the President. So we shall have seen quasi-royalty, British and American both in one week." (April 9, 1874, II, 429.)

"Sir Canon Kingsley, LL.D., of London, Chaplain to the Queen," said a post card advertisement, "will deliver his great lecture on the 'Norse-Discoverers of America' at the First Congregational Church, Wednesday evening, April 8, 1874. . . . The Boston papers speak of it in terms of high commendation. The Canon has yielded to an urgent request and returns to Washington solely for the sake of giving this lecture. Admission, seventy-five cents."

At Baltimore, on April 12, Kingsley finally consented to preach, and had of course a huge congregation. New York again and the beginning of the journey westward; Cornell—a narrowly averted railway accident on the way to Ithaca; Niagara Falls; Hamilton—the "Westminster Abbey" lecture; Toronto; Detroit; St. Louis—the lecture on "Westminster Abbey" and then, in response to a special request signed by a score of leading citizens, a second lecture, the one on "Ancient Civilization."

At Omaha began the expedition organized by Cyrus Field and J. A. C. Gray of New York. The party travelled, sixteen in all, in a "magnificent Pullman car." Salt Lake City, May 15; Kingsley preached in the newly consecrated Episcopal Church. Brigham Young, Rose records, sent to offer him "the tabernacle to lecture or preach in, but of this offer he of course took no notice whatever."

Carson City, Virginia City, Sacramento where Kingsley lectured again. Then the party went through the Yosemite Valley by stage and horseback. On Whitsunday Kingsley preached in a little parlour at Black's. On May 29 he was in San Francisco and a few days later lecturing to enthusiastic students at Berkeley, the whole college turning out to hear him. In San Francisco he caught a cold so severe that he was urged by the doctors to get away as rapidly as possible to a warmer and drier climate. In Denver, after a trying journey, he met providentially his brother George, the big-game hunting doctor. He diagnosed the illness at once as pleurisy and sent Kingsley down to Colorado Springs where he was nursed and cared for by Dr. and Mrs. W. A. Bell. By July he was well enough to explore the surrounding country and to preach to a church crowded with young Englishmen who rode in twenty miles from distant ranches to hear him. He gave, too, his Westminster Abbey lecture, and one of his auditors has recorded with delight how there alighted on his MS. an insect of a species apparently new to him, how he caught it deftly, examined it minutely and set it free again without once interrupting the eloquent torrent of his discourse.

"I cannot believe," Kingsley wrote his wife from Glen Eyrie on July 14, "that I shall see you within twenty-one days; and never longed so for home. . . . I am so glad you like Westminster. Yes! we shall rest our weary bones there for a while before kind death comes, and, perhaps, see our grand-children round us there. Ah! please God *that*! I look forward to a blessed quiet autumn, if God so will, having had a change of scene, which will last me my whole life through, and has taught me many things." (II, 444.)

The American journey delighted Kingsley but its rigours and his severe illness left him weary rather than refreshed. At home again he rushed too eagerly into parish work through a hot summer and when he went up to Westminster in September he had an alarming liver attack which prevented his preaching as often as he had expected to do during his residence. In October Mrs. Kingsley was taken dangerously ill and that anxiety added to his own weariness made the Abbey preaching, though it was as successful and his congregations as large as before, an increasing strain. It was with genuine relief that he delivered his last sermon on November 29 and took his wife down to Eversley. The journey was too trying for her, her condition became really alarming, and the doctors were constrained to tell him that there was no possibility of her recovery.

For weeks while she lived on the border between life and death Kingsley devoted all his love and energy to comforting and strengthening her for the passage. Like the Kingsley courtship the record of those last weeks bears witness to a perverse generation that the elaborate deathbed scenes of Victorian novels are actually stark realism. There was daily prayer and daily reading of the psalms and gospels; there was talk of the eternal nature of married love, the certainty of reunion, the blessed possibility that years of separation might seem to one who dwelt with Christ as only the passage of a moment. All the happinesses of earth were gathered up and relived, letters looked over, souvenirs examined, scenes recalled, favourite poems read aloud once more: "The Intimations of Immortality," Arnold's "Buried Life," certain passages from Shakespeare and, again and again, Milton's "Ode to Time." That intense desire of the nineteenth century to assure itself of the importance of the individual rose up in all its strength at the approach of death. Even more violently than the romantics the mid-Victorians strove to maintain their separate personalities, perhaps because they felt sweeping down upon them, when science had opened the flood gates, the engulfing idea of the common life of the race. It was never enough to be a part of all that they had met; what they had met must become a part of them. Nothing from their personal experience must ever be lost. So their passion for mementoes. They cherished bits of silk and locks of hair; they gathered roses from Tintern Abbey, ivy from Goethe's grave; and these they treasured up in their cabinets and attics as bulwarks for their individuality. They found no rest unless they could believe in a paternal God, counting the sparrows.

> Then long Eternity shall greet our bliss
> With an individual kiss.

On December 28 the cough, from which Kingsley who had not been thinking of his own health was suffering, developed into pneumonia. He welcomed it almost; he had long been ready to lay down the burden of life and it was his dearest wish that he and his wife might die together. She made him promise, however, to fight for life for his children's sake and for days they lay in adjoining rooms communicating now and then by little penciled notes. His daughters, his curate, his nurse and the servants who watched in the sick-room treasured the phrases they heard him utter during those weeks which did not seem to him, he said, three days: "It is all right. All under rule." "No more fighting—no more fighting." "How beautiful God is."

Once, when left alone for a moment, he leaped out of bed, ran into his wife's room and sat by her bed holding her hand. "Don't speak," he said, "this is heaven." But the exertion brought on a terrible fit of coughing and he was warned that another such exposure would be fatal. He submitted and made a gallant fight for life. A London doctor was called down to help the local medical man and the Prince of Wales sent his own physician, but Kingsley's body was too weakened and weary to bear the long strain. Early in the morning of January 23 he was heard repeating the words of the burial service in a clear strong voice. Before noon he died, so quietly and peacefully that his daughter and the family nurse who were in the room scarcely knew that he had gone. He believed, it was thought, that his wife had died just before him. She recovered, however, and lived till 1891.

"The Abbey is open to the Canon and the Poet," telegraphed Dean Stanley but "there was no hesitation with those who knew his own feelings" and at Eversley he was buried on January 28, 1875.

Osborne, January 24, 1875

Dear Mrs. Kingsley,

Though personally unknown to you you must allow me to express to you my *deepest deepest* sympathy in your overwhelming loss coming too on you in the midst of illness—and my true concern at the loss we have *all* sustained in your dear Husband!

He was noble, loyal, warmhearted, talented and chivalrous—and *such* can ill be spared! I shall never forget his kind sympathy when I first saw him after my terrible bereavement, and he wrote some beautiful, touching lines in a book of mine, which perhaps you do not know. If so, I will send them to you! He was so truly attached to our son, and took so great an interest in him.

But why do I speak of what *I* feel when it is you and your children who have lost everything!

May God support and sustain you, as well as the blessed thought of re-union, which is our greatest help in the hour of separation!

Your dear Husband's memory will ever be gratefully cherished by me.

My warm sympathy I ask also to express to your dear and devoted daughters, and to your sons.

Pray believe me always,
Yours sincerely
Victoria R.

BIBLIOGRAPHY OF CHARLES KINGSLEY'S WORKS

THIS bibliography is intended to indicate the extent of Kingsley's literary output year by year and also to identify the reviews, articles and poems which he published anonymously in various periodicals. A great many of these which were not republished in book form have not hitherto been attributed to him and the list is probably not yet complete; items have been included only when internal evidence or references in letters made their authorship indubitable. American editions are not included nor are reissues of works to which no new material by Kingsley himself was added. Detailed bibliographical information on Kingsley's works may be found in the elaborate and excellent *Charles Kingsley and Thomas Hughes,* First Editions in the Library at Dormy House, Pine Valley, New Jersey, described with Notes by M. L. Parrish, London, 1936. Constable.

? 1836

Translation of *The Beheading of John the Baptist,* a sermon by Friedrich Wilhelm Krummacher, Religious Tract Society. London (anon.)

1847

A Sermon preached at Eversley, Hants., on Sunday morning, 18th April 1847. London, printed at the request of Sir John Cope and at his expense

1848

The Saint's Tragedy; or, the True Story of Elizabeth of Hungary, Landgravine of Thuringia, Saint of the Romish Calendar, with a Preface by Professor Maurice. London, Parker

A Sermon preached at Hawley Church, April 30, 1848, in Behalf of the New Church at York Town, published by request. The Profits arising from the sale of this will be appropriated towards the Building. Wokingham and London, Parker

Apr. "Why Should We Fear the Romish Priests?" (anon.) *Fraser's Magazine*
May 6 "Workmen of England" (anon.); "The National Gallery," I. (Parson Lot) *Politics for the People*

May 13	"Old and New—a Parable" (verse) (anon.) (*Poems*, 1858, 2nd ed.); "Letters to the Chartists," 1. (Parson Lot) *Politics for the People*
May 20	"Old Saws New Set, 1. A Greek Fable to an English Moral" (verse) (anon.); "The National Gallery," 2. (Parson Lot) *Politics for the People*
May 27	"Old Saws New Set, 2. England for the English, 3. The Golden Goose" (verse) (anon.) "Letters to the Chartists," 2. (Parson Lot) *Politics for the People*
June 17	"Letters to the Chartists," 3. (Parson Lot) *Politics for the People*
July 1	"The British Museum" (Parson Lot) *Politics for the People*
July-Dec.	"Yeast; or, The Thoughts, Sayings, and Doings of Lancelot Smith, Gentleman" (anon.) (see 1851) *Fraser's Magazine*

1849

Twenty-Five Village Sermons. London, Parker
2. "On English Composition," 3. "On English Literature," *Introductory Lectures, delivered at Queen's College, London*. London, Parker (*Literary and General Lectures and Essays, 1880*)

Jan.	"The Bothie of Toper-Na-Fuosich" (anon.) *Fraser's Magazine*
Mar.	"The Poetry of Sacred and Legendary Art" (anon.) (*Miscellanies*, 1859, I) *Fraser's Magazine*
Apr.	"Recent Novels" (anon.) *Fraser's Magazine*
May	"Recent Poetry and Recent Verse" (anon.) *Fraser's Magazine*
July	"North Devon," 1. (anon.) (*Miscellanies,* 1859, II) *Fraser's Magazine*
Dec.	"North Devon," 2. (see above) *Fraser's Magazine*

1850

Alton Locke, Tailor and Poet. An Autobiography. (anon.) London, Chapman and Hall. 2 vols.
Cheap Clothes and Nasty (Parson Lot). London, Pickering; Cambridge, Macmillan

Jan.	"Sir E. B. Lytton and Mrs. Grundy" (anon.) *Fraser's Magazine*
Feb.	"North Devon," 3. (see 1849) *Fraser's Magazine*
Apr.	"The Poet's Question" (verse) (C. K.) (*Poems*, 1858, "Dartside") *Fraser's Magazine*
June	"Readable and Unreadable" (anon.) *Fraser's Magazine*
Sept.	"Tennyson" (anon.) (*Miscellanies,* 1859, I) *Fraser's Magazine*

Sept. 21 "Robert Owen's First Principles" (letter) *Leader*
Nov.   "The Agricultural Crisis" (anon.) (*Miscellanies*, 1859, II) *North British Review*
Nov. 2   "The Day of the Lord" (verse) (Parson Lot) (*Poems*, 1858); "Thoughts on the Frimley Murder," 1. (Parson Lot) *Christian Socialist*
Nov. 2   "Alton Locke" (letter) *Record*
Nov. 9   "Bible Politics: or God Justified to the People," 1. (Parson Lot) *Christian Socialist*
Nov. 16   "Thoughts on the Frimley Murder," 2. (Parson Lot) *Christian Socialist*
Nov. 23   "Bible Politics," 2. (Parson Lot) *Christian Socialist*
Nov. 30   "Thoughts on the Frimley Murder," 3. (Parson Lot) *Christian Socialist*
          "Evidence against the Universities" (letter) (A Cambridge First-Class Man and Country Rector) *Spectator*
Dec.   "The Church-Bells Were Ringing" (verse) (C.K.) (*Poems*, 1858, "A Parable from Leibig") *Fraser's Magazine*
Dec. 14   "My Political Creed" (Parson Lot) *Christian Socialist*
Dec. 28   "Thoughts on the Frimley Murder," 4. (Parson Lot) *Christian Socialist*

1851

Yeast: A Problem. Reprinted, with corrections and additions, from *Fraser's Magazine* (anon.) London, Parker (see 1848)
The Application of Associative Principles and Methods to Agriculture: A Lecture, delivered on behalf of the Society for Promoting Working Men's Associations, On Wednesday, May 28, 1851. London, Bezer
The Message of the Church to Labouring Men. A Sermon, Preached at St. John's Church, Charlotte Street, Fitzroy Square, On the Evening of Sunday, June the 22nd, 1851. London, Parker

Jan. 11   "A Christmas Carol" (verse) (Parson Lot) (*Poems*, 1858) *Christian Socialist*
Jan. 25   "The Reform that the Universities need" (letter) (A Cambridge First-Class Man and Country Rector) *Spectator*
Jan. 28   "*The Edinburgh Review* and Christian Socialism" (letter) (F. D. Maurice, *Reasons for Cooperation*. London, Parker, 1851) *Morning Chronicle*
Feb. 8   "Bible Politics," 3. (Parson Lot) *Christian Socialist*
Feb. 15   "The Church *versus* Malthus," 1. (Parson Lot) *Christian Socialist*
          "University Reform" (letter) (A Cambridge First-Class Man and Country Rector) *Spectator*
Feb. 22   "Bible Politics," 4. (Parson Lot) *Christian Socialist*
Mar. 8   "Bible Politics," 5. (Parson Lot) *Christian Socialist*
Mar. 15   "Bible Politics," 6. (Parson Lot) *Christian Socialist*

Mar. 22	"Bible Politics," 7. (Parson Lot) *Christian Socialist*
Mar. 29	"The Church *versus* Malthus," 2. (Parson Lot) *Christian Socialist*
Apr. 5	"The Church *versus* Malthus," 3. (Parson Lot) *Christian Socialist*
Apr. 12	"The Church *versus* Malthus," 4. (Parson Lot) *Christian Socialist*
Apr. 19	"Bible Politics," 8. (Parson Lot) *Christian Socialist*
Apr. 26	"Bible Politics," 9. (Parson Lot) *Christian Socialist*
May	"The Prevailing Epidemic" (anon.) *Fraser's Magazine*
	"The Water Supply of London" (anon.) (*Miscellanies*, 1859, II) *North British Review*
May 21	"The Review of *Yeast*" (letter) (The Author of *Yeast*) *Guardian*
July	"Little Books with Large Aims" (anon.) *Fraser's Magazine*
July 5	"The Nun's Pool" (the Author of *Yeast*) *Christian Socialist*
July 12	"The Nun's Pool" (the Author of *Yeast*) *Christian Socialist*
July 19	"The Nun's Pool" (the Author of *Yeast*) *Christian Socialist*
Aug. 2	"The Nun's Pool" (the Author of *Yeast*) *Christian Socialist*
Aug. 9	"The Nun's Pool" (the Author of *Yeast*) *Christian Socialist*
Aug. 23	"The Nun's Pool" (the Author of *Yeast*) *Christian Socialist*
Aug. 30	"The Nun's Pool" (the Author of *Yeast*) *Christian Socialist*
Sept. 13	"The Ugly Princess" (verse) (*Poems*, 1858) *Christian Socialist*
Sept. 27	"Sonnet" (C. K.) (*Poems*, 1858, "The baby sings not on its mother's breast") *Christian Socialist*
Oct. 11	"Three fishers" (verse) (*Poems*, 1858) *Christian Socialist*
Nov.	"Burns and His School" (anon.) (*Miscellanies*, 1859, I) *North British Review*
Nov. 1	"A Thought from the Rhine" (verse) (*Poems*, 1858) *Christian Socialist*
Nov. 15	"The Long Game," 1. (Parson Lot) *Christian Socialist*
Nov. 22	"The Long Game," 2. (Parson Lot) *Christian Socialist*
Nov. 29	"The Long Game," 3. (Parson Lot) *Christian Socialist*
Dec.	"This Year's Song Crop" (anon.) *Fraser's Magazine*

1852

Phaethon; or, Loose Thoughts for Loose Thinkers. Cambridge, Macmillan

Sermons on National Subjects, Preached in a Village Church. London, Griffin

Who Are the Friends of Order? A Reply to Certain Observations in a Late Number of *Fraser's Magazine* on the so-called "Christian Socialists." London, Lumley, and Bezer

Jan.-Dec. "Hypatia: or, New Foes with an Old Face" (the Author of *Yeast,* and *The Saint's Tragedy*) (see 1853) *Fraser's Magazine*
Feb. "The Last Buccanier" (verse) (*Poems,* 1858) *Fraser's Magazine*
June 28 "Parson Lot's Last Words"; "Epicedium" (verse) (*Poems,* 1858, "On the Death of a Certain Journal") *Christian Socialist*
July 17 "The Christian Socialists" (letter) *Spectator*

1853

Hypatia: or, New Foes with an Old Face, reprinted from *Fraser's Magazine.* London, Parker, 2 vols.
Jan.-Apr. "Hypatia: or, New Foes with an Old Face" (the Author of *Yeast,* and *The Saint's Tragedy*) (see 1852) *Fraser's Magazine*
Oct. "Alexander Smith and Alexander Pope" (anon.) (*Miscellanies,* 1859, I) *Fraser's Magazine*
Nov. "Thoughts on Shelley and Byron" (anon.) (*Miscellanies,* 1859, I) *Fraser's Magazine*

1854

Alexandria and Her Schools. Four Lectures Delivered at the Philosophical Institution, Edinburgh, with a Preface. Cambridge, Macmillan
Sermons on National Subjects, Second Series. London and Glasgow, Griffin
Who Causes Pestilence? Four Sermons with Preface. London and Glasgow, Griffin [reprinted from *Sermons on National Subjects,* 1852]
Preface, *Theologia Germanica,* Dr. Pfeiffer, ed., tr. from the German by Susanna Winkworth. London, Longman
Jan. "Lord Palmerston and the Presbytery of Edinburgh" (anon.) *Fraser's Magazine*
Feb. "Poems by Matthew Arnold" (anon.) *Fraser's Magazine*
June "Frederick Tennyson's Poems" (anon.) *Fraser's Magazine*
Nov. "The Wonders of the Shore" (anon.) (see 1855, *Glaucus*) *North British Review*

1855

Westward Ho! or, the Voyages and Adventures of Sir Amyas Leigh, Knight, of Burrough, in the County of Devon, in the Reign of Her Most Glorious Majesty Queen Elizabeth. Rendered into Modern English by Charles Kingsley. Cambridge, Macmillan, 3 vols.
Glaucus; or, The Wonders of the Shore. Cambridge, Macmillan (see 1854)

Sermons for the Times. London, Parker
Brave Words for Brave Soldiers and Sailors (tract) (anon.) (*True Words for Brave Men,* 1878). Cambridge, Macmillan
n. d. *Sermons for Sailors* (see 1885)
2. "The Country Parish," *Lectures to Ladies on Practical Subjects.* Cambridge, Macmillan (*Sanitary and Social Lectures and Essays, 1880*)

May   "Sir Walter Raleigh and His Time" (anon.) (*Miscellanies,* 1859, I) *North British Review*
July   "Sydney Smith" (C. K.) *Fraser's Magazine*
Sept.   "Tennyson's Maud" (anon.) *Fraser's Magazine*

1856

The Heroes; or, Greek Fairy Tales for My Children, 8 illustrations by the Author. Cambridge, Macmillan
A Sketch of the Author's Life, *Paraguay, Brazil, and the Plate,* by Charles B. Mansfield. Cambridge, Macmillan
Alton Locke, Tailor and Poet, An Autobiography, with Preface Addressed to the Working Men of Great Britain. London, Chapman and Hall (see 1850)
Glaucus; or, The Wonders of the Shore. Cambridge, Macmillan, 3rd ed. corrected and enlarged (see 1855)

May   "Plays and Puritans" (anon.) (*Miscellanies,* 1859, II) *North British Review*
Aug.   ? "An Epistle" (verse) (C. K.) *Fraser's Magazine*
Sept.   "Hours with the Mystics" (C. K.) (*Miscellanies,* 1859, I) *Fraser's Magazine*
Nov.   "Mansfield's Paraguay, Brazil, and the Plate" (anon.) (*Miscellanies,* 1859, II) *Fraser's Magazine*
        "Froude's History of England" (anon.) (*Miscellanies,* 1859, II) *North British Review*

1857

Two Years Ago. Cambridge, Macmillan, 3 vols.
Preface, *The History and Life of the Reverend Doctor John Tauler of Strasbourg; with Twenty-Five of His Sermons,* tr. from the German by Susanna Winkworth. London, Smith, Elder
Oct. 3   "Tom Brown's School Days" (anon.) *Saturday Review*

1858

Andromeda and Other Poems. London, Parker
Pamphlet, no title, letter, Oct. 19, 1858, to Rev. W. M. on Esau
Jan.   "A Mad World, My Masters," by a Sanitary Reformer (C. K.) (*Miscellanies,* 1859, I) *Fraser's Magazine*

Apr. "My Winter Garden," by a Minute Philosopher (C. K.) (*Miscellanies,* 1859, I) *Fraser's Magazine*
Sept. "Chalk-Stream Studies," by a Minute Philosopher (C. K.) (*Miscellanies,* 1859, I) *Fraser's Magazine*

1859

Miscellanies, reprinted chiefly from *Fraser's Magazine* and the *North British Review.* London, Parker, 2 vols.
The Good News of God: Sermons. London, Parker
The Massacre of the Innocents, an address delivered at the first public meeting of the Ladies National Association for the Diffusion of Sanitary Knowledge. London, Partridge (*Miscellanies,* 1859, II)
Preface, *The Fool of Quality: or, the History of Henry Earl of Moreland,* by Henry Brooke. London, Smith, Elder, 2 vols.
Yeast: A Problem, 4th ed. with a new Preface. London, Parker
Glaucus; or, the Wonders of the Shore, 4th ed. corrected and enlarged. Cambridge and London, Macmillan (see 1855)
Jan. "The Knight's Leap at Alternach" (verse) (C. K.) (*Poems,* 1872) *Fraser's Magazine*
July "The Irrationale of Speech," by a Minute Philosopher (C. K.) (1864) *Fraser's Magazine*

1860

The Limits of Exact Science as Applied to History. An Inaugural Lecture, delivered before the University of Cambridge. Cambridge and London, Macmillan
The Example of the Early Navigators, A Sermon Preached in the Church of St. Olave, Hart Street, on Trinity Monday, June 4, 1860. London, Parker
Why should we Pray for Fair Weather? A Sermon. Preached in Eversley Church, August 26th, 1860. London, Parker
Preface, Bunyan's *Pilgrim's Progress,* with illustrations by Charles Bennett. London, Longman
Feb. "Song" ("Hark, hark, hark") (anon.) (*Poems,* 1884, "The Knights' Return") *Fraser's Magazine*

1861

Town and Country Sermons. London, Parker

1862

Ode Performed in the Senate-House, Cambridge, on the tenth of June 1862. Composed for the Installation of His Grace the Duke of Devonshire, Chancellor of the University. Set to music by W. Sterndale Bennett, Mus. Doc., Professor of Music. Cambridge and London, Macmillan

198 Bibliography of Charles Kingsley's Works

Speech of Lord Dundreary in Section D on Friday Last. On the Great Hippocampus Question (anon.) Published by Private Request. Cambridge and London, Macmillan
A Sermon on the Death of His Royal Highness the Prince Consort, Preached at Eversley Church December 22nd, 1861. London, Parker
Alton Locke, Tailor and Poet, An Autobiography. New edition. With a New Preface "To the Undergraduates of Cambridge." Cambridge and London, Macmillan (see 1850)
Apr. 11 "The Emigration of Women" (letter) *Times*
Aug.-Dec. "The Water-Babies: A Fairy Tale for a Land-Baby" (see 1863) *Macmillan's Magazine*
Nov. 18 "North and South" (letter) *Times*
Nov. 22 "North and South" (letter) *Times*

1863

The Water-Babies: A Fairy tale for a Land-Baby. London and Cambridge, Macmillan (leaf B 1, with L'Envoi was suppressed by Kingsley during the printing and appears in only a few copies) (see 1862)
The Gospel of the Pentateuch. A Set of Parish Sermons, with a Preface [addressed to the Rev. Canon Stanley], published by request. London, Parker
Jan.-Mar. "The Water-Babies: A Fairy Tale for a Land-Baby" (see 1862) *Macmillan's Magazine*
Jan. "The Monks and the Heathen" *Good Words*
Jan. 3 "George Hartwig's *The Tropical World*" (C. K.) *Reader*
Jan. 17 "C. A. Gordon, *China from a Medical Point of View* (C.K.) *Reader*
Feb. 7 "W. R. Grove, *The Correlation of Physical Forces*" *Reader*
Feb. 14 "Roger Ascham, *The Schoolmaster*" (C. K.) *Reader*
Aug. 29 "W. B. Lord, *Sea-Fish and How to Catch Them*" (C. K.) *Reader*
Sept. 12 "Wellington College" (letter) *Times*
Oct. "Henrietta Browne's Picture of the Sister of Charity" *The Fine Arts*

1864

The Roman and the Teuton A Series of Lectures delivered before the University of Cambridge. Cambridge and London, Macmillan
"What, Then, Does Dr. Newman Mean?" A Reply to a Pamphlet lately published by Dr. Newman. London and Cambridge, Macmillan
The Irrationale of Speech, by a Minute Philosopher, reprinted from *Fraser's Magazine* for July 1859. London, Longman (C. K.) (variant title page: *Hints to Stammerers*)
Jan. "Froude's History of England, Vols. VII and VIII (C. K.) *Macmillan's Magazine*

Mar. "The Song of the Little Baltung" (verse) (*Poems*, 1872) *Fraser's Magazine*

1865

David: Four Sermons preached before the University of Cambridge. London and Cambridge, Macmillan
Jan.-Dec. "Hereward, the Last of the English" (see 1866) *Good Words*

1866

Hereward the Wake, "Last of the English." London and Cambridge, Macmillan, 2 vols. (see 1865)
The American Lectureship (broadside)
The Proposed American Lectureship (broadside)
The Temple of Wisdom, a Sermon preached to the Boys of Wellington College, All Saints' Day, 1866. London, Macmillan
June "Superstition," a Lecture delivered at the Royal Institution, April 24 (*Health and Education*, 1874) *Fraser's Magazine*
July "Science," a Lecture at the Royal Institution (*Health and Education*, 1874) *Fraser's Magazine*
"From the Ocean to the Sea" (*Prose Idylls*, 1873) *Good Words*

1867

Three Lectures delivered at the Royal Institution, on the Ancien Regime as it Existed on the Continent before the French Revolution. London, Macmillan
The Water of Life, and Other Sermons. London, Macmillan
National Rifle Association, *A Sermon* preached at the Volunteer Camp, Wimbledon on Sunday Morning, 14th July 1867, printed at the request of the Association. London, Eyre and Spottiswoode
May "The Fens" (*Prose Idylls*, 1873) *Good Words*
June "A Charm of Birds" (*Prose Idylls*, 1873) *Fraser's Magazine*
Nov. ? "The Birds of Norfolk" *Fraser's Magazine*

1868

The Hermits, Sunday Library for Household Reading No. II, Part 1, April; Part 2, May; Part 3, June. London, Macmillan
Discipline, and other Sermons. London, Macmillan
Jan. "Christmas Day" (verse) (*Poems*, 1872) *Good Words*
Feb. "Leaves from the Journal of Our Life in the Highlands" *Fraser's Magazine*
Sept. "Rondelet, the Huguenot Naturalist" (*Health and Education*, 1874) *Good Words*

Oct.   "Vesalius, the Anatomist" (*Health and Education,* 1874) *Good Words*
Nov.-Dec. "Madam How and Lady Why" (see 1869, 1870) *Good Words for the Young*
Dec.   "George Buchanan, Scholar" (*Health and Education,* 1874) *Good Words*

1869

God's Feast, A Sermon preached for the Industrial Schools, Cambridge, in the Church of St. Mary the Great, March 7, 1869. London and Cambridge, Macmillan

The Two Breaths, reprinted from *Good Words,* published by the Ladies Sanitary Association. London, Jarrold (*Health and Education,* 1874)

Women and Politics, reprinted from *Macmillan's Magazine,* published by the London National Society for Women's Suffrage. London, Spottiswoode

The Address on Education, read before the National Association for the Promotion of Social Science, at Bristol, on the 1st October, 1869, by the Rev. Charles Kingsley, President of the Education Department of the Association. London, Head (100,000 copies distributed)

Jan.-Oct. "Madam How and Lady Why" (see 1868, 1870) *Good Words for the Young*
Feb.   "The Self-Education of Young Men, a Village Sermon" *Good Words*
May   "Thrift, a Lecture to Ladies" (*Health and Education,* 1874) *Good Words*
July   "The Two Breaths, a Lecture" (*Health and Education,* 1874) *Good Words*
Oct.   "Women and Politics" *Macmillan's Magazine*

1870

Madam How and Lady Why or First Lessons in Earth Lore for Children. London, Bell and Daldy (see 1868, 1869)

Jan.   "To Boys" (Preface to *Madam How and Lady Why*) *Good Words for the Young*
      "The Air-Mothers" (see 1874, "Pure Water") (*Health and Education,* 1874) *Good Words*
Mar.-Oct.-Dec. "Letters from the Tropics" (*At Last,* 1871) *Good Words*
June   "The Legend of La Brea" (verse) (*Poems,* 1884, 2nd ed.) *Macmillan's Magazine*
Nov.   "Letter from Canon Kingsley" (on land for army Manoeuvres) *Macmillan's Magazine*

1871

At Last: A Christmas in the West Indies. London and New York, Macmillan, 2 vols. with illustrations (see 1870)

n. d. *Letter to Young Men on Betting and Gambling.* London, Society for Promoting Christian Knowledge

n. d. *Letter to a Public School Boy, on Betting and Gambling.* London, Society for Promoting Christian Knowledge

Feb. 22   "The Rev. Charles Kingsley, M.A., Canon of Chester, on Chester Races, Betting and their Attendant Evils" (letter) *Chester Courant*

Mar.   "The Natural Theology of the Future," a Paper read in the Hall of Sion College, Jan. 10, 1871 (*Scientific Lectures and Essays*, 1885) *Macmillan's Magazine*

May   "Grots and Groves," a Lecture delivered at the King's School, Chester (*Health and Education*, 1874) *Good Words*

June   "Physical Science," a Lecture to a Class of Young Men (Preface to *Town Geology*, 1872) *Good Words*

"The Mango-Tree" (verse) (*Poems*, 1878) *Macmillan's Magazine*

"The Wind and the Rain" *Good Words for the Young*

1872

Town Geology. London, Strahan

Poems; Including The Saint's Tragedy, Andromeda, Songs, Ballads, etc., Collected Edition. London, Macmillan

Jan.-July   "Town Geology" *Good Words*

Jan.   "Mr. Helps as an Essayist" *Macmillan's Magazine*

May   "Frederick Denison Maurice. In Memoriam" *Macmillan's Magazine*

1873

Plays and Puritans, and Other Historical Essays. London, Macmillan

Prose Idylls, New and Old. London, Macmillan

Frederick Denison Maurice, a Sermon Preached in Aid of the Girls' Home, 22 Charlotte Street, Portland Place. London, Macmillan

Jan.   "The Science of Health" (*Health and Education*, 1874) *Good Words*

Jan.-Feb.-May   "Winter in the Rocky Mountains," Canon Kingsley, ed. (1874) *Good Words*

Feb. 26   "Canon Kingsley" (letter) *Guardian*

June-July   "Spring in Mexico," Canon Kingsley, ed. (1874) *Good Words*

Oct.   "The Priest's Heart" (verse) (*Poems*, 1878) *Macmillan's Magazine*

1874

Health and Education. London, Isbister
Westminster Sermons. London, Macmillan
David: Five Sermons, 2nd ed. enlarged. London, Macmillan
No. 3, "The Peace of God," *Plain Preaching to Poor People*, Edmund Fowle, ed. London, Skeffington
Preface and ed., *South by West or Winter in the Rocky Mountains and Spring in Mexico* [by Rose Kingsley]. London, Isbister (see 1873)

Jan.   "Nausicaa in London; or, the Lower Education of Woman" (*Health and Education*) *Good Words*
Feb.   "The Tree of Knowledge" (*Health and Education*) *Good Words*
Mar.   "Pure Water; or, a Substitute for Latin Verses" (continuation of "The Air-Mothers," 1870) (*Health and Education*) *Good Words*

1875

Lectures Delivered in America in 1874. London, Longmans

Feb.   "The Lord Coming to His Temple" (sermon) (*All Saints' Day*, 1878) *Good Words*
Mar.   "All Saints' Day" (sermon) (*All Saints' Day*, 1878) *Good Words*
Apr.   "God is Our Refuge" (sermon) (*All Saints' Day*, 1878) *Good Words*
July   "On the Peace of God" (sermon, elaborated version of that in *Plain Preaching*, 1874) (*All Saints' Day*, 1878) *Good Words*
Oct.   "On Charity" (sermon) *Good Words*

1876

Mar.   "Prepare to Meet thy God" (sermon) *Good Words*

1877

Letters to Young Men on Betting and Gambling. London, King (see 1871)

1878

Poems; Including The Saint's Tragedy, Andromeda, Songs, Ballads, etc. Collected Edition. London, Macmillan (additions to 1872 ed.)
All Saints' Day and Other Sermons, Wm. Harrison, ed. London, Kegan Paul
True Words for Brave Men, a Book for Soldiers' and Sailors' Libraries. London, Kegan Paul (see 1855)

1880-1885

Collected Works, 28 vols. London, Macmillan

1880

Poems, Collected Works, Vol. I. London, Macmillan (additions to 1878 ed.)

Historical Lectures and Essays, Collected Works. Vol. XVII. London, Macmillan

Sanitary and Social Lectures and Essays, Collected Works. Vol. XVIII. London, Macmillan

Literary and General Lectures and Essays, Collected Works. Vol. XX. London, Macmillan

Out of the Deep: Words for the Sorrowful, from the writings of Charles Kingsley [Fanny E. Kingsley, ed.]. London, Macmillan (some material not heretofore published)

1882

May   "Fireside Sundays," No. II *Good Words*

1884

Poems, Vol. I, "The Saint's Tragedy"; Vol. II, "Andromeda" and Miscellaneous Poems. London, Macmillan (additions to 1880 ed.)

Daily Thoughts Selected from the Writings of Charles Kingsley by His Wife. London, Macmillan (some material not heretofore published)

1885

Scientific Lectures and Essays, Collected Works. Vol. XIX. London, Macmillan

Sea Sermons. London, Kegan Paul (identical with *Sermons for Sailors,* see 1855)

1887

From Death to Life Fragments of Teaching to a Village Congregation with Letters on the Life after Death, by Charles Kingsley, edited by His Wife. London, Macmillan (some material not heretofore published)

1901

"Speech," Charles Kingsley at the Dinner in his Honour, February 15, 1872, *Speeches at the Lotos Club,* arranged by John Elderkin, Chester S. Lord, Horatio N. Fraser. New York, Privately Printed

1912

Words of Advice to School-Boys. Collected from hitherto unpublished notes and letters of the late Charles Kingsley, edited by E. F.

Johns with a Preface by Lucas Malet. London, Simpkin; Winchester, Warren

1916

The Tutor's Story an unpublished novel by the late Charles Kingsley revised and completed by his daughter Lucas Malet (Mrs. Mary St. Leger Harrison). London, Smith, Elder

INDEX

abolition, 135-6
Agassiz Museum, 184
Ainsworth, Harrison, 77
Albert, Prince, 82, 114, 115, 144, 147, 152
Alcibiades, 169-70
Aldershot, 14
"Alexander Smith and Alexander Pope," 138-9
Alexandria and Her Schools, 115-16
Alton Locke, 11, 51, 56, 57, 72-81, 96, 126, 127, 131, 137-8, 149, 163, 178
America, 21, 46, 73, 96, 106, 107, 135-6, 150, 171, 180, 183-7
American lectureship at Cambridge, 150
ancestry, 2, 32
"Ancient Civilization," 184, 185, 186
Andromeda, 45, 139, 140-1
Apologia, 153-61
Argemone Lavington (character), 18, 19, 52, 53, 56
Armada, 121-2
army, 14, 118-19
Arnold, Matthew, 93, 166-7, 187
Arnold, Thomas, 9, 26, 78, 101
art, opinions on, 22, 26, 53-4, 87, 97-8, 138
artists, 22, 72, 113, 124, 131-3, 139-40
Ashburton, Lord, 165
Associations, 32, 66-7, 71, 88
Astley, Sir Francis, 52
Athanasian creed, 22, 130, 164
Athenaeum, 7, 47, 123, 149
At Last, 182-3

Barnack, 6, 7
Beheading of John the Baptist, The, 12
Bell, W. A., 186
Bennett, Charles H., 97
Benson, E. W., Archbishop of Canterbury, 146, 176

betting, 16, 179
Biarritz, 159
"Bible Politics," 69, 70
Bideford, 117, 118, 119, 121, 127
Birmingham, 127
Blackwell, Elizabeth, 181
Blomfield, C. J., Bishop of London, 84, 85
Bowles, Samuel, 185
Bowles, T. Gibson, 168
Boys' History of England, 172
Bramshill, 29, 30, 34
Brave Words, 118-19
Bremer, Fredrika, 56, 93, 166
Brimley, George, 132-3; letters to, 55, 80
Bristol, 8, 59
"British Museum, The," 63, 64
British Museum, 32
Brontë, Anne, 92
Brontë, Charlotte, 92
Brooke, Henry, 97
Brooke, Sir James, Rajah of Sarawak, 119
Brown, W. Henry, 6 n.
Browning, Robert, 48, 95, 120
Bryant, William Cullen, 185
Buckland, William, 26
Bullar, John, letters to, 71, 94, 126, 141
Bunbury, Sir Charles, letters to, 180, 183
Bunsen, Baron, 45, 75, 96, 141, 180
Bunyan, John, 97, 133

Cadogan, Lord, 11
Cambridge, University, 2, 14-23, 29, 77-8, 101-2, 104, 105, 106, 108-9, 114, 122, 147-52, 159, 166, 171, 172
Campbell, E. P., letter to, 104
Canada, 185
canonry: of Chester, 176; Middleham, 175; Westminster, 183; Worcester, 175

Index

Carlyle, Thomas, 22, 73, 79, 93
Catholicism, 20-1, 38, 45, 53, 54, 55, 57, 97, 101, 107, 130, 131, 153-60
Caxtons, The, 92
Cazamian, Louis, 73
Chambers's Journal, 141
Chanter, Mrs. J. M., 4
Chaplain to the Prince of Wales, 151
Chaplain to the Queen, 3, 143-4, 147
Chapman and Hall, 51, 73, 112
Charter, 60, 61-2, 74
Chartism, 3, 8, 59-71, 79
Chartist riots, 59-61
Cheap Clothes and Nasty, 67, 76
Chelsea, 11-13, 33, 38, 47
Cheshire, 2, 81, 138
Chester, 81, 176, 178-80, 182, 183; see also J. S. Howson
Chester Archaeological Society, 81, 179
Chester Courant, 179
Chester Guardian, 179
Chester Natural Science Society, 179-80
children, see Grenville, Mary, Maurice, Rose Kingsley
chloroform, 104
cholera, 10, 76-7, 127-8
Christian Socialism, 3, 8, 59-71, 79-81, 82-5, 88-9
Christian Socialist, 32, 39, 47, 58, 66-7, 68-71, 88, 100-1, 140
Christian Socialists, 29, 38, 39, 59, 88-90
Church of England Review, 113-14
"Church *versus* Malthus, The," 69, 70
Cirencester, 106
Civil War, American, 135-6, 150
Claude Mellot (character), 53, 54-5
Clifton, 8, 9
Clough, Arthur Hugh, 91, 92
Clovelly, 7, 107, 121
Coleridge, Derwent, 9, 47, 106; letter to, 31
Coleridge, Mrs. Derwent, 12
Coleridge, John Duke, 56
Coleridge, Samuel Taylor, 22
Colorado, 106, 107, 184, 186
Commonwealth, 74, 167
Coningsby, 55
Conington, John, 62; letters to, 43, 55
conversion, 11, 21-3
Cooper, Thomas, 73-5, 165, 167; letter to, 119

cooperative associations, 32, 66-7, 71, 88
Cope, Sir John, 28, 29, 30
Cope, Sir William, 35, 160
Cotton, J., 121
Crimean War, 52, 117-19, 123, 124-5, 129, 132, 135, 180
Cumins, Maria, 171-2
Currie, Raikes, letter to, 175
"Cyrus, the Servant of the Lord," 184

damnation, 130, 143, 144
Darling, the History of a Wise Woman, 40, 169
Darwin, Charles, 21, 129, 165-6
David, 145, 172
"David's Weakness," 172
Davidson, John, 174 n.
Davies, J. Llewellyn, 102, 167
democracy, 90, 150
demoniac possession, 176-7
depression, 119, 123-5
Desmoulins, Camille, 79-80, 117
Devon, 3, 6, 7, 23, 36, 43, 58, 91, 117, 119-20, 121; see also Bideford, Clovelly, Torquay
Dickinson, Lowes, *frontispiece,* 38, 168
Disraeli, Benjamin, 55, 175
dissent, 39, 45, 63, 75-6, 131 and n., 162
dogs, 35, 69, 117
Drake, Sir Francis, 120
drama, 41, 45-7
dreams, 11, 78-9
Drew, G. S., 82, 84-6
Dublin Review, 43
Dufferin, Lord and Lady, 185

Eclectic Review, 123
Economic Review, 29, 38, 39, 59-60
Edinburgh, Philosophical Institute of, 115-16
Edinburgh Review, 80
education, theories of, 99-104
Eliot, George, 93, 100, 110
Ellis, S. M., 4
Elsley Vavasour (character), 131-2, 140
Emerson, Ralph Waldo, 69, 96, 110-12, 114
Emma, Queen of the Sandwich Islands, 166
English Review, 43, 47, 48

Esau, 51-2, 67, 135
essays, 8, 45, 46-7, 50, 54, 91, 139, 142, 159
Essays and Reviews, 149
Evans, Mary Ann, 93, 100, 110
Eversley, 24, 28-36, 39, 99, 100, 103-4, 107, 146, 163, *facing* 168, 171, 176-7, 184, 187, 189
Exhibition of 1851, 82

feet as symbols, 109-10
Fens, 6, 7, 16, 91
Field, Cyrus, 186
Fields, James T., 184
"First Discoverers of America, The," 185, 186
fishing, 1, 3, 6-7, 30, 134-5, 177
Fool of Quality, 97
France, 159, 168, 180
Franco-Prussian War, 168, 180
Fraser's, 43, 47, 50-1, 54, 55, 57, 77, 88-9, 91, 95, 111-13, 123, 127, 139 n., 140, 141, 153
Freeman, E. A., 168
Freemont election, 135
Frimley murder, 67-70
"From the Ocean to the Sea," 159
Froude, Anthony, 20, 36-8, 93, 121, 141, 153, 154, 155, 157, 159, 174
Froude, Mrs. Anthony, 20, 38
"Froude's History of England," 154

Gainsborough, Lady, 25
gambling, 16, 179
Gaskell, Mrs., 92, 166
gentleman, the, 31, 95, 105, 153-61
Geological Society, 129
Geological Survey, 185
geology, 15, 26, 103, 129, 179-80, 185
Germany, 86-8, 168, 180
Gladstone, William Ewart, 176, 183
Glaucus, 115, 144, 171
Goderich, Lord, afterwards Earl De Grey and Ripon, letter to, 104
Goethe, 92, 124
Good Words, 1, 91, 145, 150, 159, 172, 182-3
Good Words for the Young, 91, 172
Gordon, Sir Arthur, 182
Gosse, Sir Edmund, 95 and n., 166
Gosse, Philip Henry, 115, 121, 129, 165, 166

Grant, President U. S., 185
Gray, Asa, 185
Gray, J. A. C., 186
"Great Cities and their Influence for Good and Evil," 8
Grenfell, Charlotte, *see* Mrs. Anthony Froude
Grenfell, Charles Pascoe, 19
Grenfell, Emily, *see* Lord Sydney Godolphin Osborne
Grenfell, Frances Eliza, *see* Mrs. Charles Kingsley
Grenville, Sir Richard, 19, 104
Guardian, 56, 123
Gurney, Archer W., letters to, 94-5, 140

Hakluyt's *Voyages,* 120, 121
Hare, Julius, Archdeacon of Lewes, 115
Harrison, William, 107, 145
Harrison, Mrs. William, v, 104, 107, *facing* 169, 169-70
Harrow, 2, 46, 106
Harvard College, 150, 184
Hawthorne, Nathaniel, 170
Health and Education, 91, 102-3
Hell, 130, 143, 144
Helps, Sir Arthur, 62, 167
Helston, 9, 11
Hereward, 6, 172-4
Hermits, The, 172
Heroes, The, 170
hexameters, 139
Hillyars and the Burtons, The, 12
Hints to Stammerers, variant title for *The Irrationale of Speech, q.v.*
Holne, 6, 23
Holyoake, George Jacob, 167-8
horses, 6-7, 10, 15, 18, 29, 30-1, 35, 52, 105, 106, *facing* 169, 173
Howson, J. S., Dean of Chester, 1, 178, 184
Hughes, Thomas, his Prefatory Memoir to *Alton Locke,* 45, 61, 66-7, 163; his Memoir in *Macmillan's Magazine,* 163-4; his *Memoir of Daniel Macmillan,* 125; expedition with Kingsley to Snowdon, 134-5; Kingsley's review of his *Tom Brown's School Days,* 94; letters to, 101, 103, 108, 118, 123, 150, 151-2, 177

Index

Hughes, Mrs. Thomas, 103
Hullah, John P., 33, 43, 138
Hunt, James, 147
Hunting, 3, 6-7, 10, 15, 18, 29, 30-1, 35, 52, 105, 106, *facing* 169
Hurlbert, W. H., 135
Hutton, Richard Holt, 158-9, 160
Huxley, Thomas Henry, 21, 129, 165, 166, 179
Hypatia, 10, 86, 88, 89, 91, 96, 108-15, 117, 128, 130, 137

Introductory Lectures Delivered at Queen's College, 65-6
Irish, 118
Irrationale of Speech, 103, 147, 153-4, 198
Irving, Washington, 96

James, John, 35
Jameson, Mrs., 91
Jane Eyre, 92
"Jehu Junior," 168
Jelf, R. W., 115
Jews, 43, 112, 114, 162
Johns, A. C., v, 9, 106

Kaulbach, 87, 97
Keate, John, 113
King's College, London, 12, 38, 50, 62, 65, 115
Kingsley, Charles, ancestry, 2, 32; family, 2; childhood, 5-6; boyhood, 7-13; health, 5, 9-11, 23, 24, 58, 141-2, 159, 183, 186, 188; Clovelly, 7-8; Chelsea, 11-13; Cambridge, 14-23; courtship, 17-28; conversion, 21-3; ordination, 23-4; marriage, 28; Eversley 24, 28-39; *The Saint's Tragedy*, 41-9; *Yeast*, 50-8; Christian Socialism, 59-71; Queen's College, 65-6; *Alton Locke*, 72-81; *The Message of the Church to Labouring Men*, 82-7; Germany, 86-8; essays and reviews, 91-8; pupils, 99-101; children, 104-7; *Hypatia*, 108-15; Edinburgh, 115-16; *Westward Ho!*, 117-25; *Two Years Ago*, 126-36; sanitary reform, 126-8; poems, 137-41; Chaplain to the Queen, 143-4; Regius Professor of Modern History, Cambridge, 147-52; tutor to the Prince of Wales, 147, 151-2; controversy with Newman, 153-61; France, 159; friendships, 162-8; *The Heroes*, 170; *The Water-Babies*, 170-2; *Hereward*, 172-4; Canon of Chester, 176, 178-80; West Indies, 182-3; America, 183-7; Canon of Westminster, 183; illness, 188; death, 188-9
Kingsley, Mrs. Charles, 3 n., 7, 38, 60, 103, 104, 115, 122, 125, 145, 146, 168; courtship, 18-21, 25-8; appearance, 19, *facing* 135; family, 19; tractarianism, 20-1, 24; converts Kingsley, 21-3; editing of his letters, 25; separation of the lovers, 25-8; marriage, 28; position in her husband's parish, 33; household at Eversley, 33-5; her annotation of *Yeast*, 53, 56; amanuensis for her husband, 58; John Martineau's description, 100; children, 104-7; her feet, 109; her attitude toward the Newman controversy, 153 n., 159; Kingsley's dependence on her, 52-3, 164-5; inspires *Water-Babies*, 170; letter about Chester, 180; dangerous illness, 187; letter from the Queen, 189; letters to, 7, 20, 21, 23, 24, 85, 93, 120, 159, 187
Kingsley, Charles, Sr., 2-3, 5, 6, 7, 21-2, 38, 47, 58, 86-7, 105, 114, 120
Kingsley, Mrs. Charles, Sr., 3, 5, 7, 19, 28, 37-8, 86-7, 114
Kingsley, Charlotte, *see* Mrs. J. M. Chanter
Kingsley, George, 3-4, 75, 128-9, 186
Kingsley, Gerald, 3
Kingsley, Grenville Arthur, 104, 106, 170
Kingsley, Henry, 4, 7, 11, 12, 77, 86-8; letter to, 150
Kingsley, Herbert, 3, 8, 9
Kingsley, Mary H., 4
Kingsley, Mary St. Leger, *see* Mrs. William Harrison
Kingsley, Maurice, 39, 95, 104, 105-6, *facing* 169, 170, 183
Kingsley, Mrs. Maurice, 106
Kingsley, Rose, 96, 104, 106-7, 109, 170, 171, 184
Kingsley, Dr. William, 185
Kingsley, General William, 2
King's School, Chester, 179

Index

Knight, John, 9
Koloff, 87
Krummacher, F. W., 12

Ladies Sanitary Association, 127
Lancelot Smith (character), 18, 19, 52, 53, 55, 56, 57, 114
Lanyard, G. S., 19
Leader, 56, 84 and n., 123
Leben Jesu, 100
lectures, 8, 14, 46, 115-16, 148, 149, 150, 184, 185, 186-7
Lees, 67, 68, 100-1
"Letters from the Tropics," 182-3
"Letters to the Chartists," 61-4
Lewes, George Henry, 93, 167
"Limits of Exact Science as Applied to History," 149
Lincoln, Abraham, 150
Lincoln's Inn, 15, 63
Linnean Society, 129
London Quarterly Review, 167, 171
London Review, 167, 171
Longfellow, Henry Wadsworth, 96, 184
"Long Game," 88
Longman, William, 97
"Lord Palmerston and the Presbytery of Edinburgh," 127
Lotos Club, 184
Louis, A. N., 114
Lowell, James Russell, 96, 135
"Lucas Malet," *see* Mrs. William Harrison
Lucas, Mary, *see* Mrs. Charles Kingsley, Sr.
Lucas, Nathan, 3, 182
Ludlow, J. M., article on the Christian Socialists in the *Economic Review,* 29, 38, 39, 59-60; 62, 70, 113, 117; letters to, 10, 53, 72, 74, 76, 88, 139
Lyell, Sir Charles, 166, 179
Lytton, Bulwer-, 56, 91, 92, 133

Macmillan, Alexander, vi, 3, 91, 122, 139, 144, 146, 149, 154-5, 157, 159-60, 166, 168, 169, 170, 171-2, 173, 174; *see also* Daniel Macmillan, *Macmillan's Magazine*
Macmillan, Daniel, 62, 125, 168; *see also* Alexander Macmillan, *Macmillan's Magazine*

Macmillan, Malcolm Kingsley, 122, 146, 169
Macmillan's Magazine, 91, 154-6, 158, 163-4, 170
Madam How and Lady Why, 172
Magdalene College, *see* Cambridge
"Malthus, The Church *versus,*" 69-70
Mansfield, Charles, 16-17, 62, 96
Marks of Barhamville, 139 n.
Marryat, Captain, 52
Marsh, Herbert, Bishop of Peterborough, 2, 5, 75
Marshall, Frederic, 103-4
Martineau, Harriet, 5, 68, 99, 166
Martineau, James, 111
Martineau, John, 16, 68-9, 99-100, 146, 164
matrimony, 20-1, 41-2, 57, 66, 109
Maud, 54, 92, 94-5, 119
Maurice, F. D., 25, 64, 76, 78, 80, 82, 89, 96, 113, 132, 140, 158, 164, 168; beginning of his friendship with Kingsley, 38-9; Preface to *The Saint's Tragedy,* 47; Reader of Lincoln's Inn, 63; King's College, 65, 115; Christian Socialists, 59-71; godfather to Kingsley's eldest son, 104, 105; *Hypatia,* 111, 114-15; letters to, 51, 70, 93, 94, 105-6, 111, 117-18, 124-5, 129, 130, 141, 151, 171
Maxwell, Sir James, 116
Mayhew, H., 67
medicine, 26, 27
Meredith, George, 51, 93
mesmerism, 176
Message of the Church to Labouring Men, The, 82-7, 88
Mexico, 96, 106, 107, 184
militarism, 14, 117-19, 180
Mill, John Stuart, letter to, 180-1
Millais, Sir John, 54
Milton, 94, 187-8
Miscellanies, 8, 46-7, 54, 91, 139
Mitford, Mary Russell, 163, 166
Moberly, George, Bishop of Salisbury, 176
Montégut, Emile, 80-1
Morning Chronicle, 67, 76-7, 80
Morris, William, 95
Mudie's Library, 7, 122-3, 125
Müller, Max, 108, 113, 148, 180
Muscular Christianity, 7, 44, 171, 172

music, 26, 33, 110, 138
"My Political Creed," 32-3
mysticism, 11, 44

"National Gallery, The," 63, 64
Negroes, 135-6, 150
Nemesis of Faith, The, 36-8
Neo-Platonism, 115; *see also Hypatia*
New Forest, 2, 39-40, 169
Newman, John Henry, 89, 153-61
Newton, Alfred, 174
North British Review, 46, 91, 115
"North Devon," 7, 54
novels, 57, 142, 169-70, 174; *see also Yeast, Alton Locke, Hypatia, Westward Ho!, Two Years Ago, Hereward*
novel, theories of, 77, 111, 133-4
"Nun's Pool, The," 58, 70

obituary, 1
O'Connor, Feargus, 75
"Oh! that we two were Maying," 42, 47, 48, 49, 138
Omphalos, 165
ordination, 23, 24, 145
Origin of Species, 21, 165-6
Osborne, Lord Sydney Godolphin, 28, 62
Oxford Movement, 20-1, 24, 31, 41, 43-4, 50, 51, 56, 78, 119, 131
Oxford Tracts, 20
Oxford University, 2, 41, 101-2, 108-9

Palmerston, Lord, 126, 127, 147
Paraguay, Brazil and the Plate, 16, 96
Paris, 159
Parker, John, 47, 50-1, 62, 88-9, 93, 97, 111-13, 140, 166; *see also Christian Socialist, Fraser's, Politics for the People*
Parker, John, the elder, 47, 50-1, 60, *see also* John Parker, *Christian Socialist, Fraser's, Politics for the People*
Parrish, M. L., 191
"Parson Lot," 63-71, 74, 88
Paul, Kegan, 41, 75, 126-7, 146
Phaethon, 45, 96, 110
Pickering, 47
Pilgrimage of Grace, The, 141, 169
Pilgrim's Progress, The, 97, 133

Pimperne, 28
Plays and Puritans, 46-7, 91
poetry, 6, 7, 9, 11, 23, 39-40, 48, 49, 50, 63, 70-1, 72-3, 86 and n., 88, 92, 95, 109, 110, 122, 129, 132, 137-41
poets, 72, 74, 113, 131-3, 137-8, 139-40, 141
Politics for the People, 57, 61-4, 66, 74, 80, 140
Potter, Horatio, Bishop of New York, 185
Powles, Cowley, 9, 36, 41, 47, 105; letter to, 11-12
prayers, 27
preaching, 128, 145-7, 186, 187
prefaces, 16, 96-7, 107
Pre-Raphaelitism, 35, 54
Prose Idylls, 91
Prospective Review, 111
pupils, 99-101
Purgatory of Suicides, The, 74
Pusey, E. B., 20, 108-9, 119, 172

Quarterly Review, 65-6, 80, 158
Queen's College, London, 57, 65-6, 80

Rabelais, 96, 163-4, 170
"Readables and Unreadables," 139 n.
Reader, 91
"Recent Novels," 77, 112
Record, 79, 177
Redpath Lyceum, 184
Regius Professorship of Modern History, Cambridge, 77-8, 147-52, 159
reviews, 46-7, 54, 77, 91-3, 94-5, 112, 139 and n.
Revue des Deux Mondes, 80-1
Reynolds, G. W., 92 and n.
Rigg, J. H., 45-6, 167
Roman and the Teuton, The, 148, 149
Ruskin, John, 54, 93-4, 97-8
Ryder, Fr. Ignatius Dudley, 158

St. Barnabas, 31
St. Elizabeth of Hungary, 20-1; *see also The Saint's Tragedy*
St. John, the Evangelist, Fitzroy Square, 82-5
St. Luke's, Chelsea, 11
"Saint Maura," 140-1
St. Neot's, 105

Index

Saint's Tragedy, The, 20-1, 25 n., 41-9, 76, 112, 113, 114, 122, 139, 140, 144
"Sands of Dee, The," 81, 137-8
Sandy Mackaye (character), 72-3, 110
sanitary reform, 32, 90, 91, 102-3, 126-8
Saturday Review, 94, 141
"Science," 102-3
science, 1, 3, 7, 9, 10, 22, 26, 45, 87, 126, 129, 145, 165-6, 174, 179-80, 182, 186-7
Scotland, 73, 115-16
Scott, Sir Walter, 92, 123
Sedgwick, Professor Adam, 15
"Self-Education of Young Men, The," 145
sermons, 39, 45, 127-8, 142, 144-7, 172, 186, 187
Sermons on National Subjects, 127-8
Shakespeare, 43, 45, 46, 48, 49, 63, 92, 122, 133, 137, 187
Shaw, F. G., 184
Shaw-Lefevre, Charles (afterwards Viscount Eversley), Speaker of the House of Commons, 68, 113
Shields, Frederic, 97-8
Smith and Elder, 97
Smith, Alexander, 118, 137, 139
Smith, J. Stores, 84 and n.
Smithsonian Institute, 185
smoking, 11, 34
Snake's Book, The, 22
Snowdon, 133-5
Society for the Promotion of Working Men's Associations, 66, 71
South America, 106
South by West, 96, 107
Spasmodic poets, 119, 131
Spectator, 43, 48, 56, 85-6, 101-2, 133, 158-9
Spenser, Edmund, 13, 120
"Stage as It Was Once, The," 46
stammer, 10, 39, 146-7, 163
Stanley, Arthur Penrhyn, Dean of Westminster, 62, 104, 108, 189
Stapleton, A. G., v, 28, 119
Stapleton, Mrs. A. G., letter to, 99
Stapleton, Edward, letter to, 180
Stapleton, Frederic, 147; letters to, 151, 159
stays, 103
Stephen, Sir James, 147

Stowe, Harriet Beecher, 92, 96, 135-6, 166
Strauss, Johan, 69, 74, 100, 101, 102
Strettell, Alfred, 66, 170
Sunday amusements, 32, 105
Swinburne, Algernon Charles, 95

Tartarus, 130, 143, 144
Tauler, John, 97
Taylor, Tom, 45, 134
teetotalism, 32
Tenant of Wildfell Hall, The, 92
Tennyson, Alfred, Lord, 24, 39, 54, 91, 92, 94-5, 114, 118, 166
Thackeray, William Makepeace, 93, 123, 125, 160, 166
Theologia Germanica, 96
"Three Fishers," 71, 86
"Thrift," 102
Ticknor and Fields, 140
Times, 19, 91, 123
Tom Brown's School Days, 94
Tom Thurnall (character), 128-9, 131, 135
Torquay, 115, 119, 121
Town Geology, 103, 180
tractarianism, 20-1, 24, 31, 41, 43-4, 50, 51, 56, 78, 119, 131
Tracts by Christian Socialists, 67
Tracts for the Times, 20
Tutor's Story, The, 169
Twain, Mark, 185
Twenty-five Village Sermons, 144
"Two Breaths, The," 103
Two Years Ago, 54, 72, 87-8, 96, 110, 126-36, 144, 169, 170

Uncle Tom's Cabin, 92, 96, 135
United States, *see* America
universities, reform of, 101-2, 167

Vanity Fair caricature, 168
Vaudois massacres, 170
Victoria, 1, 35, 108-9, 114, 143-4, 151, 152, 175-6, 183; letter from, 189
Village Sermons, Twenty-five, 80, 122, 144

Wales, 132-5
Wales, Prince of, 108, 147, 151-2, 188, 189
Wallace, Alfred Russell, 21

war, opinions on, 117-19, 123, 124-5, 168, 180
Ward, Wilfrid, 153 n., 158
Warner, Susan, 171-2
Water-Babies, The, 138, 170-2, 179
Wellesley, Gerald, Dean of Windsor, 47; letter to, 147
Wellington College, 104, 105
West Indies, 3, 182-3
"Westminster Abbey," 184, 186-7
Westminster Abbey, 32, 145, 168, 183, 187, 189
Westminster Review, 93, 121, 149
Westward Ho!, 109, 117-25, 126, 131, 182
What, Then, Does Dr. Newman Mean?, 157-8
Whitman, Walt, 96
Whittier, John Greenleaf, 184-5
Who Are the Friends of Order?, 89
"Who Causes Pestilence?", 127-8
"Why Should We Fear the Romish Priests?", 51
Wilberforce, Samuel, Bishop of Oxford, 108-9

Winchester, deanery of, 175
Winkworth, Susanna, 96, 97
Winton House, v, 106
"Woman's Work in a Country Parish," 33
women, Kingsley's "knowledge" of, 52-3, 56, 123
women's rights, 180-1
"Wonders of the Shore, The," see *Glaucus*
Wood, Sir Charles, 113
Wood, Peter, 175
Woolner, Thomas, 168
Woolwich, 14
Wordsworth, William, 47, 168, 187
Working Men's College, 89, 93
Wright, Thomas, 173
writing, method of, 57-8, 121-2

Yeast, 15-16, 18, 19, 22, 28, 29, 50-8, 66, 70, 79, 80, 99, 109, 112, 113, 153
Yorke, Marie, see Mrs. Maurice Kingsley
Yorkshire, 141, 169-70
Young, Brigham, 186